EVERYONE'S MONEY BOOK

ON RETIREMENT PLANNING

JORDAN E. GOODMAN

Dearborn™
Trade Publishing
A **Kaplan Professional** Company

Vice President and Publisher: Cynthia A. Zigmund
Editorial Director: Donald J. Hull
Senior Managing Editor: Jack Kiburz
Interior Design: Lucy Jenkins
Cover Design: Design Alliance, Inc.
Typesetting: the dotted i

Published by Dearborn Trade Publishing, a Kaplan Professional Company

Printed in the United States of America

02 03 04 05 06   10 9 8 7 6 5 4 3 2 1

Library of Congress Cataloging-in-Publication Data

Goodman, Jordan Elliot.
    Everyone's money book on retirement planning / Jordan E. Goodman.
        p.   cm.
    Includes index.
    ISBN 0-7931-5378-6 (pbk.)
    1. Finance, Personal.   2. Retirement—Planning.   3. Retirement income—Planning.   I. Title.
    HG179 .G6753 2002
    332.024'01—dc21

                        2002006183

Contents

List of Figures

Preface

Americans are living longer. It's not uncommon to see people living into their 80s, 90s, and even reaching the century mark. In fact, 100-year-olds are the fastest-growing age group in the nation. Those who say good-bye to the 9-to-5 grind at age 65 may have 20 or more years in retirement. Trouble is, they'll also need more in the retirement kitty to support that new lifestyle. The monthly check from Social Security will help, but it likely won't take care of everything. That old standby, the traditional company pension paid for by your company, continues to disappear from the financial landscape. Increasingly, the onus is on *you* to prepare for your golden years to make sure they *are* golden.

How well you manage your finances will determine whether you have the means to fulfill the dreams that you finally have time to pursue, be it traveling, spending more time with family, continuing your education, or moving into that beachfront property you've always wanted. On the other hand, you could wind up impoverished. According to a recent report from the American Association of Retired Persons (AARP), 40 percent of Americans over age 60, regardless of their current economic circumstances, will experience poverty at some point in their later years.

It's an ominous statistic. You don't want to be one of the millions of Americans in poverty. Neither do most people. With approximately 76 million Americans now age 50 and over, retirement is suddenly not so far away. It's not surprising, then, that retirement has become such a hot topic. A plethora of information is available—from books, Web sites, seminars, magazines, newsletters, and software. You don't have to search hard to find advice on the subject. Discussions of retirement are so prevalent that many Gen Xers, unlike their parents and grandparents, are already at least entertaining the notion of what they want later in life.

Though there's no shortage of information, that's not to say it's being put to good use. According to many surveys, for the most part people are not saving or not saving enough for retirement, because they are operating blindly—they haven't calculated how much money they need to save. Many are consumed with instant gratification, whereas others are trying to make ends meet and think they can't afford to look beyond today to tomorrow. If it weren't for employer-sponsored plans such as 401(k)s, some would have no retirement stash at all.

REALITY CHECK

What seems to have gotten lost in all the retirement hubbub is that you can start small. Even saving $20 a week, or $1,040 a year, has the potential of growing to $50,000 in 25 years, assuming a 5 percent rate of return. Most everyone can salt away 20 bucks a week if they really want to. What's important is to get started saving—and the sooner the better. Time works like magic, growing your money in ways you might never imagine, thanks to the wonders of compounding. But the truth is that even late starters—those in their mid-50s—are better off than those who don't plan or put aside any savings.

The good news is that you've picked up this book. That's a valuable first step. Your next move will be more challenging. First, you have to set goals. What's the best-case scenario? How would you really like to spend your retirement years? What matters most? Perhaps the biggest questions are: How much will it take to finance your dreams and where will the money come from? And if there's a shortfall, what are your options?

For many people, investing is still a mystery. How do you choose the right savings vehicles? What are the risks and potential rewards? How do you tap your investments once you've retired?

I'll help you answer the many questions surrounding your retirement. There is much to be considered. If you're given an early retirement offer, do you accept it? What are the financial implications? Once you're no longer under your employer's wing, how will you continue to protect yourself through life, health, disability, and long-term care insurance? How much will you need, and where can you find the best deals? What can you expect from Medicare and Medicaid?

RETIRE WITH STYLE

Then there's the whole issue of quality of life—enjoying retirement. One of the biggest questions is: Where will you live? There are a host of housing options. I'll explain the advantages and limitations of each so you can decide for yourself which is likely to be your best bet. Retirement is also a time of opportunity—to continue your education, explore hobbies, volunteer, travel, or do whatever else makes you happy. I'll explore those areas, too.

Without question, the notion of retirement is exhilirating and overwhelming at the same time. There's much to be sorted out. That's what this book is for. Each chapter is written simply and contains additional resources, such as links to organizations, Web sites, and publications that will help you along. I trust that this retirement book is unlike any other you find on the market in its comprehensiveness and ability to help you meet your retirement goals.

Acknowledgments

Everyone's Money Book on Retirement Planning would not have been possible without the generous contributions and extremely hard work of many talented people. Foremost among the contributors is finance writer Sheryl Nance-Nash, who expertly pulled together the threads of this book into a wonderful and comprehensive resource on retirement planning.

I also would like to thank each of the following highly esteemed experts for his or her input: Elaine Bedel, CFP, Bedel Financial, Indianapolis, Ind.; Gayle Buff, CFP, Buff Capital Management, Newton, Mass.; John Clark, public relations, Social Security Administration; Robert Davis, president and CEO, Long-Term Care Quote, Chandler, Ariz.; Jack Dolan, public relations, American Council of Life Insurers, Washington, D.C.; Danielle Grush, public relations, Centers for Medicare & Medicaid Services, Region II; Joe Luchok, public relations, Health Insurance Association of America, Washington, D.C.; Ken Scholen, National Center for Home Equity Conversion, St. Paul, Minn.; Ed Slott, *Ed Slott's IRA Advisor* newsletter, Rockville Centre, N.Y.; Jeffrey Speicher, public relations, Pension Benefit Guaranty Corporation; Hersh Stern, Annuity Shopper, Monroe TWP, N.J.; and Michael Terry, CFP, Financial Asset Management Corporation, New York, N.Y.

And finally, it's my pleasure to acknowledge reprint permission kindly granted by the following: Carol Anderson of CWA/ITU Negotiated Pension Plan; Letitia Findeison, legal administrator of The Vanguard Group, Valley Forge, Penn.; John Greaney of RetireEarlyHomePage.com; Kien Liew of Pensionbenefits.com, Plano, Tex.; and Ed Slott of *Ed Slott's IRA Advisor,* Rockville Centre, N.Y.

CHAPTER 1

Figuring Out What You Need

It's OK to dream. Think big. What's the best-case scenario? What would a perfect retirement look like? It ideally starts at what age? To plan for retirement, you have to know what you want. Set goals.

Two big pieces of the retirement puzzle are pinpointing when you want to retire and trying to figure out how long you can expect to live. According to the Employee Benefit Research Institute (EBRI), half of the men reaching age 65 have an additional life expectancy of approximately 17 years, and half the women reaching age 65 can expect to live another 21 years. In fact, increasingly male and female centurians are becoming more common. People tend to underestimate their longevity. The EBRI survey showed that almost 20 percent of workers expect their retirement to last 10 years or less, and an additional 15 percent expect their retirement to last from 11 to 19 years. Sixteen percent were unable to even guess. Of course, you must consider your health and your family medical history to draw realistic conclusions. What's the bottom line? Retirement could be much longer than you imagine. Your assets will need staying power. You don't want to outlive your money.

Once you've visualized the dream, it's time to figure out how you can make the dream a reality. How much money will it take? What resources will you be able to draw on? And if you come up short, how best can you play catch-up?

Ready, set, go.

GETTING STARTED

The best place to start is here and now. Financial planners typically say you can expect to spend anywhere from 60 to 100 percent of what you spend during your working years. How much you'll need depends on how lavish your dreams are. If you're like most people, you have a rough idea of where your money goes. But wild guesses can be wildly wrong. If you're completely clueless, get a notebook and begin keeping a diary of all your spending for a few weeks. Keep track of monthly bills, groceries, magazines, dry cleaning, movies, gifts, transportation costs, trips to Starbucks for coffee . . . everything. Glean information from your checkbook and your credit card statements. After several weeks you'll be able to produce an average monthly figure for expenses. To help you accurately determine how much you have coming in and going out, look at Figure 1.1.

You've got a good grasp now of your current needs. What's likely to change by the time you're ready to call it quits? Your children will be grown and on their own; the mortgage may have vanished, though there will be maintenance and taxes; and you won't have all the expenses associated with working. But while you're striking things off the list, realize there'll be new expenses to contend with. Remember, you'll have the time to enjoy more evenings out, travel, continue your education, or play golf as if there's no tomorrow. What will your to-do list cost?

For a rough idea of your expenses in retirement, use the worksheet in Figure 1.2 or the tools on several Web sites mentioned in the Resources section of this chapter. The worksheet is designed to adjust your working years' level of expenses to your retirement years' level of expenses and to factor in a long-term inflation rate of 4.5 percent. The savings called for in item 2 include all regular savings plus contributions to retirement plans such as 401(k)s and individual retirement accounts (IRAs). The worksheet's sample figures assume an annual income of $50,000, an annual savings of $5,000, a 70 percent level of retirement spending, and 20 years remaining before retirement.

The Impact of Inflation

As you can see from the worksheet in Figure 1.2, inflation is a factor to be reckoned with. Although inflation's been a relatively tame beast in the past decade, it could again rear its ugly head. You'll have to consider the impact of inflation on your estimates for your retirement cost of living and your investment returns in retirement. Your retirement kitty can cover your lifestyle comfortably if inflation stays mild, but be conscious of what an upsurge in inflation could mean. The impact of inflation increases over time, and you have to take into consideration not just the expected rate of inflation but such things as how many years you have until you retire and how long you expect to be in retirement.

Figure 1.1　Monthly Budgeting Worksheet

MONTH _____　　　　YEAR _____

Income	Budget	Actual	YTD Budget	YTD Actual
Earned Income	$_____	$_____	$_____	$_____
Self-Employment Income	_____	_____	_____	_____
Family Income	_____	_____	_____	_____
Government Income	_____	_____	_____	_____
Retirement Income	_____	_____	_____	_____
Investment Income	_____	_____	_____	_____
Other Income	_____	_____	_____	_____
TOTAL INCOME	$_____	$_____	$_____	$_____

Expenses

Fixed Expenses

	Budget	Actual	YTD Budget	YTD Actual
Automobile-Related	$_____	$_____	$_____	$_____
Family	_____	_____	_____	_____
Home-Related	_____	_____	_____	_____
Insurance	_____	_____	_____	_____
Savings and Investments	_____	_____	_____	_____
Taxes	_____	_____	_____	_____
Utilities	_____	_____	_____	_____
Other	_____	_____	_____	_____
Total Fixed Expenses	$_____	$_____	$_____	$_____

Flexible Expenses

	Budget	Actual	YTD Budget	YTD Actual
Children	$_____	$_____	$_____	$_____
Clothing	_____	_____	_____	_____
Contributions and Dues	_____	_____	_____	_____
Education	_____	_____	_____	_____
Equipment and Vehicles	_____	_____	_____	_____
Financial and Professional Services	_____	_____	_____	_____
Food	_____	_____	_____	_____
Home Maintenance	_____	_____	_____	_____
Medical Care	_____	_____	_____	_____
Miscellaneous	_____	_____	_____	_____
Recreation and Entertainment	_____	_____	_____	_____
Savings and Investments	_____	_____	_____	_____
Travel and Vacations	_____	_____	_____	_____
Other	_____	_____	_____	_____
Total Flexible Expenses	$_____	$_____	$_____	$_____
TOTAL EXPENSES	$_____	$_____	$_____	$_____
TOTAL INCOME LESS TOTAL EXPENSES	$_____	$_____	$_____	$_____

Figure 1.2   Retirement Expenses Worksheet

		Example	Your Situation
1.	Present Gross Annual Income	$50,000	$ 122000
2.	Present Annual Savings	$ 5,000	$ 5000
3.	Current Spending (Subtract item 2 from item 1.)	$45,000	$ 117000 .7
4.	Retirement Spending Level (between 60% and 80%, depending on your assumptions of lifestyle)	70%	70 %
5.	Annual Cost of Living (in present dollars) If You Retired Now (Multiply item 4 by item 3.)	$31,500	$ 81900.0 3
6.	4.5% Inflation Factor (from table below)	2.4	3.0
7.	Estimated Annual Cost of Living (in future dollars) at Retirement (Multiply item 6 by item 5.)	$75,600	$245700

Years until Retirement	Inflation Factor
40	5.8
35	4.7
30	3.7
25	3.0
20	2.4
15	1.9
10	1.6
5	1.2

For example, if your living expenses are $25,000 today and inflation is 4 percent, in 10 years, you'd need $37,000; in 15 years, $45,000; and in 20 years, more than $56,000 to pay those bills. If, however, inflation jumped to 8 percent, that $25,000 would have to be $54,000 in 10 years, more than $79,000 in 15 years, and more than $116,000 in 20 years (see Figure 1.3). You get the picture. Inflation could be your biggest enemy.

Figure 1.3   Impact of Inflation

Cost of Living Based on 4% Inflation				Cost of Living Based on 8% Inflation			
Today	*10 Years*	*15 Years*	*20 Years*	*Today*	*10 Years*	*15 Years*	*20 Years*
$25,000	$37,000	$45,000	$56,900	$25,000	$54,000	$79,250	$116,500

WHERE WILL THE MONEY COME FROM?

If you want to take a page from current retirees' playbook, consider the 2001 Retirement Confidence Survey published by the Employee Benefit Research Institute, the American Savings Education Council, and Mathew Greenwald & Associates. How are current retirees footing the bill for their retirement adventure? The largest sources of income are:

Social Security	42%
Employer-sponsored plans	23%
Personal savings	21%
Other government income	5%
Sale of home or business	3%
Employment	1%

Almost half of all retirees—47 percent—report that their current household income after retirement (including Social Security, money provided through an employer, money drawn from savings, etc.) is lower than it was just before they retired; 20 percent say it is higher; and about 31 percent say it is the same.

Back to your circumstances. With a general idea of how much money you will need each year in retirement, examine your potential sources of income. The three most likely sources are (1) Social Security, (2) your employer's pension plan and 401(k)s, and (3) personal retirement investment accounts, such as IRAs or other personal savings. The amount of assets you build up in these types of accounts depends on how much you can contribute and your investment choices. You can see now why it's essential to estimate how much you will accumulate based on your expected future contributions and your expected future rates of return from various investments. You'll be able to determine which types of investments are best suited for you when you match those numbers with your estimates for how much you will need for a comfortable retirement.

The Social Security Administration estimates your benefits in current dollars, based on your earnings and years of service. Your company's employee benefits department can tell you in today's dollars what you should expect to receive from your pension, based on your current age and salary level. Adjust both the pension and Social Security figures by the same 4.5 percent inflation rate used in the Retirement Expenses Worksheet (Figure 1.2). To calculate the amount of savings and investments you will need to make up the difference, subtract the adjusted pension and Social Security amounts from your projected annual living expenses.

Finally, to estimate the amount of capital you must amass to generate that level of annual investment income, assuming a 5 percent rate of return, multiply the number by 20. (For example, you need $20,000 in capital to produce $1,000 in interest if the capital earns 5 percent annually.) If you want to assume a rate of return higher than 5 percent, multiply by a smaller number. For example, multiply by 10 if you want to assume a 10 percent average annual return (because $10,000 will produce $1,000 in interest at 10 percent).

Using the assumptions in the Retirement Expenses Worksheet, you would therefore need to amass $312,000 over the next 20 years until retirement if you want to maintain a lifestyle similar to your current lifestyle (see the Capital Accumulation Worksheet in Figure 1.4).

Of course, many factors can change the capital you have to accumulate. If your pension or Social Security benefit doesn't rise as fast as inflation, for example, you will require more in private savings. However, if you earn a higher return on your investments, you can save less.

The next step is to figure out how much money you must save each year before retirement to accumulate the needed capital. The amount of money calculated in item 8 in the Capital Accumulation Worksheet (Figure 1.4) is not all the money you need to fund your retirement. It is the amount needed to fund your first year of retirement. To keep pace with inflation, you must increase your savings by at least 5 percent a year until you reach retirement age. The Annual Savings Worksheet (Figure 1.5) will help you determine how much money you must save each year to meet this goal. The sample

---

Figure 1.4   Capital Accumulation Worksheet

		Example	Your Situation
1.	Estimated Annual Cost of Living (in future dollars) at Retirement (item 7 from Retirement Expenses Worksheet)	$ 75,600	$245,700
2.	Annual Pension Income	10,000	_____
3.	Inflation-Adjusted Pension Income (Multiply item 2 by appropriate inflation factor in Figure 1.2.)	24,000	_____
4.	Annual Social Security Benefit	15,000	_____
5.	Inflation-Adjusted Social Security Benefit (Multiply item 4 by appropriate inflation factor.)	36,000	_____
6.	Inflation-Adjusted Pension and Social Security Income (Add items 3 and 5.)	60,000	_____
7.	Amount by which Expenses Exceed Pension and Social Security Income (Subtract item 6 from item 1.)	15,600	_____
8.	Needed Capital (Multiply item 7 by 20.)	$312,000	$_____

figures assume an after-tax rate of return of 7.5 percent on all investments beginning 20 years before retirement.

After running your numbers through the three worksheets (Figures 1.3, 1.4, and 1.5), you should have a sense of how much money you will need to save and invest each year to meet your retirement savings goal. If you would like to apply different rates of return and inflation rates or change other factors, check out software on the market that is designed to help you calculate how much you need to save for retirement. Some personal finance programs, such as Quicken and Microsoft Money, also have retirement planning sections. You can also find tools for retirement planning on such Web sites as Fidelity Investments <www.fidelity.com>, MSN MoneyCentral <www.moneycentral.com>, or the Mutual Fund Education Alliance <www.mfea.com>.

Figure 1.5   Annual Savings Worksheet

		Example	Your Situation
1.	Capital Needed to Fund Retirement (item 8 from Capital Accumulation Worksheet)	$312,000	$_____
2.	Current Investment Assets (value of stocks, bonds, mutual funds, etc.)	$ 30,000	$_____
3.	7.5% Appreciation Factor (from table below)	4.2	_____
4.	Appreciation of Your Investment Assets until Retirement (Multiply item 2 by item 3.)	$126,000	$_____
5.	Other Assets Required by Retirement Age (Subtract item 4 from item 1.)	$186,000	$_____
6.	Savings Factor for Years until Retirement (from table below)	.0231	_____
7.	Savings Needed over the Next Year (Multiply item 5 by item 6.)	$ 4,296	$_____

Years until Retirement	7.5% Appreciation Factor
40	18.0
35	12.6
30	8.8
25	6.1
20	4.2
15	3.0
10	2.1
5	1.4

Years until Retirement	Savings Factor
40	.0044
35	.0065
30	.0097
25	.0147
20	.0231
15	.0383
10	.0707
5	.1722

WHAT IF YOU COME UP SHORT?

What if the numbers are a little daunting, and you don't see how you'll be able to reach your goals?

First, see where you can do more today. You did a monthly budget—where's the fluff, the waste, and where can you cut back? Making only a few adjustments, such as brown-bag lunches, energy proofing your home and appliances to save on utility bills, taking fewer or less exotic vacations, limiting the number of times per week you eat out, and the like, can free up more money you can sock away in your employer-sponsored retirement plan or savings outside of work. For instance, say you're 40 and salt away $50 a week. By the time you're 65, your kitty could exceed $206,000, assuming an 8 percent average annual return. What you want to do is max out on tax-deferred accounts. Ideally, you should be striving to save 15 to 20 percent of your gross income.

How else can you play catch-up? Reduce your debt. Vow to pay off those high-interest credit cards. Contact an organization like the Debt Relief Clearinghouse at 800-779-4499 or <www.debtreliefonline.com> to help you consolidate your debt at a much lower interest rate and get out of debt in 2 to 4 years instead of 20 or more. That money going down the drain could go a long way toward funding your retirement.

Make saving easy on yourself. Systematically set aside money every month. Have money deducted from your paycheck or bank account. What you don't see you can't spend foolishly. Then, too, you'll benefit from *dollar cost averaging,* a systematic way of putting away money regularly into stocks or mutual funds regardless of the investment's current price. With dollar cost averaging, you most often wind up buying more shares at low prices than at high prices. It's also a lot easier than trying to determine when a stock has hit its low or high point. See Figures 1.6 and 1.7.

> *Hot Tip: Dollar cost averaging is a system of investing a regular amount of money on a set schedule regardless of the price of the investment at the time. Dollar cost averaging usually results in your buying more shares at low prices than at high prices.*

Find out if your employer's plan permits you to also make contributions on an after-tax basis. If so, it may make sense to take advantage of that opportunity. Though you don't reduce your current taxable income, you still get the benefit of those earnings growing tax deferred, which means they will accumulate faster than earnings in fully taxable investment accounts.

Move on. How much house do you need? If your home has appreciated in value, consider whether you want to sell it and buy a cheaper one. With tax law

Figure 1.6   Investing $10,000 All at the Same Time

Month	Amount Invested	Share Price	Shares Purchased	Cumulative Shares	Cumulative Market Value
January	$10,000	$50	200	200	$10,000
February	0	45	0	200	9,000
March	0	40	0	200	8,000
April	0	35	0	200	7,000
May	0	30	0	200	6,000
June	0	25	0	200	5,000
July	0	30	0	200	6,000
August	0	35	0	200	7,000
September	0	40	0	200	8,000
October	0	45	0	200	9,000
November	0	50	0	200	10,000
Total	$10,000	$50*	200	200	$10,000

*Average price

Figure 1.7   Investing $10,000 in a Dollar Cost Averaging Strategy

Month	Amount Invested	Share Price	Shares Purchased	Cumulative Shares	Cumulative Market Value
January	$ 1,000	$50	20	20	$ 1,000
February	1,000	45	22.2	42.2	1,899
March	1,000	40	25	67.2	2,688
April	1,000	35	28.5	95.7	3,350
May	1,000	30	33.3	129	3,870
June	1,000	25	40	169	4,225
July	1,000	30	33.3	202.3	6,069
August	1,000	35	28.5	230.8	8,078
September	1,000	40	25	255.8	10,232
October	1,000	45	22.2	278	12,510
November	0	50	0	278	13,900
Total	$10,000	$37.5*	278	278	$13,900

*Average price

changes, you won't have to worry about capital gains on the first $500,000 in profit if you're a married couple filing jointly and $250,000 if you're single. And with interest rates the lowest in years, look into refinancing. You may even want to refinance into an automatic rate cut (ARC) loan, where the rate falls when rates drop but remains unchanged when rates rise. You can find out more about ARC loans at 888-ARCLOAN or <www.arcloan.com>. Through refinancing, you may be able to significantly reduce your monthly payments. Plug the savings into your retirement accounts. Also consider a *reverse mortgage.*

Hot Tip: Reverse mortgages offer a way to tap some of the equity in your home to provide additional retirement income.

Ask yourself tough questions. First, are you willing to consider delaying retirement to give yourself more time to save or to accumulate more pension benefits? The longer you wait to tap Social Security, the better. Proportionally, you'll receive more. Second, is working part-time for a while during retirement an option you could live with? You'll benefit on a couple of fronts; not only will it reduce the amount you have to save before you retire, but income from a job lowers the amount you must withdraw from your retirement stash, thus helping to decrease the possibility that you'll run out of money. With recent changes in the laws, you no longer have to worry about being penalized by a reduction in your Social Security benefits. Third, are you or your spouse up for taking on a second job with an eye toward using that money specifically to invest for retirement?

You have a lot of options. What's important is to get on and stay on track. If you're like most people, you have multiple financial goals. It's not as if the only thing you have to worry about is retirement. You may be contributing to your children's college education, trying to save for a second home, or financially supporting your parents. Even though these are all noble goals, they should not be considered your first order of business—that honor should go to preparing for retirement. Whether you've got a good head start or are playing catch-up, keep your eye on the retirement prize.

RESOURCES

Books, Booklets, and Pamphlets

Baby Boomer Retirement: 65 Ways to Protect Your Future, by Don Silver (Adams Media Corp., 57 Littlefield St., Avon, MA 02322; 508-427-7100; 800-872-5627; www.adamsmedia.com). Suggests five steps every baby boomer should be doing right now.

Charles Schwab Smart Retirement Guide (101 Montgomery St., San Francisco, CA 94104; 800-225-8570; www.schwab.com). Prepares you to answer such questions as how much income you'll need to retire and whether your current retirement portfolio will cover your expenses.

Reverse Mortgages

Home is more than where the heart is. It can also be a source of retirement income. For households with net assets of $100,000 to $250,000, the value of their homes represents 43 percent of their wealth, according to a recent study from the Consumer Federation of America.

Tapping that gold mine is an option. If you own your home free and clear, consider a reverse mortgage. Single-family, one-unit dwellings are eligible properties for any type of reverse mortgage. However, you'll need to inquire whether two-, three-, or four-unit, owner-occupied dwellings—condominiums, manufactured homes, and other types of dwellings—can be used for a reverse mortgage. Instead of borrowing against your equity and paying interest, you contract with a bank to convert some of your home equity to cash while you retain ownership. These are called reverse mortgages because they are the opposite of traditional mortgages—the bank pays you. You can use the money for anything you want, though it is prudent to use it for such living expenses as taxes, insurance, heat, or food.

With a reverse mortgage you can take your proceeds in a lump sum, in monthly checks, through a line of credit you can tap into whenever you want, or possibly a combination of the three options. The amount you can borrow depends on your age (you must be 62 or older), the value of the equity in your home, and the interest rate charged by the lender. Some loans charge a fixed rate of interest, whereas others charge a variable rate. When obtaining a reverse mortgage, you normally must pay closing costs and insurance premiums and sometimes a monthly service fee. The reverse mortgage comes due when you die, sell the home, or move permanently. At that point, you or your heirs must pay off the loan, or the bank will take title to your home.

Reverse mortgages increase the amount of interest you owe every month. Over time, the interest owed can become considerable and your equity stake can shrink dramatically. However, a reverse mortgage is a good way to use the equity in your home if you don't mind leaving your heirs a far smaller estate when you die.

All payments you receive from a reverse mortgage (technically, they are loan advances) are considered nontaxable income. Therefore, they do not lower your Social Security or Medicare benefits. On the other hand, the interest you pay on reverse mortgages is not tax deductible until you pay off part of your total reverse mortgage debt.

You have a choice of several basic types of reverse mortgages:

Single purpose. These mortgages are generally usable for one specific purpose only, such as making home repairs or paying property taxes, for example. These specialized mortgages are not widely available and usually are not geared to high-income homeowners. Single-purpose reverse mortgages are often offered by state and local government agencies, and payment is typically a single lump sum that is to be used as specified. Because they are for a one-time use, the amount of cash you'll receive is usually much lower than you'll receive with other types of reverse mortgages.

Federally insured home equity conversion mortgages. You need not pay off a Federal Housing Administration (FHA)–insured reverse mortgage as long as you live in your home. You can change your payment options from monthly advances to a line of credit at any time at little or no cost, and you can use the proceeds for any purpose. Generally, these loans provide greater total cash advances than other types of reverse mortgages and offer a wider choice of cash advance options. The FHA guarantees your payments even if the lender defaults.

Proprietary. You can use proprietary reverse mortgages for any purpose. These loans are more expensive than other types of reverse mortgages and are offered by banks, private lenders, and mortgage companies. They are usually guaranteed by the private companies that develop them.

Choosing a reverse mortgage that's best for you requires further investigation, but the choice depends primarily on your particular situation, what types of loans are available to you, and your personal preferences. To help you sort out your options, get a copy of the booklet *Home Made Money: A Consumer's Guide to Reverse Mortgages* published by the American Association of Retired Persons (AARP) (601 E St., N.W., Washington, DC 20049; 800-209-8085) for reverse mortgage information. The AARP also has a considerable amount of information on its Web site about reverse mortgages, including calculators and other useful tools at <www.aarp.org/revmort>. Another good resource for more detailed information on how reverse mortgages work and which institutions currently grant them is the National Center for Home Equity Conversion (360 N. Robert, Suite 403, St. Paul, MN 55101; 651-222-6775; www.reverse.org).

Don't Die Broke: How to Turn Your Retirement Savings into Lasting Income, by Margaret A. Malaspina (Bloomberg Press, 400 College Rd., Princeton, NJ 08542; P.O. Box 888, Princeton, NJ 08542; 609-279-3000, www.bloomberg.com). Offers suggestions for creating a lasting retirement income, lowering potential taxes, and building an estate that can be passed along.

Ernst & Young's Retirement Planning Guide: Take Care of Your Finances Now . . . and They'll Take Care of You Later, by Robert J. Garner and William J. Arnone (John Wiley & Sons, 1 Wiley Dr., Somerset, NJ 08875; 212-850-6000; 800-225-5945; www.wiley.com). Highlights the key financial issues you need to consider during your preretirement and retirement years.

Feathering Your Nest: The Retirement Planner, by Lisa Berger (Workman Publishing Co., 708 Broadway, New York, NY 10003; 212-254-5900; 800-722-7202; www.workman.com). Explains how to map out your retirement needs, invest prudently, take care of estates and wills, minimize taxes in retirement, and live a rewarding lifestyle when retired.

Home Made Money: A Consumer's Guide to Reverse Mortgages, published by the American Association of Retired Persons (601 E St., N.W., Washington, DC 20049; 800-424-3410; www.aarp.org). AARP also has information on its Web site about reverse mortgages, including calculators and other useful tools, at <www.aarp.org/revmort>.

How to Plan for a Secure Retirement, by Barry Dickman and Trudy Lieberman (Consumer Reports Books, P.O. Box 10637, Des Moines, IA 50336; 800-500-9760). Helps you estimate your income and expenses in retirement; also covers health care plans, housing options, and estate planning.

How to Retire Young and Rich, by Joseph Coyle (Warner Books, 1271 Avenue of the Americas, New York, NY 10020; 212-522-7200; www.twbookmark.com). Provides basics on planning for and enjoying retirement.

Last Chance Financial Planning Guide: It's Not Too Late to Plan for Your Retirement If You Start Now, by Anthony Spare and Paul Ciotti (Prima Publications, 1815 N. Fort Myer Dr., Suite 1020, Arlington, VA 22209; 703-528-7701; www.primacentral.org). For the over-40 generation without a substantive retirement program, explains how to determine retirement income needs and build portfolios quickly to make up for lost time.

Savings Fitness: A Guide to Your Money and Your Financial Future. An informative booklet offered by the U.S. Department of Labor <www.dol.gov/dol/pwba> and the Certified Financial Planner Board of Standards <www.cfp-board.org>. Call 800-998-7542 or 866-275-7922 for the free publication. The Board of Standards also offers a financial planning resource kit; call 888-237-6275 for more information.

Scudder Investments (2 International Pl., Boston, MA 02110-4103; 800-322-2282; www.aarp.scudder.com). Offers many useful booklets, and the Web site has worksheets and other tools to help you plan for retirement.

Set for Life: Financial Peace for People over 50, by Bambi Holzer (John Wiley & Sons, 1 Wiley Dr., Somerset, NJ 08875-1272; 212-850-6000; 800-225-5945; www.wiley.com). Provides straightforward, practical advice on financial planning and how to develop tomorrow's income by setting realistic financial goals today.

Take Charge!: A Woman's Guide to a Secure Retirement, by Edie Milligan (Alpha Books/Pearson Education, 201 W. 103rd St., Indianapolis, IN 46290; 800-428-5331). Seeks to provide tools to demystify retirement planning for women and show them how to find the way to a financially secure future.

The New Working Woman's Guide to Retirement Planning: Saving and Investing Now for a Secure Future, by Martha Priddy Patterson (University of Pennsylvania Press, 4200 Pine St., Philadelphia, PA 19104-4011; 215-898-6261; www.upenn.edu). Explains why women's retirement needs are different from those of men. Advises women on how to plan for retirement with an emphasis on financial planning.

Software

Harvest-Time (The Advisors Edge, 2814 W. 15th St., Suite 1, P.O. Box 15638, Panama City, FL 32406; 800-397-1456; www.theadvisorsedge.com). Helps you calculate how much you must save to enjoy a comfortable retirement.

Trade Associations

American Savings Education Council (2121 K St., N.W., Suite 600, Washington, DC 20037; 202-775-9130; www.asec.org). Undertakes initiatives to raise public awareness about what is needed to ensure long-term personal financial independence.

National Center for Home Equity Conversion (360 N. Robert, Suite 403, St. Paul, MN 55101; 651-222-6775; www.reverse.org). Provides valuable information about reverse mortgages.

Web Sites

Deloitte & Touche, *Principles of Retirement Planning/Retirement Planning Process* <www.dtonline.com/prptoc/PRPPLAN.htm>. Helps with identifying personal goals, gathering data, evaluating goals, and identifying obstacles along with developing strategies for goal achievement, among other topics.

Fidelity Investments <www.fidelity.com>. Provides valuable information to aid you in retirement planning.

MSN MoneyCentral <www.moneycentral.com>. Provides a life expectancy calculator in the planning/retirement section.

Mutual Fund Education Alliance <www.mfea.com>. In the retirement section, lets you calculate your annual living expenses, analyze how much you may receive from Social Security and the impact of pensions, calculate the value of current investments, and determine annual investment requirements.

Northwestern Mutual <www.northwesternmutual.com>. Click on the calculator section and pull up the Longevity Game, an interactive lifestyle and health awareness quiz that will give you a general idea of how long you may live past retirement.

Oppenheimer Funds <www.oppenheimerfunds.com>. The retirement planning channel on the home page contains the Retirement Resource Center, which provides practical advice about retirement, including tools for figuring out how much you will need, and information about individual retirement accounts, estate planning, and more.

Quicken.com <www.quicken.com/retirement>. Includes advice and information on 401(k) plans, IRAs, and other tax-deferred plans; offers advice on investments and links to financial planners all over the country.

CHAPTER 2

Social Security

An important aspect of the retirement income calculation is the amount that you will receive from Social Security. Don't believe the prophecies that the Social Security system will go broke and people now paying into it will receive no benefits. Millions of voters, including those receiving Social Security and those paying Social Security taxes, will make sure that politicians don't scrap the system. Social Security is still a sacred cow of sorts. The trouble is that benefit checks depend on money flowing in. The ratio of workers to retirees continues to shrink as baby boomers head into retirement. In the 1930s, when it was designed, the purpose of Social Security was to be a safety net, but not the only net. Keep that in mind. Be assured, too, that Social Security rules will change in coming years. Already, as of January 1, 2001, workers who have reached full retirement age (age 65 in 2001) are allowed to earn unlimited income without their benefits being reduced. This, of course, is good news for you. Following are just a few ways in which Social Security will be or may be altered:

- *A means test may allocate a smaller benefit to higher-income people.*
- *You will be penalized for retiring earlier than age 65.* Even under today's law, you receive only 80 percent of your full Social Security benefit amount if you retire at age 62. Under current rules, starting in the year 2000, this percentage will drop annually until it reaches 70 percent by the year 2022. It is possible that the percentage will drop even more than that as Congress seeks ways to trim Social Security spending.

- *The minimum age for receiving full Social Security benefits will rise gradually from age 65 to 67 starting in the year 2003.* This affects people born in 1938 and later. For example, if you were born in 1940, your minimum retirement age will be 65½. If you were born in 1950, your minimum retirement age will be 66. If you were born in 1960 or later, you will be eligible for full retirement benefits at age 67. In the future, the minimum age will probably be extended even further.

- *You will be encouraged to retire later.* A special credit is given to those who delay retirement beyond their full retirement age. This credit, which is a percentage added to your Social Security benefit amount, varies depending on your date of birth. The rate increases until it reaches 8 percent per year for people turning 65 in 2008 or later. This incentive might be sweetened even more over time.

- *You may pay higher taxes on Social Security benefits.* You must pay tax on as much as 85 percent of your benefits if your modified adjusted growth income (which includes tax-exempt municipal bond interest) plus one-half of your Social Security benefit exceeds $44,000 for married couples filing jointly or $34,000 for all other filers except married couples filing separately. Married couples filing separately are also subject to the 85 percent threshold when modified adjusted gross income is greater than $0.

- *The percentage of your retirement pay that Social Security is designed to replace will likely be reduced from the current 24 percent to 20 percent or less.*

- *Social Security payroll taxes will increase from the current 7.65 percent for employees to as much as 15 to 20 percent.* How high these tax rates can be pushed without causing a taxpayer revolt remains uncertain.

All of these changes mean that Social Security will probably make up an increasingly smaller percentage of your retirement income in the years ahead.

To be eligible to receive Social Security, you must work and pay taxes into the system. As you work, you can earn Social Security credits, up to four quarters of credit per year. In 2002, you receive one quarter of credit for each $870 you earn during the year; the dollar amount is indexed to the national average wage annually. Most people need 40 credits, or ten years of work, to qualify for Social Security. These extra credits do not increase the size of your benefit. Only the amount of income that you earn increases your check.

If you would like a current estimate of your Social Security benefit amount based on your pay level, years of work, and age of retirement, write or call the Social Security Administration (SSA) (6401 Security Blvd., Randalstown, MD 21235; 800-772-1213; www.ssa.gov).

Ask the SSA to send you its *Request for Earnings and Benefit Estimate Statement,* also known as Form SSA-7004-SM. A copy of the form appears in Figure 2.1. Once you complete and mail back the form, you will receive your payment history and a table of the benefits you may expect. Also know that the statement is automatically mailed out annually to anyone who is over 25 and not receiving Social Security benefits. The form usually arrives approximately three months before the recipient's birthday. You can also request this form by visiting Social Security's Web site at <www.ssa.gov/mystatement>. While you're on the site, click on Benefit Planners to get more help in planning for a comfortable retirement. You'll be able to estimate your benefits based on different assumptions about your future earnings or when you plan to stop working. You'll also learn more about disability and survivors benefits and what they could mean to you and your family.

Hot Tip: *Though you can speak to a service representative from 7 AM to 7 PM on business days, the lines are busiest early in the week and early in the month. If you can wait, call at other times and be sure to have your Social Security number handy if you don't know it by heart.*

Look over the Social Security statement that is mailed to you annually. You may find that your employer has not reported all your earnings or that the Social Security Administration has not credited your wages to the correct Social Security number. If you find a discrepancy, point it out to the administration and back up your claim with past W-2 forms from your employer. You want to receive every penny you deserve when you retire.

The table in Figure 2.2 shows what you and your spouse might expect to collect from Social Security if you both retire at full retirement age and have the same steady lifetime earnings. The calculations assume that you and your spouse are the same age. Your spouse may qualify for a greater or lesser retirement benefit based on his or her work record.

WHEN TO TAP SOCIAL SECURITY

Just as deciding when to retire is a major decision, so is deciding when to tap your Social Security benefits.

You may start receiving benefits as early as age 62. However, if you start your benefits early, they are reduced five-ninths of 1 percent for each month before your "full" retirement age. For example, if your full retirement age is 65 and you sign up for Social Security when you're 64, you will receive 93 percent of your full benefit. At age 62, you would get 80 percent. Note, however, that the reduction will be greater in future years as the full retirement age increases. Beginning in the year 2003, the age at which full benefits are

Figure 2.1   Request for Earnings and Benefit Estimate Statement

SOCIAL SECURITY ADMINISTRATION

Request for Earnings and Benefit Estimate Statement

Thank you for requesting this statement.

After you complete and return this form, we will--within 4 to 6 weeks--send you:

- a record of your earnings history and an estimate of how much you have paid in Social Security taxes, and
- estimates of benefits you (and your family) may be eligible for now and in the future.

We're pleased to furnish you with this information and we hope you'll find it useful in planning your financial future.

Social Security is more than just a program for retired people. It helps people of all ages in many ways. Whether you're young or old, male or female, single or with a family--Social Security can help you when you need it most. It can help support your family in the event of your death and pay you benefits if you become severly disabled.

If you have questions about Social Security or this form, please call our toll-free number, 1-800-772-1213.

Kenneth A. Apfel

Kenneth S. Apfel
Commissioner of Social Security

Mailing Address

Social Security Administration
Wilkes Barre Data Operations Center
PO Box 7004
Wilkes Barre PA 18767-7004

About The Privacy Act

Social Security is allowed to collect the facts on this form under Section 205 of the Social Security Act. We need them to quickly identify your record and prepare the earnings statement you asked us for. Giving us these facts is voluntary. However, without them we may not be able to give you an earnings and benefit estimate statement. Neither the Social Security Administration nor its contractor will use the information for any other purpose.

Paperwork Reduction Act Notice and Time It Takes Statement

The Paperwork Reduction Act of 1995 requires us to notify you that this information collection is in accordance with the clearance requirements of section 3507 of the Paperwork Reduction Act of 1995. We may not conduct or sponsor, and you are not required to respond to, a collection of information unless it displays a valid OMB control number. We estimate that it will take you about 5 minutes to complete this form. This includes the time it will take to read the instructions, gather the necessary facts and fill out the form.

Figure 2.1 (continued)

Form Approved
OMB No. 0960-0466

SP

Request for Earnings and Benefit Estimate Statement

☐ Please check this box if you want to get your statement in Spanish instead of English.

Please print or type your answers. When you have completed the form, fold it and mail it to us. (If you prefer to send your request using the Internet, contact us at http://www.ssa.gov)

1. Name shown on your Social Security card:

_____ _____
First Name   Middle Initial

_____
Last Name Only

2. Your Social Security number as shown on your card:

☐☐☐ – ☐☐ – ☐☐☐☐

3. Your date of birth (Mo.-Day-Yr.)

☐☐ – ☐☐ – ☐☐☐☐

4. Other Social Security numbers you have used:

☐☐☐ – ☐☐ – ☐☐☐☐
☐☐☐ – ☐☐ – ☐☐☐☐

5. Your sex: ☐ Male   ☐ Female

For items 6 and 8 show only earnings covered by Social Security. Do NOT include wages from State, local or Federal Government employment that are NOT covered for Social Security or that are covered ONLY by Medicare.

6. Show your actual earnings (wages and/or net self-employment income) for last year and your estimated earnings for this year.

A. Last year's actual earnings: *(Dollars Only)*

$ ☐☐☐,☐☐☐.☐0

B. This year's estimated earnings: *(Dollars Only)*

$ ☐☐☐,☐☐☐.☐0

7. Show the age at which you plan to stop working.

☐☐ *(Show only one age)*

8. Below, show the average yearly amount (not your total future lifetime earnings) that you think you will earn between now and when you plan to stop working. Include performance or scheduled pay increases or bonuses, but not cost-of-living increases.

If you expect to earn significantly more or less in the future due to promotions, job changes, part-time work, or an absence from the work force, enter the amount that most closely reflects your future average yearly earnings.

If you don't expect any significant changes, show the same amount you are earning now (the amount in 6B).

Future average yearly earnings: *(Dollars Only)*

$ ☐☐☐,☐☐☐.☐0

---

9. Do you want us to send the statement:
- To you? Enter your name and mailing address.
- To someone else (your accountant, pension plan, etc.)? Enter your name with "c/o" and the name and address of that person or organization.

_____
Name

_____
Street Address (Include Apt. No., P.O. Box, or Rural Route)

_____
City   State   Zip Code

Notice:
I am asking for information about my own Social Security record or the record of a person I am authorized to represent. I understand that if I deliberately request information under false pretenses, I may be guilty of a Federal crime and could be fined and/or imprisoned. I authorize you to use a contractor to send the statement of earnings and benefit estimates to the person named in item 9.

▲ **Please sign your name (Do Not Print)**

_____
Date   (Area Code) Daytime Telephone No.

Form SSA-7004-SM Internet (6-98) Destroy prior editions

payable will increase in gradual steps from 65 to 67. The following table (Figure 2.3) lists the steps.

There are advantages and disadvantages to taking your benefit before your full retirement age. The downside is that your benefits are permanently reduced. The upside is that you collect benefits for a longer period of time.

Figure 2.2   Approximate Monthly Benefits If You Retire at Full Retirement Age and Had Steady Lifetime Earnings

Your Age in 2002	Your Family	$20,000	$30,000	$40,000	$50,000	$60,000	$70,000	$84,900 or more
45	You	$ 876	$1,143	$1,409	$1,574	$1,699	$1,824	$1,977
	You, Spouse	1,314	1,714	2,113	2,361	2,548	2,736	2,965
55	You	876	1,143	1,409	1,574	1,697	1,815	1,925
	You, Spouse	1,314	1,714	2,113	2,361	2,545	2,722	2,887
65	You	820	1,072	1,323	1,453	1,536	1,611	1,660
	You, Spouse	1,230	1,608	1,984	2,179	2,304	2,416	2,490

Note: The accuracy of these estimates depends on your actual earnings which may vary significantly from those shown here.
Source: Social Security: Understanding the Benefits, a booklet by the Social Security Administration.

Figure 2.3   Age to Receive Full Social Security Benefits

Year of Birth	Full Retirement Age
1937 or earlier	65
1938	65 and 2 months
1939	65 and 4 months
1940	65 and 6 months
1941	65 and 8 months
1942	65 and 10 months
1943–54	66
1955	66 and 2 months
1956	66 and 4 months
1957	66 and 6 months
1958	66 and 8 months
1959	66 and 10 months
1960 and later	67

Source: Social Security Administration.

And if you're really strapped for cash, you may have few choices other than turning to Social Security. It's a big decision. Contact Social Security several months before you decide to retire.

Because we can only gaze with a crystal ball without any certainty, base your decision on such factors as your risk tolerance and other likely sources of income. It's not prudent to sell tax-deferred investments to pay for retirement expenses and lose years of tax-deferred growth if you can collect Social Security benefits. By the same token, if you have significant nonretirement assets and can afford to live off this money, your best choice may be to delay tapping your Social Security benefits.

Your choice impacts your spouse. If your spouse will collect payments based on your entitlements, delaying when you receive your benefits leads to a larger survivor's benefit.

If you keep up the "9 to 5" beyond your full retirement age and don't sign up for Social Security until later, you'll come out ahead in two ways. First, your extra income usually will increase your "average" earnings; and the higher your average earnings, the higher your benefit. Second, a special credit is given to those who delay retirement beyond their full retirement age. This credit, which is a percentage added to your Social Security benefit amount, varies depending on your date of birth. For those reaching full retirement in 2001, the rate is 6 percent per year. That rate gradually increases in future years, until it reaches 8 percent per year for people reaching full retirement age in 2008 or later. You no longer earn this special credit after you reach age 70.

What Records Will You Need?

Be ready to prove your eligibility for Social Security benefits. What the Social Security Administration may ask depends on the circumstances of your claim. But here's a partial list of what you can expect to be asked to show:

- Your Social Security number
- Your birth certificate
- Proof of U.S. citizenship or lawful alien status if you were not born in the United States
- Your spouse's birth certificate and Social Security number if he or she is applying for benefits based on your record
- Marriage certificate (if signing up on a spouse's record)
- Your most recent W-2 form, or your tax return if you're self-employed

Hot Tip: *Social Security benefits are generally paid by direct deposit. Be sure to have your checkbook or account statement with you when you apply to ensure that your monthly benefit is deposited correctly into your account.*

How to Avoid Unpleasant Tax Surprises

You may be unaware that Uncle Sam can tax your Social Security checks. What determines whether you have to pay tax on your benefits? Whether you owe money depends on whether your income reaches a high enough level. If you file a federal tax return as an individual and your combined income—that is, your and your spouse's adjusted gross income plus nontaxable interest plus one-half of your Social Security benefits—is between $25,000 and $34,000, you may have to pay taxes on 50 percent of your Social Security benefits. If your combined income is above $34,000, up to 85 percent of your Social Security benefits is subject to income tax. If you file a joint return, you may have to pay taxes on 50 percent of your benefits if you and your spouse have a combined income that is between $32,000 and $44,000. If your combined income is more than $44,000, up to 85 percent is subject to taxes. If you're married but file a separate return, you probably will pay taxes on your benefits. Although you're not required to have federal taxes withheld, you may find it easier to do so than making quarterly estimated tax payments.

To have federal taxes withheld, you can get a W-4V form from the IRS by calling the toll-free number (800-829-3676) or by visiting <www.ssa.gov>. Once you complete the form, you can return it to your local Social Security office in person or by mail. You can find the Social Security office nearest you via the Web or by calling 800-772-1213.

Another way to beat the tax man is to be savvy about how you tap your retirement accounts. Those mandatory annual withdrawals from traditional individual retirement accounts (IRAs) can cost you come tax time. If your withdrawals are big enough you'll boost your modified adjusted gross income and land squarely in a higher federal tax bracket. So be mindful of this when taking money from your retirement accounts.

Supplemental Security Income (SSI)

For those with extremely low incomes and few assets, an additional source of retirement funds is Supplemental Security Income (SSI). The SSI program is run by the Social Security Administration, though benefits are paid from the U.S. Treasury, not the Social Security Trust Fund. To qualify for SSI, you must be a U.S. citizen living in the United States, and you must be 65 years or older, blind, or disabled. The maximum income you can receive from private or government pensions or earn from a job differs by state. When totaling assets, the Social Security Administration does not include the value of your home, your car, or many of your personal belongings. Instead, it focuses on assets in bank and brokerage accounts and cash.

If you qualify for SSI, your benefit depends on how much you earn and where you live. However, the basic national benefit, which changes over time, is $545 a month for one person and $780 a month for a couple. Many states augment this basic benefit as well. SSI is also available for nonretired people, including children with disabilities. To learn more about the rules for qualification and benefit levels in your state, contact a local Social Security office or call the Social Security Administration (800-772-1213; www.ssa.gov).

Here's a closer look at what Social Security considers when determining whether you are disabled:

1. **Are you working?**
   If you are and your earnings average more than $780 a month, you generally cannot be considered disabled.
2. **Is your condition "severe"?**
   Your condition must interfere with basic work-related activities for your claim to be considered. If it does not, Social Security will find that you are not disabled.
3. **Is your condition found in the list of disabling impairments?**
   Social Security maintains a list of impairments for each of the major body systems that are so severe they automatically mean you are disabled. If your condition is not on the list, Social Security will have to decide if it is of equal severity to an impairment on the list.
4. **Can you do the work you did previously?**
   If your condition is severe, but not at the same or equal level of severity as an impairment on the list, then Social Security will determine if it interferes with your ability to do the work you previously did. If it doesn't, your claim will be denied.
5. **Can you do any other type of work?**
   If you cannot do the work you did in the past, Social Security will want to see if you can adjust to other work. It'll take into account your medical condition, age, past work experience, and any transferrable skills you may have. If you cannot adjust to other work, your claim will be approved. If you can adjust, your claim will be denied.

DISABILITY BENEFITS

In addition to regular Social Security retirement benefits, you can collect disability benefits if you become disabled. The government defines disability as a physical or mental impairment that is expected to keep you from doing substantial work (earning $780 or more a month) for at least a year. You can receive disability benefits until age 65, after which they automatically convert to retirement benefits, but the amount remains the same. Figure 2.4 notes the monthly disability benefit you might receive from Social Security based on your work and earnings history.

Certain members of your family may qualify for benefits on your record; for example, your spouse who is 62 or older, or any age if he or she is caring for a child of yours who is younger than 16 or disabled and also receiving checks. Also, your disabled widow or widower age 50 to 60 may qualify. However, the disability must have started before your death or within seven years after your death. (If your widow or widower caring for your children receives Social Security checks, she or he is eligible if she or he becomes disabled before those payments end or within seven years after they end).

Figure 2.4   Approximate Monthly Benefits If You Become Disabled in 2002 and Had Steady Lifetime Earnings

Your Age in 2002	Your Family	$20,000	$30,000	$40,000	$50,000	$60,000	$70,000	$84,900 or more
25	You	$ 876	$1,143	$1,409	$1,574	$1,699	$1,824	$1,921
	You, Spouse and Child	1,314	1,714	2,114	2,361	2,549	2,737	2,882
35	You	876	1,143	1,409	1,574	1,699	1,824	1,932
	You, Spouse and Child	1,314	1,714	2,114	2,361	2,549	2,737	2,899
45	You	876	1,143	1,409	1,574	1,699	1,824	1,918
	You, Spouse and Child	1,314	1,714	2,114	2,361	2,549	2,737	2,878
55	You	876	1,143	1,409	1,574	1,684	1,783	1,847
	You, Spouse and Child	1,314	1,714	2,114	2,361	2,527	2,674	2,771
64	You	839	1,095	1,351	1,487	1,572	1,648	1,689
	You, Spouse and Child	1,259	1,643	2,027	2,231	2,359	2,473	2,547

Note: The accuracy of the illustrated amounts depends on your pattern of actual earnings, which may vary significantly from those shown here.

Source: Social Security: Understanding the Benefits, a booklet by the Social Security Administration.

SURVIVORS BENEFITS

Social Security will also provide regular income to your family if you die, no matter how old you are or whether you have accumulated enough work-credit hours. Not everyone is entitled to *survivors benefits,* however. Family members can collect if they are one of the following:

- Widow or widower at least 60 years old
- Widow or widower at least 50 years old who is disabled
- Widow or widower of any age who cares for a child 16 years old or younger or a disabled child receiving Social Security benefits
- Unmarried child younger than age 18
- Unmarried child younger than age 19 who is enrolled in an elementary or a secondary school full-time
- Unmarried child 18 years or older who has a severe disability that started before he or she reached age 22
- Parent who depended on the deceased for at least half of his or her income
- Ex-spouse who is at least 60 years old (or 50 years old and disabled) and was married to the deceased for at least ten years before the divorce
- Ex-spouse of any age if he or she still cares for a child eligible for benefits on the deceased's record

A family's survivors benefits can total between 75 and 100 percent of the basic Social Security retirement benefit, depending on several factors. However, survivors can receive no more than between 150 and 180 percent of the basic monthly total survivors benefit. If the combined benefits from all family members exceed that amount, the total survivors benefit will be reduced proportionately.

The table in Figure 2.5 contains several examples of the benefits your surviving spouse and children might receive, depending on your age, your number of children, and your level of earnings when you die.

Social Security is an important part of your retirement pie. Take it upon yourself to swim through the rules and regulations that apply to the various programs. You want to be sure that you receive all that's due you. In retirement, you can't afford to leave any money on the table.

RESOURCES

Books, Booklets, and Pamphlets

Bankroll Your Future: How to Get the Most from Uncle Sam for Your Retirement Years—Social Security, Medicare, and Much More, by Ellen Hoffman (New-

Figure 2.5   **Approximate Monthly Survivors Benefits for Your Family If You Had Steady Lifetime Earnings and Die in 2002**

Your Age in 2002	Your Family	$20,000	$30,000	$40,000	$50,000	$60,000	$70,000	$84,900 or more
35	Spouse, one child	$1,314	$1,714	$2,114	$2,361	$2,549	$2,737	$2,912
	Spouse, two children	1,461	2,116	2,473	2,756	2,975	3,194	3,398
	One child	657	857	1,057	1,180	1,274	1,368	1,456
	Spouse aged 60	626	817	1,008	1,125	1,215	1,304	1,388
45	Spouse, one child	1,314	1,714	2,114	2,361	2,549	2,737	2,880
	Spouse, two children	1,461	2,116	2,473	2,756	2,975	3,194	3,361
	One child	657	857	1,057	1,180	1,247	1,368	1,440
	Spouse aged 60	626	817	1,008	1,125	1,215	1,304	1,373
55	Spouse, one child	1,314	1,714	2,114	2,361	2,527	2,674	2,771
	Spouse, two children	1,461	2,116	2,473	2,756	2,949	3,121	3,234
	One child	657	857	1,057	1,180	1,263	1,337	1,385
	Spouse aged 60	626	817	1,008	1,125	1,204	1,274	1,321

Note: The accuracy of the illustrated amounts depends on your pattern of actual earnings, which may vary significantly from those shown here.

Source: Social Security: Understanding the Benefits, a booklet by the Social Security Administration.

market Press, 18 E. 48th St., New York, NY 10017; 212-832-3575; 800-233-4830; www.newmarketpress.com). Information about hundreds of federal laws that affect retirement, including Social Security, Medicare, Medicaid, pension plans, and tax aspects of retirement planning.

2001 Mercer Guide to Social Security and Medicare, by Robert Treanor, Robert Myers, and Dale Detlefs (William M. Mercer Inc., 1166 Avenue of the Americas, New York, NY 10036; 212-345-7000; www.mercer.com). Covers such topics as the Senior Citizen's Freedom to Work Act, your rights, knowing when to file, and working while collecting Social Security.

Nolo's Guide to Social Security Disability: Getting & Keeping Your Benefits, by David A. Morton III, M.D. (Nolo Press, 950 Parker St., Berkeley, CA 94710; 510-549-1976; 800-992-NOLO; www.nolo.com). An attempt to demystify the program and an explanation in plain English what Social Security disability is; how to prove a disability; and how age, education, and work experience affect benefits.

The Only Retirement Guide You'll Ever Need, by Kathryn and Ross Petras (Simon & Schuster, 100 Front St., Riverside, NJ 08075; 212-698-7000; 800-223-2348; www.simonsays.com). A comprehensive guide to retirement planning, including sections on investments, insurance, IRAs, Social Security, health care, working in retirement, estate planning, and housing options.

Social Security Benefits Handbook (Social Security Benefits Handbook, 2d ed.), by Stanley A. Tomkiel (Sourcebooks Trade, 1935 Brookdale Rd., Suite 139, Naperville, IL 60563; www.sourcebooks.com). Advice on how to deal with the Social Security Administration, highlighting eligibility requirements, the disability program, Medicare, and more.

Social Security, Medicare & Government Pensions: Get the Most Out of Your Retirement & Medical Benefits, by Joseph Matthews and Dorothy Matthews Berman (Nolo Press, 950 Parker St., Berkeley, CA 94710; 510-549-1976; 800-992-NOLO; www.nolo.com). A guide showing those over age 55 how to maximize benefits and make sure they get what they are entitled to.

The Social Security Statement and Your Retirement, from the American Association of Retired Persons Investment Program's Financial Library (AARP Investment Program from Scudder Investments, 2 International Place, Boston, MA 02110-4103; 800-322-2282; www.aarp.scudder.com). A guide that sorts out the rules for receiving Social Security benefits, with particular emphasis on the impact of early retirement on lifetime Social Security benefits.

Social Security: The Inside Story: An Expert Explains Your Rights and Benefits, by Andrew Landis (Crisp Publications, 1200 Hamilton Ct., Menlo Park, CA 94025; 800-442-7477; www.crisplearning.com). A guide to the Social Security and Medicare systems that covers histories, eligibility requirements, payment computations, claims process, and family, survivor, and disability benefits.

Your Rights over Age 50 (American Bar Association, 541 N. Fairbanks Ct., Chicago, IL 60611-3314; 312-988-5000; www.abanet.org). A pamphlet in question-and-answer format covering such topics as age discrimination in employment, credit, higher education, pensions, Social Security, Medicare, and Medicaid.

Trade Associations and Government Agencies

National Academy of Social Insurance (1776 Massachusetts Ave., N.W., Suite 615, Washington, DC 20036; 202-452-8097; www.nasi.org). A nonprofit, nonpartisian research and education organization made up of the nation's leading experts on Social Security, Medicare, and other insurance programs that sponsors numerous conferences and events on these topics.

National Committee to Preserve Social Security and Medicare (10 G St., N.E., Washington, DC 20002; 202-216-8376; www.ncpssm.org). A grassroots organization devoted to retirement issues that provides in-depth analysis of Capitol Hill action, personal retirement finances, and health care.

National Organization of Social Security Claimants' Representatives (6 Prospect St., Midland Park, NJ 07432; 201-444-1415; 800-431-2804; www.nosscr.org). A group of lawyers who specialize in resolving disability and SSI benefits claims problems with the Social Security Administration and will represent you, usually on a contingency-fee basis, if you have been denied benefits.

National Senior Citizens Law Center (1101 14th St., N.W., Suite 400, Washington, DC 20005; 202-289-6976; www.nsclc.org). A group of practicing lawyers that lobbies for legal services programs on behalf of the elderly and specializes in litigation, research, lobbying, and training lawyers on such issues as age discrimination, guardianship, home care, mandatory retirement, Medicaid, Medicare, nursing homes, pensions, Social Security, and SSI.

Social Security Administration (6401 Security Blvd., Baltimore, MD 21235; 410-965-7700; 800-772-1213; www.ssa.gov). The federal agency that regulates distribution of Social Security benefits to eligible Americans and also administers programs for the aged, the blind, and dependents. For a free copy of the *Social Security Handbook* and any one of over 100 free booklets and pamphlets on Social Security, disability, Medicare, SSI, retirement, and other related subjects, go to the Web site <www.ssa.gov> and download them or write to Public Information Distribution Center (Social Security Administration, P.O. Box 17743, Baltimore, MD 21234, 410-965-0945).

Web Sites

Socialsecurity.com <www.socialsecurity.com>. Provides up-to-date Social Security and retirement information.

SocialSecurityInfo.com <www.socialsecurityinfo.com>. (Denver Tax Software, P.O. Box 5308, Denver, CO 80217-5308; 303-796-7780.) Provides answers to such questions as current wage limits, the different ways reform might come about, and how reforms might affect you. You can download free software that will show you what your personal benefits might be under numerous situations.

The Social Security Network <www.socsec.org>, c/o The Century Foundation, 41 E. 70th St., New York, NY 10021; 212-452-7743. A resource for information, analysis, and expert commentary on the Social Security debate.

CHAPTER 3

Pensions

No matter the amount of Social Security benefits you qualify for, the amount, as a sole source of income, will fall far short in helping you realize your dream retirement. You will need a regular source of pension income to enhance your lifestyle. Pensions come in two forms: (1) one that your employer provides without any contribution from you, and (2) one to which you contribute part of your earnings during your working years either through your employer or through a separate plan, such as an individual retirement account (IRA) or a Keogh account. (More on these in Chapter 4.) In the best of all worlds, you would have both types of pensions.

For now, though, let's look at what your employer can do for you. The idea of an employer providing a retirement plan for its employees started in the United States in 1759 when the Presbyterian Church created a fund to care for the widows and children of ministers. More than a century later, in 1875, American Express formed the first corporate pension plan. Now, hundreds of thousands of companies offer pension plans, and tens of millions of workers are covered. Pension plans have grown to become one of the biggest pools of assets in the United States that are worth trillions of dollars. As such, pension plans are among the largest and most influential investor classes in the country because they own billions of dollars worth of stocks, bonds, real estate, and other assets.

The basic idea behind a traditional benefit pension plan is that the company sets aside a certain amount of money in a trust fund for each employee every year. It then invests the money wisely so that it will grow; and when you retire, the plan pays you a monthly pension benefit. The employer not only puts up all the money that goes into the pension fund, but it also hires money managers to invest it for both capital growth and regular income, which is distributed to the pensioners. From the employer's point of view, all contributions to the pension plan are deductible as a business expense, thus providing a big tax break for the company. In addition, all the capital gains, dividends, and interest earned by the company's pension fund accumulate tax free. Pension money is taxed only when it is paid to employees, who must report it as regular income in the year they receive it. Today, many modern defined benefit plans also offer the option of a lump sum distribution.

If you work for a company, government agency, or nonprofit organization that provides a traditional defined benefit pension plan, you are fortunate. Many such plans are being cut back or eliminated because they are expensive to fund and administer. For those employees who qualify, defined benefits can provide a substantial portion—from 10 to 40 percent—of your total retirement income. The amount you receive often depends on how many years you worked for your employer and your salary in your final few years at the company. The longer you worked for the employer and the higher your salary, the fatter your monthly pension check.

THE LOWDOWN ON PENSIONS

Defined benefit pension plans are so named because they guarantee in advance the size of your monthly pension benefit. There's little to guess about. You know what you can expect to receive. The company is responsible for funding the pension plan and choosing managers to invest the funds to earn a high return at a reasonable level of risk. The money managers invest in stocks, bonds, real estate, money market securities, venture capital, or other vehicles to produce a return high enough to make the promised payments to pensioners.

To qualify for a pension, you must work for your employer a certain number of years to become vested. Being vested means you have completed enough years of service to be entitled to the benefits. Under current law, most plans allow you to become fully vested after five years, which is known as *cliff vesting*. Alternatively, you can become vested on a graduated vesting schedule over seven years, during which time you are 20 percent vested after the first three years and then vested 20 percent more in each subsequent year. Typically, earning a year of service requires working at least 1,000 hours that year, or the equivalent of about 20 hours a week. Those hours are defined as time you were paid or were entitled to be paid, including vacation days, sick days, and back-pay days.

Don't assume, however, that just because your company has a pension plan that you're in it. Be sure. Talk to your benefits department. The pension laws allow employers to exclude people from their pension plans, usually by job category. And the rules can be whimsical. The guidelines provide that companies can exclude up to 30 percent of their employees for any reason. You'll also want to find out whether your pension has a Social Security offset, which means your pension benefit is reduced by the amount of your Social Security benefit.

Companies use several formulas to determine the size of employees' pension benefits. The best pension plan averages your salary for your final three or five years of work, when your income should be at its peak. A less generous plan averages your salary over your entire career. You will receive the lowest benefit if your pension plan pays a flat dollars-per-month amount for every year you worked at the company, an arrangement usually used for union members. In anticipating the size of your pension benefit, know which of these methods of calculations your company uses.

Here's a more in-depth look at the ways your company may determine your monthly pension benefit:

- *Flat benefit formula plans* pay a flat dollar amount each month at retirement. The more years you worked at a company, the higher the monthly payment. Such plans are typically offered to hourly and unionized workers, whose benefits are specified in collective bargaining agreements.
- *Career-average formula plans* average the income you earned over your entire career at a company to determine your monthly payment. In some cases, you receive a percentage of your pay for every year you participated in the pension plan. Other companies average your yearly salary for as long as you took part in the pension plan. Your benefit is then determined by a specified percentage of your career-average pay multiplied by the number of years you worked at the company.
- *Final-pay formula plans,* which generally produce the highest monthly payments, average your income for your last few years (typically five) at a company, when you probably earned your peak salary. Once you retire, you receive a payment based on a percentage of these average earnings multiplied by the number of years you worked at the firm.

Both career-average and final-pay formula plans are usually offered to professionals in nonunion situations, though some unions manage to obtain these more favorable calculation methods through bargaining agreements.

Your retirement benefit is determined not only by one of these formulas but also by your age when you retire. In general, the later you retire, the higher your monthly payment. If you bow out at age 55, you will receive a much smaller payout than you would at age 65 because the company figures you will collect that payment for a much longer time. In some cases, when a company encourages workers to retire early (before age 65), it offers credit for a few extra years of service that you have not actually worked. For example, if you are 58 years old, the company might give you pension benefits as if you were age 62 to induce you to retire. On the other hand, if you work beyond age 65, you may qualify for a deferred retirement benefit, which can be more than the payment that the 65-year-olds receive. But no matter when you retire, your plan must begin paying benefits by age 70½, and you must pay income tax on those payments every year.

A series of congressional laws and IRS rules limit the amount that a pension plan can pay you in any year. When the maximum was first defined in the 1970s, it was 100 percent of your average pay for your three highest earning years, up to $75,000. With recent changes in the law, starting in 2002, the annual defined benefit limit increased to $160,000. In addition, the dollar limit will no longer be adjusted based on the Social Security retirement age. Instead, the dollar limit will be reduced for benefits beginning before age 62, or increased for benefits beginning after age 65.

To get a sense of what you might receive, contact your employee benefits department. You should get a yearly statement from the department detailing all your benefits, including your pension. If you don't receive one, request a personalized benefits statement, which will describe your monthly pension benefit starting at age 65 if you were to leave the company today. If you are young or haven't been at the company very long, the benefit may not amount to much; however, if you stay several years, or even decades, the benefits can grow substantially.

By all means keep those statements. File them away with other important documents. It's not a bad idea to keep a record of each year's salaries, bonuses, and other such information. These could prove crucial if problems arise in the future. Face it, pension administrators are only human. Mistakes happen. Your employer may overlook such key factors as overtime and bonuses when determining your pension, or your information could get lost in a company merger. Lots of things could go wrong. You want backup material to prove your case.

WHEN A PENSION PLAN TERMINATES WITH INSUFFICIENT FUNDS: ARE YOU PROTECTED?

If the company goes out of business and the pension plan terminates without sufficient funds to pay all benefits, the federally backed *Pension*

Ten Common Causes of Errors in Pension Calculation

1. All relevant information, such as commissions, overtime, and bonuses (if these were to be included in your plan) was not included in calculating your benefits.
2. The calculation was not based on all your years of service with the company or all your work within different divisions.
3. The plan administrator used an incorrect benefit formula, such as an incorrect interest rate.
4. The plan used wrong Social Security data in calculating your benefits.
5. Basic information, such as your birthdate or Social Security number, was incorrect.
6. Your company merged with another company or went out of business, and confusion exists over which pension benefits you qualify for.
7. Assets in your account were improperly valued.
8. Your employer failed to make required contributions on your behalf.
9. Basic mistakes were made in the mathematical calculations.
10. You failed to update your personnel office about changes (marriage, divorce, death of spouse) that may affect your benefits.

Source: U.S. Department of Labor's Pension and Welfare Benefits Administration.

Benefit Guaranty Corporation (PBGC) will step in as trustee for the plan. However, the PBGC does impose a maximum annual pension benefit of about $35,000, which increases with inflation every year. (See Figure 3.1.) With defined benefit plans, therefore, you don't have to worry very much about how the pension fund is invested because your basic benefit is guaranteed under almost all circumstances.

Examples of the maximum guarantee for a single-life annuity with no survivor benefits for retirement at ages 65, 62, 60, or 55 are shown in Figure 3.1. The maximum is lower if the benefit is paid in a form other than for a single-life annuity, such as a form that provides for survivors benefits. The pension benefit that the PBGC can pay depends on your age, the provisions of your plan, the form of your benefit, the legal limits on what the PBGC can guarantee, and amounts the PBGC recovers from employers for plan underfunding. That's not to say, however, that you shouldn't keep your eyes and ears open for irregularities.

Figure 3.1   PBGC Maximum Monthly Guarantees

Year Plan Terminated	Monthly Guarantee			
	Age 65	Age 62	Age 60	Age 55
2002	$3,579.55	$2,827.84	$2,326.71	$1,610.80
2001	3,392.05	2,679.72	2,204.83	1,526.42
2000	3,221.59	2,545.06	2,094.03	1,449.72
1999	3,051.14	2,410.40	1,983.24	1,373.01
1998	2,880.68	2,275.74	1,872.44	1,296.31
1997	2,761.36	2,181.47	1,794.88	1,242.61
1996	2,642.05	2,087.22	1,717.33	1,188.92
1995	2,573.86	2,033.35	1,673.01	1,158.24
1994	2,556.82	2,019.89	1,661.93	1,150.57
1993	2,437.50	1,925.63	1,584.38	1,096.88
1992	2,352.27	1,858.29	1,528.98	1,058.52
1991	2,250.00	1,777.50	1,462.50	1,012.50
1990	2,164.77	1,710.17	1,407.10	974.15

Source: Pension Benefit Guaranty Corporation.

Know the rules and your rights spelled out in ERISA (Employee Retirement Income Security Act). The Department of Labor and the Pension and Welfare Benefits Administration offer some useful reminders. The money must be invested in your interest. Your pension money is supposed to be working for you and everybody else covered by the plan—not for people who set up, run, or provide services to the plan. The people managing the fund are not allowed to use the money for themselves, for their relatives, or for their business. They must make investments solely in the interest of plan participants.

Pension managers are not permitted to spend excessive amounts on plan business trips, offices, furniture, or other plan expenses. If they are paid full-time as union or company employees, it is unlawful for them to also receive compensation from the plan except for reimbursement of expenses properly and actually incurred. Pension managers are generally not allowed to put all assets of the pension plan in a single investment, such as one stock or real estate in a single location. They are typically expected to spread the money among a variety of investments so there is less chance that one poor investment exposes the entire pension fund to a risk or large losses. Finally, your pension money must be invested wisely and carefully. Pension fund managers must use care, skill, and prudence to protect your money; although they will take risks, the risks should be reasonable.

You're probably wondering how you would know if your plan was sidestepping the rules. Glad you asked. Under federal law your pension plan is required to give you information about plan investments. The plan must automatically provide you with a summary of its finances for each year or a written notice of your right to receive that summary, which is called a Summary Annual Report, or SAR. In addition, if you ask for the summary in writing, you must be given a copy of the full annual report and financial statements that the plan files with the government. Plans covering 100 or more participants generally use a Form 5500 and those with fewer than 100 participants can use Form 5500-C/R. These forms usually must be filed with the government within 7 months after the end of the calendar year or other 12-month period your plan uses for financial reporting purposes.

The SAR will indicate how well your pension plan's investments have performed. You should be able to glean whether the plan's investments have lost large amounts of money during a year; the plan's total administrative expenses for the year; a list of items that can alert you to questionable financial arrangements with individuals or organizations closely connected to the plan; and if any money loaned by the plan has not been paid back on time. Even though the SAR can signal potentially troublesome areas, it is only a summary. You may also want to take a look at the plan's complete annual report and financial statements. The SAR will tell you how to get a copy. (See Figure 3.2 for a sample Summary Annual Report and Figure 3.3 for Sources of Plan Information.)

Although you may be assured of receiving pension payments, you are by no means guaranteed that those payments, combined with Social Security, will adequately fund your retirement. Most pension benefits are fixed at the time you retire, so inflation slowly erodes the value of the benefits. (A few generous pension plans provide a cost-of-living adjustment for benefits, but don't count on it.) In addition, companies looking for ways to cut expenses can institute payment formulas that will reduce your benefit.

In the most extreme cases, companies will terminate their pension plans altogether and substitute an annuity purchased from an insurance company that will provide a fixed benefit, which is usually less than you would have earned from the pension plan directly. Such a substitution also replaces the ultimate backing of your pension payment from the federal PBGC with that of the insurance company. Although no one used to worry about this, such a replacement did affect thousands of pensioners whose annuities were backed by Mutual Benefit Life Insurance and Executive Life Insurance, when those firms were taken over by regulators in the early 1990s. Even though no pen-

Figure 3.2   Sample Summary Annual Report

June 2001

TO ALL PARTICIPANTS:

We are pleased to provide you with this summary of the annual report for the CWA/ITU Negotiated Pension Plan, EIN 13-6212879-001, for the year ended December 31, 2000. The annual report has been filed with the U.S. Department of Labor's Pension and Welfare Benefits Administration, as required under the Employee Retirement Income Security Act of 1974 (ERISA).

BASIC FINANCIAL STATEMENT
Benefits under the Plan are provided from the Plan's assets held in trust. The Plan had total income of $63,479,966, which includes employer contributions of $18,693,746, investment earnings of $44,622,929 (including the change in market value of investments), and other income of $163,291.

The Plan had total expenditures of $80,762,194, which includes benefits paid to participants and beneficiaries of $78,498,164 and administrative expenses of $2,264,030. A total of 44,013 persons were participants or beneficiaries of the Plan at the end of the Plan year, although not all of these persons had yet earned the right to receive benefits.

The value of the Fund decreased by $17,282,228 during 2000. As a result, the net assets available to pay benefits at December 31, 2000 were $1,090,291,152 compared to $1,107,573,380 at December 31, 1999. This is the amount available to continue paying pensions to current pensioners and to provide future benefits for participants not yet retired.

MINIMUM FUNDING STANDARDS
The actuary's statement shows the Plan is adequately funded in accordance with the minimum funding standards of ERISA.

SUMMARY PLAN DESCRIPTION
Your rights to benefits under the Plan are set forth in the Summary Plan Description (SPD). If you would like to receive a copy of the current SPD (revised as of March 2001) or a previous version, please contact the Plan Office and it will be sent to you without charge. You can also access the SPD on the Plan's web site at www.cwaitu.com.

NEW TRUSTEES OF THE PLAN
During the year 2000, James Artz was appointed as Employer Trustee and Wayne Mitchell was appointed as Union Trustee.

Fraternally,

William J. Boarman, Chairman

Figure 3.2   (continued)

YOUR RIGHTS TO ADDITIONAL INFORMATION

You have the right to receive a copy of the full annual report, or any part thereof, upon request to the Plan Administrator at the address shown on the previous page. The charge to cover copying costs will be $.25 per page. The following items are included in that report:

1. An Auditor's report
2. Financial information and information on payments to service providers
3. A list of assets held for investment
4. A list of transactions involving more than 5% of Plan assets
5. Information regarding the common/collective trusts in which the Plan participated
6. Actuarial information regarding funding of the Plan

You have the right to receive from the Plan Administrator, or request and at no charge, a statement of the assets and liabilities of the Plan and accompanying notes or a statement of income and expenses of the Plan and accompanying notes, or both. If you request a copy of the full annual report from the Plan Administrator, these two statements and accompanying notes will be included as part of that report.

You have the legally protected right to examine the annual report at the Fund Office located at 225 S. Union Blvd., Second Floor, Colorado Springs, CO. You can view the annual report at the U.S. Department of Labor in Washington, DC, or you can obtain a copy from the U.S. Department of Labor upon payment of copying costs. Requests to the Department of Labor should be addressed to: Public Disclosure, Room N5638, Pension & Welfare Benefit Programs, U.S. Department of Labor, 200 Constitution Ave., NW, Washington, DC 20210.

TO ALL PARTICIPANTS WHO HAVE REACHED AGE 65
OR WILL REACH AGE 65 WITHIN THE NEXT YEAR

If you are a vested participant in the Plan, age 65 or older, and are retired from the industry, you are eligible for a pension benefit and you should obtain an application from the Plan. If you continue to work past 65 in the printing industry, in the same trade or craft and the geographic area covered by the Plan, and you work more than the number of days per month set forth in Section 7.03 of the Plan, you can begin to receive a pension when you stop working by filing an application for pension with the Plan Office. Plan provisions require you to begin receiving your pension on April 1 of the year following the date you reach 70½, even if you continue to work. You will need to apply then.

If you are age 65 or over and have not yet applied for a pension, the Plan will presume you have continued to work after age 65 until the time you apply unless you inform the Plan in writing once each year that you have been unemployed the previous twelve months or that your employment has been outside the industry, your trade, craft, or the Plan's geographic area. Applicable Department of Labor regulations on this subject may be found in Section 2530.203-3 of Title 29 of the Code of Federal Regulations. If you believe that you are entitled to begin benefit payments, you should write to the Plan Administrator.

TO ALL PENSIONERS REGARDING TAX WITHHOLDING

This is a reminder that you may choose whether or not to have taxes withheld. Benefits under the Plan are taxable income to the recipient. (The IRS may charge a penalty if your tax withholding or estimated tax payments are not sufficient to cover your tax liability.) If you desire withholding, please advise the Plan Office in writing of the dollar amount. If you have made an election previously, it will remain in effect until changed or revoked, which you may do by notifying the Plan Office.

If you have not made an election, we will use the classification of a married individual claiming three withholding allowances to determine whether or not to withhold federal tax from your pension. This will NOT result in any tax withholding unless your monthly pension from this Plan exceeds $1,280. If no change in withholding is desired, do not respond to this reminder.

Figure 3.3 Sources of Plan Information*

Type of document	Who you can get it from	When you can get it	Your cost
Summary Plan Description (SPD): This summary of your pension plan tells you what the plan provides and how it operates.	Plan Administrator	Upon written request	*Reasonable charge*
		Automatically within 90 days of your becoming covered under the plan	*Free*
		Automatically every 5 years if your plan is amended	*Free*
		Automatically every 10 years if your plan has not been amended	*Free*
	Department of Labor	Upon request	*Copying charge*
Summary of Material Modifications (SMM): This summarizes material changes to your plan.	Plan Administrator	Automatically within 210 days after the end of the plan year for which the plan has been amended or modified (distribution of a revised SPD satisfies this requirement)	*Free*
	Department of Labor	Upon request	*Copying charge*
Summary Annual Report: This summarizes the annual financial reports that most pension plans file with the Department of Labor.	Plan Administrator	Automatically within 9 months after the end of the plan year, or 2 months after the due date for filing the annual report.	*Free*
Annual Report (Form 5500 Series): Annual financial reports that most pension plans file with the Department of Labor.	Plan Administrator	Latest annual report upon written request	*Reasonable charge*
	Department of Labor	Upon request	*Copying charge*
Individual Benefit Statement: A statement describing your total accrued and vested benefits is required to be provided by most pension plans.	Plan Administrator	Upon written request once every 12 months	*Free*
Documents and instruments under which the plan is established or operated: This includes, for example, the plan document, collective bargaining agreement, trust agreement, SPD, SMM, and latest annual report.	Plan Administrator	Upon written request	*Reasonable charge*
		Available for inspection upon request	*Free*
Disclosure Notice: Plan administrators with plans less than 90% funded must inform you about the plan funding level and limits on PBGC's guarantees.	Plan Administrator	Within 2 months after the due date for filing the annual report	*Free*

Documents filed with the Labor Department can be obtained by contacting the U.S. Department of Labor, PWBA, Public Disclosure Facility, Room N5638, 200 Constitution Ave., N.W., Washington, DC 20210; 202-219-8771.

What Happens When the PBGC Takes Over My Plan?

- The PBGC reviews your plan's record to determine what benefits each person will receive.
- If you are already retired and receiving benefits, the PBGC will continue paying you without interruption during its review. These payments will be an *estimate* of the benefits that the PBGC can pay under the insurance program, and they may be less than you were receiving from your plan.
- If you have not yet retired, the PBGC will pay you an estimated benefit when you become eligible.

Once the PBGC completes its review, it informs you in writing what your pension amount will be and what rights you have to appeal the decision.

---

sioner's payments were terminated, some payments were reduced, and many retirees were frightened about the possibility of losing their pension income.

PAYOUT OPTIONS

As long as you are vested, your spouse will receive pension benefits if you die. Ask your benefits department how much your spouse might get in survivors coverage if you were to die before retirement. Usually, the benefit is half the amount you would have received once retired, and it is paid starting in the year you would have stopped working, usually age 65. This is known as a *preretirement survivors annuity.* If your spouse signs a document waiving the right to this annuity, the two of you will earn a larger pension benefit when you retire. However, if you die before retirement, your widow will not receive a pension from the company. Usually, it is not a good idea to take this risk, which could leave your spouse without pension income on which he or she had been counting.

Most pension plans also continue payments to spouses once the primary employees die if they opt for *joint and survivor payout.* If you are married or if someone depends on your income, you may want to select this option, which pays a fixed amount until both you and your spouse or dependent die. When you die, your spouse or dependent receives *qualified joint and survivor annuity* (QJAS) payments until he or she dies. These payments are usually less than the amount you received, but by law they cannot be less than

50 percent of your payment. Because both you and your spouse or dependent may live a long time, the joint and survivor plan offers the lowest monthly payment. However, it is also the safest plan because it ensures that your spouse or dependent will receive a monthly income after you are gone.

Most insurance agents advise you to choose a straight life annuity pay-out option instead of the joint and survivor option, a strategy often called *pension maximization.* Even though the straight life choice pays a higher monthly amount, it ceases payments once you die. Insurance salespeople advocate taking a portion of the higher payments and buying an insurance policy to provide capital to cover your spouse's needs once you die. This may sound good in theory, but it is usually not so in practice. Here's why: The cost of the insurance policy, which includes large sales commissions, can consume most or all of the extra income provided by the straight life annuity. And the size of the death benefit may not adequately support your spouse for the rest of his or her life; therefore, your spouse will have to manage the money to produce extra income, which he or she may not have the expertise to do. It is therefore safer to choose the joint and survivor plan to make sure your spouse is covered until death. (See Chapter 7 for more on annuities.)

The size of your pension benefit should weigh heavily in your decision to leave your employer for another. Every time you hook up with a new company, you start at square one in accumulating pension credits. The pension benefit you receive from your former employer is locked at the level earned when you left the company.

If you leave your present company for another, you may be offered the option to receive your pension benefit in a *lump sum,* which should be rolled over into the new firm's plan or an IRA. When you accept a lump sum, you receive an amount that is discounted from today's dollar based on an assumed rate of return. Ask your employer what this rate of return is. If you think you can beat the return by investing on your own, consider taking the lump sum, but if you fear that you won't do as well, you might leave the money with your employer's plan.

In addition, complex rules mandate how that lump sum will be taxed. Under some conditions and if you were born before 1936, you may be able to qualify for a favorable form of taxation called *ten-year averaging,* which greatly reduces your tax bite. However, you will not qualify for this kind of taxation once you've rolled the cash into an IRA. You must be extremely careful to make sure that the lump sum is deposited directly into an IRA through a *trustee-to-trustee transfer,* or the IRS will withhold 20 percent of the cash.

The decision to take all of your pension money at once is extremely complicated, so consult a qualified financial planner before you grab what may look like a huge chunk of cash. In many cases, you have no option in taking a lump sum: you must wait until retirement age to begin drawing payments from the plan. If, by chance, you return to a former employer, you will again earn pension credits, and depending on how long you were away, you may not be penalized much for your absence. In any case, for most people who depend on that monthly pension check, it is far safer to opt for an annuity than to take on the responsibility of investing the lump sum.

Other payout options may include "life only," which means income stops at your death, or "period certain and life," which means that during the "period certain," which is often ten years, you (or your spouse if you die during the period) receive a specific amount. Once the period is over, you continue to receive the amount, but your spouse receives nothing if you die first.

CASH BALANCE PLANS

One of the latest trends in pensions is the growing popularity of cash balance plans, particularly among large employers. A cash balance plan is a defined-benefit plan that defines the benefit in terms that are more characteristic of a defined-contribution plan. These hybrid plans are defined benefit plans insured by the PBGC and subject to laws such as ERISA, the Age Discrimination in Employment Act (ADEA), and the Internal Revenue Code.

The retirement benefit in a cash balance plan is generally described in terms of a hypothetical account balance that looks like the account balance in a 401(k) plan. In this hypothetical account, a worker accumulates pay credits (usually a percentage of pay) and interest credits (either a fixed rate or a variable rate that is linked to an index such as the one-year Treasury bill rate). Increases and decreases in the value of the plan's investments do not directly affect the benefit amounts promised to participants. The investment risks and rewards of plan assets are borne solely by the employer.

When a participant becomes entitled to receive benefits under a cash balance plan, the benefits that are received are defined in terms of an account balance. For example, assume that you have an account balance of $100,000 when you reach age 65. If you decide to retire at that time, you would have the right to an annuity. Such an annuity might be approximately $10,000 per year for life. In many cash balance plans, however, you could instead choose (with the consent of your spouse) to take a lump sum benefit equal to the $100,000 cash balance.

In addition to generally permitting you to take your benefits in a lump sum at retirement, cash balance plans often permit vested participants to choose (again, with the nod of your spouse) to receive your accrued benefits in lump sums if you terminate employment prior to retirement age. That's an option usually not offered in traditional defined benefit plans.

CASH BALANCE VERSUS TRADITIONAL DEFINED BENEFIT PLANS

Like traditional defined benefit plans, benefits in cash balance plans don't depend on how much a worker is willing or able to contribute, the employer bears the investment risk, plans must offer an annuity with a survivor benefit, and benefits are insured by the PBGC.

They differ, however, in the following ways: workers can know the value of their benefits and tend to understand them better when expressed as a hypothetical individual account; younger workers and shorter-service workers, who are often women, can receive higher benefits; and workers who do not spend their full careers with one employer have more portable benefits that can be transferred to another plan. But there is a downside to cash balance plans. They frequently offer a single, lump sum payment, which you may be tempted to spend rather than roll over into another retirement account, and, generally, cash balance plans don't offer subsidized early retirement benefits and thus make it harder for workers to retire early.

Many cash balance plans are conversions from traditional defined benefit plans. Conversions generally involve a change from a traditional final average-pay plan, where benefits are based on workers' average pay at the end of their careers when their earnings often are higher, to a career-average balance plan, where benefits are based on workers' average pay for their entire career, which likely will be a lower amount. Furthermore, in these cases, long-time employees receive less under a cash balance plan than they would have received under a traditional defined benefit plan unless the employer provides transition protections.

If you want to know how the change from a traditional to a cash balance plan will affect you, contact your benefits department. The law requires that once such a plan has been put in place, your employer must provide a personalized statement showing your new balance and old balance within 60 days of your request.

You could be given the choice of staying with the old formula or converting to the new cash balance plan. Make that decision with great care. Take into account your retirement expectations, when you hope to begin receiving benefits, and the chance that your needs may change. Compare all the terms and options available to you under the cash balance package with those you already have. Look at each option under each plan formula. Consider, too, the specifics of your retirement benefit, such as how your accrued benefit (including the value of any early retirement subsidy) is defined under each formula, the current value of your accrued benefit under each formula, and the benefit's value as an annuity at normal retirement age or as a lump sum distribution. Factor in how your choice will affect survivors benefits. Don't forget to compare the value of other related benefits that may be offered under either choice. Some traditional pension plans, for example, provide an offset or subsidy if you retire prior to the age at which your Social Security benefits begin, or offer credit for service also covered by a disability benefit plan. To change or not is a big decision, so consult a financial advisor. (See the case study below.)

Pensions aren't the most exciting creatures, but do devote time to learning all you can about them and stay on top of your own pension. You want to avoid nasty surprises come retirement day.

Case Study

Are You Better Off Retiring under a Cash Balance Plan or a Traditional Pension Plan?

Depending on your career goals and personal circumstances, the two examples below should help you in making your decision.

Example 1—New Employee

Assume a new employee is hired at age 25 at a starting annual salary of $36,000 with an annual pay increase of 4 percent.

Example 1 compares lump sum value at attained ages under a cash balance plan and under a traditional pension plan running parallel for the entire career of the newly hired employee. The table below provides the employee with the answer.

Example 1—New Employee

Attained Age	25	35	45	55	65
Cash Balance Account at Attained Age	$0	$27,960	$91,441	$225,008	$ 493,623
Traditional Lump Sum Value at Attained Age	0	15,848	84,839	346,595	1,310,674

Conclusion for Example 1—New Employee

A cash balance plan works better for younger, mobile employees with short-term career horizons. Because of the heavy loading in latter years under a traditional pension plan, it is better to retire under a traditional pension plan with longer years of service.

(continued)

Example 2—Career Employee

Assume that a career employee in the traditional pension plan at age 55 with 30 years of service experiences the conversion of this plan to a cash balance plan. The employee was given the right to stay in the traditional plan. Which is the better choice? The table below provides the employee with the answer.

Example 2—Career Employee

Attained Age	55	65
Cash Balance Account at Attained Age	$346,595	$ 711,300
Traditional Lump Sum Value at Attained Age	346,595	1,310,674

Conclusion for Example 2—Career Employee

This example clearly shows it is better for a career employee to retire under the traditional pension plan.

Assumptions Used in Both Examples

Cash Balance Plan

The cash balance account is credited with 5 percent of pay and 6 percent of annual interest.

Traditional Pension Plan

The lump sum value is calculated using single-life pension commencing at the normal retirement age of 65 based on the following benefit formula:

2% × Years of Employment × Final 5-Year Average Pay × Lump Sum Factor

The lump sum factor is calculated based on GATT mortality table and 6 percent annual interest rate.

Final Note

No two pension plans are alike, and no two employees are similar, so you have to compare the numbers based on your personal information.

RESOURCES

Books, Booklets, and Pamphlets

A Predictable Secure Pension for Life (Pension Benefit Guaranty Corp., 1200 K St., N.W., Washington, DC 20005; 202-326-4000; www.pbgc.gov). A thorough examination of the different types of pensions that exist and the insurance available for each plan type.

Finding a Lost Pension (Pension Benefit Guaranty Corp., 1200 K St., N.W., Washington, DC 20005; 202-326-4000; www.pbgc.gov). Explains the steps to take to find a lost pension from earlier working life.

Fundamentals of Employee Benefit Programs, 5th Edition (Employee Benefit Research Institute, 2121 K St., N.W., Suite 600, Washington, DC 20037-1896; 202-659-0670; www.ebri.org). Comprehensive book explaining all employee benefits.

The New Working Woman's Guide to Retirement Planning: Saving and Investing Now for a Secure Future, by Martha Priddy Patterson (University of Pennsylvania Press, 4200 Pine St., Philadelphia, PA 19104-4011; 215-898-6261; www.upenn.edu). Describes how to accumulate retirement savings in 401(k) plans, pension plans, and other company retirement plans.

The Pension Book: What You Need to Know to Prepare for Retirement, by Karen Ferguson and Kate Blackwell (Arcade Publishing, 141 Fifth Ave., New York, NY 10010; 212-475-2633; www.arcadepub.com). Explains how to get the most from your pensions and otherwise prepare for retirement.

Pensions in the Public Sector, by Olivia S. Mitchell (editor) and Edwin C. Hustead (editor) (University of Pennsylvania Press, 4200 Pine St., Philadelphia, PA 19104-4011; 215-898-6261; www.upenn.edu). A thorough examination of all aspects of pensions in the private, public, and academic sectors.

Positioning Pensions for the Twenty-First Century, by Michael S. Gordon (editor), Olivia S. Mitchell (editor), and Marc M. Twinney (University of Pennsylvania Press, 4200 Pine St., Philadelphia, PA 19104-4011; 215-898-6261; www.upenn.edu). Leading economists, actuaries, labor and corporate pension experts, and policy specialists join to examine where pensions have succeeded and failed in the past, and where they will go in the future.

The Promise of Private Pensions: The First Hundred Years, by Steven A. Sass (Harvard University Press, 79 Garden St., Cambridge, MA 02138; 617-495-2480; 800-448-2242; www.hup.harvard.edu). Traces the creation of the pension system, which proved far more complicated than anyone had assumed.

Public Policy Toward Pensions, by Sylvester J. Schieber (editor) and John B. Shoven (editor) (MIT Press, 20th Century Fund Books, 5 Cambridge Center, Cambridge, MA 02142-1493; 617-253-5646; www.mitpress.mit.edu). Pension policy predicted to emerge as one of the key economic issues of the next decade, and a guide to the debate provided.

Your Guaranteed Pension (Pension Benefit Guaranty Corp., 1200 K St., N.W., Washington, DC 20005; 202-326-4000; www.pbgc.gov). Useful question-and-answer booklet about pensions, including a monthly payout table.

Trade Associations and Government Agencies

The American Academy of Actuaries (1100 17th St., N.W., 7th Floor, Washington, DC 20036; 202-223-8196, www.actuary.org), a public policy and professional organization steers you to members who specialize in pensions and offers a free nationwide referral service.

American Association of Retired Persons (AARP) (601 E. St., N.W., Washington, DC 20049: 800-424-3410; www.aarp.org). A valuable resource for issues facing retirees, including pension-related information on its Web site.

The American Society of Pension Actuaries (4245 N. Fairfax Dr., Suite 750, Arlington, VA 22203; 703-516-9300; www.aspa.org), a national organization devoted exclusively to pensions, whose members include actuaries, attorneys, consultants, and other professionals.

The Coalition for Retirement Security (P.O. Box 19812, Washington, DC 20036; www.pensions-r-us.org). A national grassroots organization that works to correct pension and health care inequities.

National Academy of Elder Law Attorneys, Inc. (1604 N. Country Club Rd., Tucson, AZ 85716; 520-881-4005; www.naela.org). Offers a directory of lawyers specializing in problems faced by retirees and a free booklet of answers to questions about finding an elder law attorney.

National Pension Lawyers Network (Gerontology Institute, University of Massachusetts Boston, 100 Morrissey St., Boston, MA 02125-3393; 617-287-7332). A national lawyer referral service for workers, retirees, widows, and people going through divorce who need legal representation in cases involving pension issues.

Pension Benefit Guaranty Corporation (1200 K St., N.W., Washington, DC 20005; 202-326-4000; www.pbgc.gov). Protects the retirement incomes of about 43 million American workers in nearly 40,000 defined benefit pension plans.

Pension Research Council (The Wharton School of The University of Pennsylvania, 3641 Locust Walk, 304 Colonial Penn Center, Philadelphia, PA 19104-6218; 215-898-7620; prc.wharton.upenn.edu). Sponsors interdisciplinary research on the entire range of private pension and Social Security programs as well as related benefits in the United States and around the world.

Pension Rights Center (1140 19th St., N.W., Suite 602, Washington, DC 20036; 202-296-3776; www.pensionrights.org). A nonprofit organization that helps educate the public about pension issues and offers a lawyer referral service for pension-related problems.

U.S. Department of Labor's Pension and Welfare Benefits Administration (200 Constitution Ave., N.W., Washington, DC 20210; 202-219-8771; www.dol

.gov/dol/pwba). Offers a copy of your pension plan's annual report and other vital information and publications about pensions.

Web Sites

Cashpensions.org <www.cashpensions.org>. An online resource for those with concerns about benefit reductions resulting from their company's pension plan changes. Provides links to legislation, litigation, and legal rights as well as articles and news.

Pensionbenefits.com <www.pensionbenefits.com>. A treasure trove of information about pensions.

CHAPTER 4

Defined
Contribution Plans

I f your employer doesn't offer a traditional defined benefit plan, it probably offers a *defined contribution plan,* which gives you the opportunity to put aside money from your salary on a tax-deferred basis until you retire. Unlike a defined benefit plan, a contribution plan does not obligate your employer to pay a certain pension benefit. Instead, you may set aside a certain contribution, which your employer may or may not match. Either way, however, you must choose among various investment options. In other words, the onus is on you—you are responsible for the ultimate size of your pension benefit. Like income from all other pension plans, investment earnings from defined contribution plans grow tax deferred; you pay Uncle Sam later when you withdraw funds rather than now as you contribute.

Your company may make its contributions to your plan in cash, which you can allocate among various investment options. Or it may give you company stock, which you can hold onto or possibly sell. Some companies offer a combination of cash *and* stock. The amount of your company's contribution is determined either by a percentage of its profits, in which case it is called a *profit-sharing plan,* or by a percentage of your salary, in which case it is called a *money-purchase plan.* In a profit-sharing plan, when your firm has a very profitable year, you might receive an additional 10 to 15 percent of your salary in your defined contribution account. However, when profits fall or the company suffers a loss, you may get 5 percent or less, or possibly nothing at all.

To qualify for participation in a company's plan, you usually must work at the company for at least one year. Once you enroll in the plan through payroll deductions, many companies will match your contribution. Their match may be as generous as 100 percent or as little as 10 percent; a typical match is 50 percent. So if you set aside 6 percent of your salary in such a plan, the company would kick in another 3 percent every year. No other investments offer such an instant 50 percent return, so you should never refuse taking it!

Any money that you contribute to a defined contribution plan is always vested, meaning that you can take it with you or roll it over into another firm's plan or an IRA if you change employers. However, to provide you with an incentive to stay, most firms make you wait three or four years before their contributions are fully vested.

Types of Plans and How They Work

The most common type of defined contribution plan is a *salary reduction plan*. If you work for a for-profit company, it is named a *401(k) plan* after the obscure section of the Internal Revenue Code that permits it. The 401(k), which is so common today, has amassed over $2 trillion in the nation's accounts, despite the fact that it has only been around since the late 1970s. If you are employed by a tax-exempt organization, such as a religious, educational, or charitable group, the defined contribution plan is called a *403(b) plan*. State and local government workers are offered *457 plans,* and federal employees can sign up for the *federal thrift savings fund.* Though these plans have their differences, they work in basically the same way.

In each of these plans, your employer deducts a percentage of your salary—usually between 2 and 10 percent, according to your wishes—and deposits the funds in your plan account. The money is deducted from your salary before being taxed at the federal, state, or local level and before Social Security taxes are deducted. Consequently, the earnings you report to the IRS on your W-2 form are lessened by the amount of your annual contribution. The money you set aside, whether or not it is matched by your employer, is invested in a range of stock, bond, and money market choices, and all investments accumulate tax deferred. You pay taxes only when you withdraw the money at retirement.

The IRS limits how much you can contribute annually to your salary reduction plan; that amount is increased each year for inflation. Currently, the limit for 401(k) and federal thrift plans is $11,000. However, with changes under the Economic Growth and Tax Relief Reconciliation Act of 2001, for 401(k)s, 403(b)s, and 457 plans, contribution limits rise to $12,000 as of 2003, and continue to increase $1,000 a year over the next few years until topping out at $15,000 in 2006. After that, the maximum deferral amount is indexed in $500 increments. (See new limits in Figure 4.1.) Another new rule permits workers aged 50 and older to make a catch-up contribution of $1,000 on top of the $11,000 maximum limit in 2002. (See Figure 4.2.) This limit will rise $1,000 a year until 2006 to $5,000, and will then be indexed to inflation.

Currently, the IRS mandates that contributions from you and your employer may not exceed the lessor of 25 percent of your pay or $35,000. The 2001 law bumps that percentage of pay limit up to 100 percent of pay and the dollar limit to $40,000. This change is great for a second-income wage earner who may be only part-time—under the new rules, 100 percent, up to the $40,000 limit, can be contributed to retirement savings.

Another significant change: In 2002, 401(k) contributions can be made on the first $200,000 of compensation. In the future, increases in inflation will trigger a rise in this limit in $5,000 increments. Also, plans such as

Figure 4.1   Qualified Employer-Sponsored Retirement Plans: Maximum Pretax Elective Deferral

Year	Limit
2002	$11,000
2003	12,000
2004	13,000
2005	14,000
2006	15,000

After 2006, the maximum deferral amount is indexed in $500 increments.

Figure 4.2   Qualified Employer-Sponsored Retirement Plans: Catch-up Elective Deferral

Year	Limit
2002	$1,000
2003	2,000
2004	3,000
2005	4,000
2006	5,000

After 2006, catch-up contributions will be indexed in $500 increments.

401(k)s can now be rolled over into a similar plan or a different plan, including a 401(k), 403(b), or IRA.

Beginning in 2005, 401(k) plans can offer a Roth 401(k) alternative. The Roth 401(k) contribution will be made using after-tax dollars versus the pretax dollars contributed to the traditional 401(k). Therefore, you will not receive an immediate income tax benefit, but the benefit the Roth 401(k) provides is tax-free earnings at retirement. Unlike the traditional 401(k), in which all distributions are 100 percent taxable, the Roth 401(k) distributions are 100 percent tax free. You need to determine which 401(k) provides the greatest benefit to you; for example, current income tax benefits versus tax-free distributions at retirement. But chances are that over the long run, taking out money tax free will likely be the best route to take.

NEW MINIMUM WITHDRAWAL RULES

Changes in the regulations also have an impact on minimum withdrawal rules. Gone are complex elections that are replaced by a single minimum withdrawal table. The table, based on your life expectancy and the life expectancy of a hypothetical person ten years younger than you, determines the amount you must withdraw.

Rules have also changed regarding how your beneficiaries will draw any remaining assets after you die. If you die before age 70½ (the age you are required to begin making minimum distributions), and you have a designated beneficiary, the beneficiary may withdraw any remaining assets based on his or her life expectancy. If you don't have a beneficiary, the assets must be withdrawn over your remaining actuarial life expectancy prior to your death. Trusts that are beneficiaries also benefit from the more relaxed rules. The trustee now has greater flexibility in managing and withdrawing the assets. If you die before age 70½, your beneficiaries also must withdraw the assets over their life expectancy; a surviving spouse is allowed to roll over the assets into an IRA of his or her own and delay distributions based on the same rules that applied to you during your lifetime. If you don't name a beneficiary, the assets must be withdrawn within five years.

WHY YOU SHOULD PARTICIPATE IN YOUR EMPLOYER'S PLAN

Simply put, 401(k)s are the greatest thing since sliced bread. Were it not for such accounts, many Americans undoubtedly would have much dimmer prospects for a comfortable retirement. The 401(k), for more than a few people, is an introduction to the world of investing in addition to its many benefits. All your savings compound undisturbed by the IRS until you withdraw the money. Think of a 401(k) as a tax shelter of sorts, too. Every dollar you save in the plan reduces the taxable income you have to report to the IRS that year. In most cases, companies put money in the pot with you, so why would you turn down free money? It's easy to save because your company automatically deducts money from your paycheck. What you don't see you won't miss; you'll learn to live taking home a bit less income. Another plus is portability. When you leave your job, you can leave the 401(k) with your former employer or take it with you by rolling it over into an IRA or into your new employer's plan.

TAKING MONEY OUT

A 401(k) does have a downside though. Because it is supposed to be for retirement, if you try to break the lock on your little Fort Knox before you reach age 59½, you'll have to pay an early withdrawal penalty plus federal and state income taxes in the year of the withdrawal. The IRS alone will hit you for a 10 percent early withdrawal penalty.

However, many plans offer a hardship withdrawal—that is, a taxable distribution without a 10 percent penalty. A hardship withdrawal is different from a loan as it does not have to be paid back. To qualify, you typically can't have an existing loan against your plan. The rules vary, but if you must pay college tuition and room and board for yourself, your spouse, or dependents; buy a principal residence; face eviction or foreclosure on your primary residence; or have unreimbursed medical expenses for yourself, your spouse, or dependents, you may be given an OK by the plan administrator.

A word of caution about borrowing from your 401(k). Although you may be able to borrow up to 50 percent of your vested account balance up to $50,000, the loan interest you pay is not tax deductible. And remember that the money is no longer working for you in your 401(k) plan. The impact of that loss over the long term could be significant. When you take a hardship withdrawal, often you can't participate in your plan for another year, though with recent changes in the law, the 12-month period is reduced to 6 months. Know, too, that if you borrow from your 401(k) and you lose or quit your job, you will be required to pay back the full amount of the loan within 60 days or face the 10 percent IRS early withdrawal penalty plus federal and state income taxes on whatever portion of the loan you don't repay.

CHOOSING INVESTMENTS

Once you see the money accumulate steadily in your account, you must allocate it among the various investment options presented. Some plans allow you to switch from one option to another every day (if you wish), whereas others limit you to quarterly or annual shifts. You usually receive quarterly written reports describing your funds' returns, and often you can call the plan's representatives or go online to learn the status of your account.

Most often you're able to choose among a variety of stock funds, bond funds, or funds that combine stocks and bonds, or money market funds. Each category may offer many options. For example, among stock funds you may be able to select aggressive, international, equity income, or index funds. Among bond funds you may be offered government, corporate, international, or junk bond funds. Some combined stock and bond options might include balanced and asset allocation funds, company stock, and *guaranteed investment contracts* (GICs), which are similar to certificates of deposits (CDs). GICs pay a fixed rate for a set time, usually one to five years, and are backed by the insurance company or bank that issued them.

You have a lot of choices. Where do you begin? How do you choose what's right for you? Well, you start by thinking about your goals. How much will you need to retire, and to what lengths are you willing to go to achieve them—simply put, how much risk can you stomach? Are you willing to bet the farm, or are you willing to settle for less if it means being able to get a good night's sleep?

Another element to factor into the equation is your time horizon. If you have 10 to 20 years until retirement, time is on your side, so you can take more risks because you won't have to tap that money very soon. You can afford to be aggressive. However, as you draw nearer to retirement and will need to withdraw the money sooner, you'll want a healthy dose of liquid, income-producing investments like CDs, short-term bonds or bond funds, or money market funds. You'll also want to scale back on investments that leave you vulnerable to a major loss of capital. You don't want to be in a position to have to sell when the market is nose-diving.

Look at how you have allocated your money outside your retirement accounts at work. If you hold mostly conservative bonds and CDs, you may want to invest pension money in more aggressive options. On the other hand, if you possess a large portfolio of aggressive stocks and mutual funds elsewhere, you may want to put more of your pension plan in conservative assets. In general, the younger you are, the more money you should invest in aggressive options; in the long run, growth-oriented vehicles like aggressive stock funds will outperform stodgy fixed-income bonds and GICs. The biggest mistake most people make is to sink most or all of their pension plan money in money market accounts, GICs, or bonds, thus depriving themselves of the potential for significant long-term gains from stocks.

What you don't want to do if you invest in stocks is to sink too much in your own company's stock. If your company matches your contribution in company stock, you will surely benefit if the firm does well. As wonderful as your company's prospects may be, you don't want to have too high a concentration of your plan's assets in your own company in case it runs into trouble. The worst thing that can happen to you, financially speaking, is that you invest most of your assets in your company's stock and its price plummets just as you are about to retire. Look no further than the plight of Enron and Global Crossing employees who had most of their money tied up in company stocks in the early 2000s as their firms plunged into bankruptcy within a few months.

ASSET ALLOCATION

You don't want all your eggs in your company's basket, nor do you want them in too few baskets. Diversity makes the difference. You do that through asset allocation, a way of spreading your money over the ideal mix of stocks, bonds, and other investments. Having a variety of assets in your portfolio reduces risk. If one class tanks, you'll have others to keep you afloat.

Diversification, or lack thereof, has become such an issue that employers are beginning to take it upon themselves to educate employees about its importance. According to a 2001 study by Hewitt Associates, nearly one-half of 401(k) participants, regardless of age, salary, or tenure, were invested in only one or two funds. The average number of funds held by 401(k) participants was 3.3. Meanwhile, 75 percent of 401(k) participants' assets were in three asset classes: employer stock, large U.S. equities, and stable value investments. Inadequate diversification was the third most common mistake, following the failure to participate early enough and not contributing enough.

If you want to get the most from your employer-sponsored plan, you have to think bigger and broader. When you're sorting through investment offerings, the different types of funds can be overwhelming. Here's a rundown of the different stock fund categories you may have to choose from.

High-Risk Funds

Aggressive growth funds. These funds buy stocks of fast-growing companies or of other companies that have great capital gains potential. Or they may buy stocks in bankrupt or depressed companies, anticipating a rebound. Such funds, also known as maximum capital gains funds, often trade stocks frequently in hopes of catching small price gains.

Foreign stock funds. These funds buy stocks of corporations based outside the United States. In addition to the usual forces affecting stock prices, fluctuations in the value of the U.S. dollar against foreign currencies can dramatically affect the price of these funds' shares, particularly over the short term.

Sector funds. Sector funds buy stocks in just one industry or sector of the economy. Some examples would be environmental stocks, oil company shares, and stocks in automakers and gold-mining companies. Because these funds are undiversified, they soar or plummet based on the fate of the industry in which they invest.

Small-company growth funds. These growth funds invest in stocks of small companies, typically those having outstanding shares with a total market value of $500 million or less. Such companies have enormous growth potential, yet the stocks the growth funds invest in are much less established—and therefore riskier—than blue chip stocks.

Special situation funds. These funds place large bets on a small number of stocks, anticipating a big payoff. The special situation the fund manager looks for might be a takeover or a liquidation of the company at a price higher than the shares currently sell for. Some funds offer venture capital financing for privately held firms, hoping to cash in when the companies offer shares to the public in the future.

Moderate-Risk Funds

Growth funds. Growth funds invest in shares of well-known growth companies that usually have a long history of increasing earnings. Because the stock market fluctuates, growth funds rise and fall over time as well, though not as much as funds holding smaller, less proven stocks.

Equity-income funds. These funds own shares in stocks that pay higher dividends than do growth funds. Whereas a growth fund's payout may be 1 percent or 2 percent, an equity-income fund might yield 4 percent or 5 percent. That higher yield tends to cushion the fund's price when stock prices fall. When stock prices rise, equity-income funds tend to increase less sharply than do pure growth funds. A slightly more aggressive version of an equity-income fund is called a *growth and income fund* or a *total return fund* because it strives for gains from both income and capital appreciation.

Index funds. These funds buy the stocks that make up a particular index to allow an investor's returns to match the index. The most popular index used is the Standard & Poor's 500. Proponents of index funds argue that because many money managers fail to match or beat the S&P 500 each year, investors can come out ahead by just matching the index. The management fees of an index fund are much lower than those of a regular stock fund because the fund manager just replicates an index and doesn't research or make decisions about which stocks to buy and sell.

Socially conscious funds. Such funds look for companies that meet certain criteria, such as advancing minority and female employees or helping clean up the environment. These funds screen out stocks of companies that are major polluters, defense contractors, or promoters of gambling or tobacco.

Low-Risk Funds

Balanced funds. Balanced funds keep a fairly steady mix of high-yielding stocks and conservative bonds, which allows the funds to pay a fairly high rate of current income and still participate in the long-term growth of stocks.

Flexible portfolio funds. These funds, also known as *asset allocation funds,* have the latitude to invest in stocks, bonds, or cash instruments, depending on a fund manager's market outlook. If the manager thinks stock prices are about to fall, the manager can shift all the fund's assets into cash instruments and thereby avoid losses. If he or she thinks stock prices are about to rise, the manager can move all the fund's assets into stocks. A flexible portfolio fund usually has money in stocks, bonds, and cash, which tends to stabilize its performance.

Utility funds. Such funds buy shares in electric, gas, telephone, and water utilities. Because all of these companies are regulated monopolies, they have steady earnings and pay high dividends. Utility funds are subject to swings in interest rates, however. Nonetheless, for a high-yielding and relatively stable stock fund, it's hard to beat a utility fund.

Another way to look at this trade-off between risk and reward is illustrated in Figure 4.3.

Self-Directed Options

In addition to providing a range of mutual funds, many companies also offer employees the opportunity to use so-called self-directed options. This allows you to buy individual stocks, bonds, and mutual funds that are not part of the standard offering to employees. If you are willing to spend the time and effort picking individual securities, you can potentially earn far higher returns than you would if you stick with the company-sponsored options. But you are also taking considerably more risk and thus have to watch your portfolio more carefully.

GUIDELINES FOR DIVIDING THE INVESTMENT PIE

So how do you figure out what's the right combo for you? Despite much talk about model portfolios, it's tough to come up with a one-size-fits-all

Figure 4.3 Trading Risk for Return: A Mutual Fund Dial

Source: The Investor's Guide to Low-Cost Mutual Funds. Reprinted by permission of The Mutual Fund Education Alliance.

plan. Old-fashioned notions such as subtracting your age from 100 and putting that number as a percent in stocks won't do you much good.

But there are some general—and more reasonable—guidelines for allocating your assets. If you're between 20 and 30 and saving for retirement, time is on your side so you can ride out market swings. Be aggressive. Financial planners say 80 to 100 percent of your portfolio should be in equities, diversified among small cap, midcap, large cap, and international equities and the rest in bond funds. That strategy often holds true, even when you're between 30 and 40. However, as you get closer to retirement, say between 40 and 50 years old, and depending on your life circumstances, it's time to scale down on equities to around 40 to 70 percent. When you hit 50 to 60 years old, you don't want to abandon stocks. In fact, you should probably always have some portion of your portfolio in stocks, but for many people the ideal allocation will be 50-50 stocks and bonds, or 60 percent stocks and the remainder in bonds and cash. Again, it depends on what you're comfortable with. Remember, though, that at 65 you may have another 20 or more years to enjoy retirement. You could spend nearly as much time in retirement as you did working. So don't completely abandon stocks or you'll lose your biggest weapon against inflation.

No matter how much money you have to play with, it's how you divvy the pot that determines whether it runneth over or quietly simmers.

Pay attention to what you're buying, especially when it comes to mutual funds. You may feel good that you've spread your money over six or seven funds, but when you put those funds' holdings under the microscope, you may find that they own very similar companies. Those similarities could be in the types of companies or the sizes of companies, for example, so you may not be as diversified as you think. Avoid redundancy. The same principle applies to loading up on too many stocks of the same type. Remember all the dot-com stocks that seemed like the deals of the century in the late 1990s? Many of those companies vanished and so did investors' capital.

Don't ignore fees and expenses. One advantage of mutual funds is that a professional is managing your money. However, you do have to pay for that privilege. Management fees and expenses have a direct and dramatic impact on your earnings over the long haul. Even a few percentage points can make a difference, costing you losses of thousands of dollars. Expenses run the gamut, so check to see what your fees are. Compare them with industry averages that you can find through an organization such as Morningstar, which rates mutual funds (225 W. Wacker Dr., Chicago, IL 60606; 312-696-6000; www.Morningstar.com). Then, too, you can check the yearly or quarterly returns on your mutual funds and compare them with similar funds listed in the newspaper.

How do you judge if your fees are too high? Some experts say expenses of 0.75 percent to 1.25 percent are acceptable, and as high as 2 percent for international funds are within the norm. If fees are eating up more than 1.5 percent of your assets, you're being taken for a ride. Annual expenses of 1 to 2 percent higher than that may not seem worth losing sleep over, but over time the results can be substantial. Assume that you are an employee with 35 years remaining until retirement and have a current 401(k) account balance of $25,000. If returns on investments in your account over the next 35 years average 7 percent, but fees and expenses reduce your average returns by 0.5 percent, your account balance will grow to $227,000 at retirement, even with no further contributions to your account. If fees and expenses are 1.5 percent, however, your account balance will grow to only $163,000. The 1 percent difference in fees and expenses would reduce your account balance at retirement by 28 percent. (See Figure 4.4.)

A Look at 403(b)s and 457 Plans

Although a 403(b) is similar to a 401(k), there are differences. One difference is that participants cannot invest in individual stocks. Instead, their choices are tax-sheltered annuity and variable annuity contracts with insurance

401(k) Mistakes to Avoid

Without question, the 401(k) for many is the primary source of funds for their retirement kitty. If you blow it with your 401(k), you can pretty much kiss your dream retirement goodbye. Here's a look of some of the top mistakes that you should avoid.

Failing to rebalance your portfolio. You certainly don't want to move in and out of your investments as a day trader does, but you also don't want to not give your initial selections another thought until retirement day. Financial gurus say that once a year you should take a hard look at your holdings: How have they done? What's happening in the market? What's changed in your life? See what, if anything, needs adjusting or pruning.

Cashing out when you change jobs. You're feeling good about that new job you'll be dashing off to, but don't lose your head. The $30,000 you've saved is not for a ticket to paradise or a fancy sports car. For one thing, that money could be whittled down by almost half by the time you pay the mandatory 20 percent federal withholding tax, the IRS's 10 percent penalty if you are under 59½, and state and local taxes—call it the case of the disappearing kitty. It's far better to roll over that money into an IRA, but be careful. If you roll over the money into an existing IRA, you won't be able to parlay that money into a new 401(k) later. This may not matter if you're 65, but it's a different story if you're 30-something. How best to handle your current 401(k) is probably a question best addressed to your financial advisor. But, generally, the benefits from rolling it over to your new employer's 401(k) are the ability to borrow the funds in the future and the little or no transaction fees when investing. The benefit of rolling it over to an IRA is that your investment options are not limited.

Putting too many eggs in one basket. You don't want to load up on your own company's stock, nor do you want too many mutual funds that look like cousins. You want a broad mix of assets to protect your growth opportunities. You'll need to spend the time to learn what you have in your portfolio, but, unfortunately, many people don't take the time. One recent survey showed that half of the survey's repondents spent six hours or less a year managing their portfolio. That kind of inattention will do nothing to boost your stash. Take advantage, too, of any employer-provided financial planning and investment advice, especially if it's free.

Figure 4.4   How 1 Percent Higher Management Fees Reduce Your Account Balance

Current Balance	Annual Returns	Annual Expenses/Fees	Balance in 35 Years
$25,000	7%	0.5%	$227,000
25,000	7	1.5	163,000

A 1 percent difference in fees and expenses would reduce your account balance at retirement by 28 percent.

companies, a custodial account made up of mutual funds, or a retirement income account set up for church employees, which can be invested in annuities or mutual funds. In a 403(b) program, the employer's involvement is not mandatory (beyond payroll), whereas with a 401(k) program the employer must set up, administer, and perform discrimination testing on the plan. Then, too, 403(b)s are subject only to ERISA regulations if there is employer involvement in setting up the program. A 403(b) is a custodial account, and a 401(k) is a trust. Another difference has to do with vesting: with a 403(b), vesting is usually automatic, whereas employees with a 401(k) may have to wait three years to be vested.

Much like a 401(k), 403(b) participants set aside money on a pretax basis through a salary reduction agreement with their employer. The contributions and earnings can grow tax deferred until withdrawal, presumably at retirement, at which time they are taxed as ordinary income. As with a 401(k), you control your destiny; it's up to you to make decisions regarding your investments. Another plus of 403(b)s is their portability. When you change jobs, you can roll over your account into another organization's 403(b) program or an IRA. Employer contributions are optional, but like the 401(k), the "match" can be anywhere from 25 to 100 percent.

Generally, the rules for taking distributions are similar to those of a 401(k) plan. Some 403(b)s allow you to borrow from your account, but you can't take a distribution from your 403(b) account until you reach age 59½, separate from service, die, become disabled, or encounter financial hardship.

A quick word about 457 plans. Along with the increase in contribution limits mentioned earlier, there's more good news on the 457 front: public sector employees can now roll their money into a new employer's plan if they take a new job in the private sector. Then, too, 457 plans can now be rolled over into an IRA. (See Figure 4.5 for a complete look at rollover options.)

Starting in 2002, those who want to make extra, catch-up contributions to compensate for missed savings opportunities can take advantage of new maximums. In 2002, the maximum is $22,000 ($11,000 regular contribution

Figure 4.5   Permitted Rollovers under the New Tax Law

Beginning in 2002, the new tax law (EGTRRA 2001) greatly expands rollovers between company plans and IRAs. The new liberalized rollover rules also apply to surviving spouses who are beneficiaries of their deceased spouse's company plans or IRAs.

Rollovers of **taxable** funds are permitted between all the plans listed in the chart below. The chart shows which plans can also roll over **after-tax** funds to other plans. Even though the new tax law permits these rollovers, company plans are not required to accept rollovers.

The numbers in the bottom of each box refer to other rollover considerations and restrictions, which are detailed following the chart.

Rollovers To:

	IRA	401(k) Plan	403(b) Plan	457 Plan
Rollovers From ⇓ **IRA**	All taxable (eligible) funds can be rolled over to other IRAs. After-tax funds rolled into IRAs from plans and nondeductible IRA contributions can be rolled over to other IRAs, but **not** to company plans.	All taxable (eligible) funds can be rolled over to a 401(k) plan. After-tax funds rolled into IRAs from plans and nondeductible IRA contributions **cannot** be rolled to a 401(k) plan.	All taxable (eligible) funds can be rolled over to a 403(b) plan. After-tax funds rolled into IRAs from plans and nondeductible IRA contributions **cannot** be rolled to a 403(b) plan.	All taxable (eligible) funds can be rolled over to a 457 plan. After-tax funds rolled into IRAs from plans and nondeductible IRA contributions **cannot** be rolled to a 457 plan.
Notes:	2,4	2,5,7,8	2,5,8	2,5,6,8,11
401(k) Plan	All taxable (eligible) funds can be rolled over to an IRA. After-tax 401(k) contributions can be rolled to an IRA.	All taxable (eligible) funds can be rolled to other 401(k) plans. After-tax 401(k) contributions can be rolled to other 401(k) plans.	All taxable (eligible) funds can be rolled over to a 403(b) plan. After-tax 401(k) contributions **cannot** be rolled to a 403(b) plan.	All taxable (eligible) funds can be rolled over to a 457 plan. After-tax 401(k) contributions **cannot** be rolled to a 457 plan.
Notes:	1,4,10	1,3,9,10	1,3,9,10	1,6,9,10,11
403(b) Plan	All taxable (eligible) funds can be rolled over to an IRA. After-tax 403(b) contributions can be rolled to an IRA.	All taxable (eligible) funds can be rolled over to a 401(k) plan. After-tax 403(b) contributions can be rolled to a 401(k) plan.	All taxable (eligible) funds can be rolled to other 403(b) plans. After-tax 403(b) contributions can be rolled to other 403(b) plans.	All taxable (eligible) funds can be rolled over to a 457 plan. After-tax 403(b) contributions **cannot** be rolled to a 457 plan.
Notes:	1,4	1,3,7,9	1,3,9	1,6,9,11
457 Plan (governmental 457 plans only)	Section 457 plans do not accept after-tax funds, so no after-tax funds can be rolled into or out of a 457 plan. The taxable plan balance can be rolled to an IRA, 401(k), 403(b), or another 457 plan. The expanded rollover rules do not apply to Section 457 plans of *nongovernmental* tax-exempt organizations.			
Notes:	1	1,7,9	1,9	1,9,11

Figure 4.5   (continued)

Rollover Considerations and Restrictions

Notes to Rollover Chart

1. Only Eligible Rollover Distributions (ERDs) can be rolled over. For distributions from plans, ERDs include all taxable plan balances **other than** Required Distributions, a series of substantially equal periodic payments (72 (t) payments), or hardship distributions. Also, distributions to plan beneficiaries (other than spouse beneficiaries) *CANNOT* be rolled over.

2. IRA distributions that are: *(a)* required distributions, *(b)* 72(t) payments and *(c)* distributions to beneficiaries from inherited IRAs (other than spouse beneficiaries) *CANNOT* be rolled over.

3. After-tax money rolled from one 401(k) to another, from one 403(b) to another or from a 403(b) to a 401(k) must be transferred by a direct trustee-to-trustee transfer. Also, the receiving plan must agree to account separately for both the taxable and the after-tax amounts rolled over. Currently, there is no provision in the new law to allow after-tax money in a 401(k) to be rolled to a 403(b), but IRS will provide guidance on this point.

4. The IRA does not need to account separately for after-tax funds rolled to the IRA from plans or from other IRAs. That is done by the IRA owner and reported to the IRS on Form 8606 "Nondeductible IRAs." Distributions from IRAs that include after-tax funds (IRA basis) are figured using the Pro Rata Rule.

5. Under the new tax law, when IRA funds are rolled to a company plan, the Pro Rata Rule does *NOT* apply. The first amounts rolled over are deemed to come from the taxable amounts in all traditional IRAs. After-tax IRA funds *CANNOT* be rolled to a company plan. This rule by-passes the Pro Rata Rule and presents an opportunity to withdraw remaining IRA basis (the nontaxable amount), or convert that basis to a Roth IRA tax free.

6. Distributions from Section 457 plans are not subject to the 10% penalty on early distributions (before age 59½). In order for Section 457 plans to accept rollovers from IRAs, 401(k)s and 403(b)s, the 457 plan must agree to separately account for the rollovers, so that any early distributions from the 457 plan that are from the rolled over funds, will be subject to the 10% penalty.

7. 10-Year Averaging and capital gain tax treatment available to those qualified plan participants born before 1936 will be lost to any qualified plan that accepts rollovers from other plans or IRAs that were not permitted under pre-EGTRRA law. Rollovers to company plans from Conduit IRAs were allowed under prior law, so Conduit IRA rollovers to plans will not cause future lump-sum distributions from the plan to lose the benefits of 10-Year Averaging or capital gain treatment. A Conduit IRA is an IRA that contains only money rolled into an IRA from a plan and earnings on that money. 10-Year Averaging and capital gain treatment are *NOT* available to distributions from Section 403(b) or 457 plans.

8. *CAUTION:* Think twice before rolling IRA money to a company plan. Even though the new law permits IRA funds to be rolled to company plans, the best retirement distribution, investment and withdrawal options are in the IRA. Once IRA funds are rolled to a company plan, they become plan assets and are subject to plan restrictions and federal laws. There are certain advantages though to rolling IRA funds into a company plan (including the by-pass of the Pro Rata Rule, among others) and those should also be evaluated.

9. *CAUTION:* Before rolling company plan money into another company plan, first consider the IRA rollover route for the reasons mentioned in #8 above.

10. *CAUTION:* Don't forget to evaluate the possible tax break for Net Unrealized Appreciation (NUA) on company stock. Before rolling funds out of a company plan to an IRA or to another company plan, find out if you may benefit from the NUA tax break.

11. *CAUTION:* There is no benefit to rolling over other plan or IRA funds into a Section 457 plan. Distribution and investment options are not as flexible as those for IRAs or other plans. The new tax law provisions should be used as an opportunity to roll money out of 457 plans.

Source: Reprinted by permission from *Ed Slott's IRA Advisor,* August 2001.

plus $11,000 catch-up). The amount will rise in $2,000 increments until maxing out at $30,000 in 2006. Also in 2002, workers who are 50 or older and more than three years from retirement but not eligible for regular catch-up are able to put in up to $1,000 above the $11,000 limit. The amount rises by $1,000 each year until 2006, when it will reach $5,000.

For most people, a defined contribution plan is among their chief resources for retirement. It's up to you to provide the care and feeding that will make it grow. Much like raising a child, you won't get a second chance; you have to get it right the first time.

RESOURCES

Books, Booklets, and Pamphlets

A Commonsense Guide to Your 401(k), by Mary Rowland (Bloomberg Press, 400 College Rd., Princeton, NJ 08542; P.O. Box 888, Princeton, NJ 08542; 609-279-3000; www.bloomberg.com). Tells readers how to get the most out of a 401(k) and how to use it as the basis of a growing portfolio to reach retirement and preretirement goals.

Building Your Nest Egg with Your 401(k): A Guide to Help You Achieve Retirement Security, by Lynn Brenner (Investors Press, Inc., P.O. Box 329, Washington Depot, CT 06794; 800-773-401(k)). Spells out how each type of investment works, how different investments can be combined to provide the return you need, and how to create an investment strategy.

The Complete Idiot's Guide to 401(k) Plans, by Wayne Bogosian and Dee Lee (Pearson Education, 1 Lake St., Upper Saddle River, NJ 07458; 800-428-5331; www.mcp.com). Describes how 401(k) plans work, how to allocate investments inside them, how to take money out of 401(k)s, and much more.

The Essential Guide to Your 401(k), by Virginia B. Morris and Kenneth M. Morris (Lightbulb Press, 112 Madison Ave., New York, NY 10016; 917-256-4900; www.lightbulbpress.com). A guide for the average consumer that shows how to create and manage an investment portfolio.

The 401(k) Millionaire, by Knute Iwaszko and Brian O'Connell (Villard Books, a division of Random House, 1540 Broadway, New York, NY 10036; 212-782-9000; www.randomhouse.com). An informative primer on the basics needed for novice investors to start parlaying 401(k) programs into formidable sums by retirement time.

401(k) Plans, by Dearborn Financial Institute, Inc. (Dearborn Trade, 155 N. Wacker Dr., Chicago, IL 60606; 312-836-4400; 800-245-2665; www.dearborntrade.com). Covers retirement plan management and pension administration as they relate to 401(k) plans.

401(k) Planning Guide: Every Employee's Guide to Making 401(k) Decisions, by Alan J. Miller (McGraw-Hill, P.O. Box 543, Blacklick, OH 43004; 800-634-3961; www.mcgraw-hill.com). Aims to take all the guesswork out of 401(k)s.

401(k) Take Charge of Your Future, by Eric Schurenberg (Warner Books, 1271 Avenue of the Americas, New York, NY 10020; 212-522-7200; www.twbookmark.com). A comprehensive guide by the former assistant managing editor of *Money* magazine to help you decide how much to save, how to evaluate your choice of funds, how to pick the best mix of investments for your needs, and when to cash out.

401(k) Today: Designing, Maintaining & Maximizing Your Company's Plan, by Stephen J. Butler (Berrett-Koehler Publishing, 235 Montgomery St., Suite 650, San Francisco, CA 94104; 415-288-0260; www.bkpub.com). Offers valuable tools that help employees understand and manage their plans as well as positively influence their company's decision making on issues of cost and quality.

How to Become a Millionaire in Your Current Job: Choose Wisely with 401(k) and IRA, by J.B. Davis (Galaxy Publishing, P.O. Box 10035, Houston, TX 77206; 800-431-1579; www.401kmillionaire.com). Explains the benefits of a 401(k) and an IRA and shows readers, even those living from paycheck to paycheck, how to save.

How to Build Wealth with Your 401(k): Everything You Need to Know to Become More Than a Millionaire over the Course of Your Working Lifetime, by Steve Merritt (Halyard Press, P.O. Box 410308, Melbourne, FL 32941; 407-634-5022). Aims to teach you everything you need to know to turn your 401(k), 403(b), 457, and other retirement benefits into accumulated riches.

IRAs, 401(k)s & Other Retirement Plans: Taking Your Money Out, by Twila Slesnick and John C. Suttle (Nolo Press, 950 Parker St., Berkeley, CA 94710; 800-992-6656; www.nolo.com). Offers specific coverage of the rules for withdrawing money from various retirement plans and covers how IRAs relate to living trusts.

J.K. Lasser's Winning Your 401(k), by Grace W. Weinstein (John Wiley, 1 Wiley Dr., Somerset, NJ 08875-1272; 212-850-6000; 800-225-5945; www.wiley.com). An in-depth guide to 401(k) plans that explains how 401(k)s work, how federal regulations and company policies affect retirement savings, how to develop investment strategies, and what happens when money is taken out.

Keys to Investing in Your 401(k) (Barron's Business Keys), by Warren Boroson (Barron's Educational Series, 250 Wireless Blvd., Hauppauge, NY 11788; 631-434-3311; 800-645-3476; www.barronseduc.com). Tells how to evaluate and improve specific 401(k) investments.

Living with Defined Contribution Pensions: Remaking Responsibility for Retirement, by Oliva S. Mitchell and Sylvester Schieber (University of Pennsylvania Press, 4200 Pine St., Philadelphia, PA 19104-4011; 215-898-6261; www.upenn.edu). Explains how 401(k)s work, asset allocation, and other 401(k) essentials.

Smart Guide to Maximizing Your 401(k) Plan, by Barbara Wagner and Barbara Hetzer (John Wiley, 1 Wiley Dr., Somerset, NJ 08875; 212-850-6000; 800-225-

5945; www.wiley.com). An all-you-need-to-know introduction to the employer-sponsored retirement plan that includes advice on how much to contribute and what you need to know about your investment options.

10-Minute Guide to 401(k) Plans, by Paul Katzeff (IDG Books/Hungry Minds, 10475 Crosspoint Blvd., Indianapolis, IN 46526; 800-434-3422; www.hungryminds. com). A guide to choosing the right investment from the options available through 401(k) plans.

T. Rowe Price Retirees Financial Guide (T. Rowe Price Associates, P.O. Box 89000, Baltimore, MD 21289-0250; 800-638-5660; 800-225-5132; www.troweprice. com). A helpful kit about retirement planning available free from T. Rowe Price, a large mutual fund marketing organization, that includes many publications.

Trade Association

Profit Sharing/401(k) Council of America (10 S. Riverside Plaza, Suite 1610, Chicago, IL 60606; 312-441-8550; www.psca.org). A nonprofit association advocating increasing retirement security through profit sharing, 401(k)s, and related defined contribution programs.

Web Sites

ey.com <www.ey.com>. The Web site for Ernst & Young. The Personal Financial Consulting section has an excellent overview of the Economic Growth and Tax Relief Reconciliation Act of 2001 and much more.

401k.com <www.401k.com>. Site sponsored by Fidelity Investments Institutional Services, where you can learn about saving for retirement with interactive education on your desktop; includes tools and other information vital to the 401(k) investor.

403bwise.com <www.403bwise.com>. A one-stop shop for just about everything you ever wanted to know about 403(b)s.

Morningstar.com <www.morningstar.com>. The funds rating service has an excellent retirement center where you can find plenty to chew on—401(k)s, 403(b)s, counting down to retirement, asset mix, portfolio protection, tools, worksheets, and more.

mPower.com <www.mpower.com>. Home to the mPower Cafe, where you'll find a treasure trove of information on 401(k)s, 403(b)s, 457 plans, and IRAs. Lots of articles, investing basics, and more.

Quicken.com <www.quicken.com>. The site boasts a comprehensive 401(k) guide.

CHAPTER 5

Self-Employed Pension Plans

W hen you are self-employed, no one looks out for your interests—except you. Because you don't have the luxury of working for a company that offers a defined benefit or contribution plan, you must take a more active role in funding your retirement. If you never set up one of the pension plans that the Internal Revenue Code allows, you will have to survive on only your personal investments and Social Security when you retire.

If you are self-employed, there's a lot you can do for yourself and your employees through various retirement plans. You can make tax-deductible contributions, which you can invest in such vehicles as stocks, bonds, mutual funds, and CDs. The funds' earnings compound tax deferred.

All the money you stash in a self-employment retirement plan must be self-employment income. That means income from freelance writing, consulting, moonlighting, arts and crafts, or from any other way you earn money through your own business. Farmers, doctors, lawyers, and other professionals who are not covered by corporate plans may also fund a self-employment plan. Some plans require you to contribute a certain amount of money every year, whereas others allow you to contribute whatever you please up to an annual maximum or nothing at all if you can't afford it or produce no self-employment income in a particular year. As with other retirement plans, you must pay a 10 percent penalty and federal and state income taxes if you withdraw funds from a self-employment retirement plan before age 59½. Therefore, invest only funds that you won't need for living expenses or emergencies before you retire.

Here's a look at several types of pension plans.

KEOGH PLANS

Named after U.S. Representative Eugene James Keogh, who first introduced the idea in the 1960s, Keogh plans come in both defined contribution and defined benefit form.

Defined Contribution

The most common type of Keogh is the defined contribution variety, of which three forms exist: money-purchase, profit-sharing, and combination.

A *money-purchase Keogh* requires you to choose a fixed percentage of your earnings and contribute that percentage every year to the plan. The percentage can be as low as 1 percent or as high as 25 percent up to a maximum of $40,000 under the Economic Growth and Tax Relief Reconciliation Act of 2001. You must contribute the money annually, no matter how profitable your business. If you don't contribute, you will be penalized by the IRS. Therefore, if you think you might have trouble meeting such a fixed obligation, consider investing in a profit-sharing Keogh.

A *profit-sharing Keogh* allows you to contribute up to 25 percent of your earnings up to $40,000 a year. However, you can contribute the full amount one year and nothing the next, depending on how your business performs each year.

A Keogh that *combines* both money-purchase and profit-sharing plans offers the option of contributing up to the maximum of $40,000 but doesn't lock you into the maximum contribution. You can start with a profit-sharing plan and then add a money-purchase plan with a set annual contribution level, such as 8 or 10 percent. In good years, you can add money to your profit-sharing plan up to the maximum of $40,000; in lean years, you can pay only the minimum.

Keogh plans are not only available if you are the sole employee of your business but you can also enroll others who work for you. Rules for other employees regarding contribution limits, percentages of salary contributed, and other matters differ slightly from those with single-worker plans. In general, you must contribute at least the same percentage of income for your employees as for yourself. Before you set up a Keogh for employees, check with a financial planner, an accountant, or an employee benefits expert to explain the rules.

Defined Benefit

This less common variety of Keogh, which can be costly to establish and administer, allows you to contribute much more than the $40,000 limit imposed on defined contribution plans. In addition, each year the amount of money you add can be significantly greater or less than the amount you invested in previous years. With the help of an actuary, you should project your defined benefit at retirement and then contribute enough money while you are still working to fund that level of benefits.

Defined benefit Keoghs are usually established by high-income people in their 50s with very successful businesses who have so far neglected to set up a pension plan. In effect, these plans allow them to catch up by investing a greater amount of capital at once to create a large pension benefit in retirement.

Other Keogh Rules

Unlike an IRA, you cannot open a Keogh account right up until the April 15 tax-filing deadline. Instead, you must establish the Keogh by December 31 of the year in which you will file for the deduction. This is a key point to remember because one of the biggest advantages of a Keogh is that all your contributions are tax deductible. Although you must open the account by the end of the year, you can make a contribution, or add to your existing account, any time up to April 15 (plus extensions) to claim the deduction in the previous year.

In general, it is difficult to withdraw cash from a Keogh before you reach 59½ if you are an employer. Employees and owners enrolled in a Keogh can borrow up to one-half their vested balance up to $50,000, which must be repaid through payroll deductions over five years.

A certain amount of paperwork goes along with establishing and maintaining a Keogh. If you deal with a reputable mutual fund company, brokerage, insurance company, or bank, it should be able to help you complete and file the necessary forms, though the firm will probably charge for the service. Accountants or financial planners can also prepare Keogh documents, such as the original application form and IRS Form 5500, which is the annual report required if the plan's assets exceed $100,000.

SIMPLIFIED EMPLOYEE PENSION (SEP) PLANS

SEPs, which combine some of the best features of IRAs and Keoghs, are even easier to establish than Keoghs and involve much less paperwork. Like an IRA, a SEP establishes an account for each participant. As in a profit-sharing Keogh, you can contribute to a SEP one year but not the next if you desire. And as with other pension plans, you must pay a 10 percent penalty plus income tax if you withdraw money from a SEP before age 59½. In addition, you cannot borrow against SEP assets in the same way such loans are banned for holders of IRAs. However, the government does not require annual filings of SEP plan assets as it does for Keoghs. You can invest the assets of a SEP with a mutual fund, bank, credit union, or brokerage.

Eligibility is attained if an employee is at least 21 years old, has worked for the firm at least three of the past five years, and has earned a certain minimum—currently $450, although the number is indexed to inflation each year. Half of your firm's employees must agree to participate before the plan can become effective. If you are the sole employee of the firm, you can set up a SEP just for yourself. Like a Keogh, a SEP allows a self-employed person to contribute up to $40,000 of his or her annual income.

As with an IRA, you can set up and fund a SEP until the April 15 tax deadline or an extension date to qualify for a tax deduction for the prior year. Therefore, if you miss the December 31 deadline for opening a Keogh, consider establishing a SEP instead. You also might look into setting up a SIMPLE (Savings Incentive Match for Employees) plan, which can be established as a SIMPLE IRA or SIMPLE 401(k) plan for firms with 100 or fewer employees.

SIMPLE IRA

Employees may sock away up to $7,000 of pretax pay per year. However, with recent changes in the laws, the limit increases to $8,000 in 2003 and $1,000 per year up to $10,000 in 2005. From 2006 through 2010, the contribution limit is indexed to inflation. Starting in 2002, you can put away an additional $500 in catch-up contributions if you are 50 or older; in 2003: $1,000; 2004: $1,500; 2005: $2,000; 2006: $2,500; and from 2007 through 2010, the catch-up contribution limit is indexed to inflation. (See Figures 5.1 and 5.2.)

Figure 5.1   SIMPLE IRA Maximums: Annual Elective Deferral Limits

Year	Limit
2001	$ 6,500
2002	7,000
2003	8,000
2004	9,000
2005	10,000
2006–2010	Indexed to inflation

Figure 5.2   SIMPLE IRA Catch-up: Annual Contribution Limits for Those 50 and Older

Year	Limit
2002	$ 500
2003	1,000
2004	1,500
2005	2,000
2006	2,500
2007–2010	Indexed to inflation

Employers are required to contribute by either matching 100 percent of their employees' contributions up to 3 percent of their annual salary, or for employees who put nothing in on their own, employers must chip in 2 percent of pay on an employee's behalf. All employees are eligible to participate if they earned at least $5,000 during any two preceding years and are expected to earn at least $5,000 in the current year. Though plan administration is minimal, small business owners can't stash much for themselves; they are limited to the same $7,000 (in 2002, for example) plus up to 3 percent of an employee's salary.

SEP IRA

The SEP IRA is similar to a regular IRA but has higher contribution limits. Contributions can vary each year at the employer's discretion, the maximum being $40,000. SEPs are fully funded by the employer, and they are required to establish accounts for nearly all employees—those who have worked for three of the past five years and earned at least $450 in the last year. Employees must be 100 percent vested immediately.

If you're self-employed, you can put away up to $40,000. SEP IRAs can be a good option for those with one to ten employees. There are no reporting requirements, and employers have only limited administrative responsibilities. Costs are low, and plans offer flexibility in the size and timing of contributions.

MAKING THE CHOICE

Although there are lots of features to consider when choosing a plan, mutual fund company T. Rowe Price has a Small Business Decision Guide

Trustee Requirements

Choosing a financial institution to maintain employees' SIMPLE IRAs is one of the most important decisions employers or employees will make. Trustees work closely with employers to receive contributions, invest them, and issue certain required information.

For SIMPLE plan purposes, only these institutions can be designated as trustees: banks, savings and loan associations, insured credit unions, insurance companies (that issue annuity contracts), or IRS-approved nonbank trustees.

Trustees must agree to the following:

- Accept and deposit contributions.
- Prepare and provide the employer with a summary description each year that includes (1) the name and address of the employer and trustee; (2) a description of eligibility requirements; (3) the benefits provided; and (4) the time and method of making salary elections and the procedure for, and effects of, withdrawals and rollovers (including the penalties for early withdrawals).
- Provide the employer with a summary description, which may be satisfied by providing the most recent copy of IRS Forms 5304 or 5305 (if these forms are used to establish the SIMPLE plans) along with the financial institution's procedures for withdrawals and transfers. (Timing is important because substantial penalties may be imposed and employers depend on receiving summary descriptions in time to notify employees of each year's election period.)
- Within 30 days after the close of each calendar year, provide each individual on whose behalf an account is maintained with a statement of the account balance and activity during the year.
- Report SIMPLE IRA information to the IRS as they do with any IRA account.
- Transfer, on request, an individual's SIMPLE IRA balance to another IRA or SIMPLE IRA without cost or penalty to the participant if trustees are designated financial institutions by agreement with the employer.

Source: U.S. Department of Labor.

that can help walk you through the process and you can get for free by calling 800-831-1067.

For those with employees. If your primary concern is to allow your employees to make salary reduction contributions, then consider the following: Choose a 401(k) if you want employees to have the ability to contribute the most money and you have flexibility in employer contributions. Or if you want the least administrative cost and hassle, go for the SIMPLE IRA.

For those without employees. If your Schedule C net income is less than $41,700 (or your W-2 wage is less than $29,600) and you want to contribute the most money possible every year, go with the SIMPLE IRA. If you're above those income limits and you want to contribute the most money possible, go with the Simplified Keogh Money-Purchase Plan. If you want to combine flexibility with maximum contributions, choose a Simplified Keogh Paired Plan. And if what matters most is the flexibility of no mandatory annual contributions, then consider a SEP IRA.

For a comparison of various small business retirement plans, see Figure 5.3.

SETTING UP YOUR PLAN

Once you've made your choice, setting up the plan is the next task and is probably the most time-consuming part of the process. A few tips when setting up a SEP or a SIMPLE IRA follow.

These are the three basic steps for setting up a SEP:

1. You must execute a formal written agreement to provide benefits to all eligible employees.
2. You must give each eligible employee certain information about the SEP.
3. A SEP IRA must be set up by or for each eligible employee.

As for a SIMPLE IRA, you must notify each employee of the following information before the beginning of the election period—generally the 60-day period immediately preceding January 1 of a calendar year (November 2 to December 31 of the preceding calendar year)—although the dates of this period are modified if you set up a SIMPLE IRA plan in midyear (for example, on July 1) or if the 60-day period falls before the first day an employee becomes eligible to participate in the SIMPLE IRA:

1. The employee's opportunity to make or change a salary reduction choice under a SIMPLE IRA plan

Figure 5.3   Small Business Retirement Savings Programs Pension & Welfare Benefits Administration Advisor

The information contained in this table is based on current interpretation of the law. Where IRS guidance is pending, assumptions have been made. Seek tax advice for additional rules and complete information.

Options / Features	SEP IRA	Payroll Deduction IRA	SIMPLE IRA	401(k)	Profit Sharing	Defined Benefit	Money Purchase Plan
Key Advantage	Easy to set up and maintain.	Easy to set up and maintain.	Salary reduction plan with little administrative paperwork.	Permits employee to contribute more than in other options.	Permits employer to create large account balances for employees.	Provides a fixed, preestablished benefit for employees.	Permits employer to make a larger contribution than through other defined contribution plans.
Employers Who Can Provide This Option	Any business that does not currently maintain any other retirement plan.	Any business with one or more employees.	Any business with 100 or fewer employees that does not currently maintain any other retirement plan.	Any business with one or more employees.	Any business with one or more employees.	Any business with one or more employees.	Any business with one or more employees.
Employer's Responsibilities	Set up plan by completing IRS Form 5305-SEP. No employer tax filing required.	Set up arrangements for employees to make payroll deduction contributions. Transmit contributions for employees to funding vehicle. No employer tax filing required.	Set up by completing IRS Form 5304-SIMPLE or 5305-SIMPLE. No employer tax filing required. Bank or financial institution does most of the paperwork.	There is no model form to establish a plan. Advice from a financial institution or employee benefit advisor would be necessary. Annual filing of IRS Form 5500 required. Also requires special testing to ensure plan does not discriminate in favor of highly compensated employees.	There is no model form to establish a plan. Advice from a financial institution or employee benefit advisor would be necessary. Annual filing of IRS Form 5500 is required.	There is no model form to establish a plan. Advice from a financial institution or employee benefit advisor would be necessary. Annual filing of IRS Form 5500. Actuary must determine funding obligations.	There is no model form to establish a plan. Advice from a financial institution or employee benefit advisor would be necessary. Annual filing of IRS Form 5500 is required.
Funding Responsibility	Employer contributions only.	Employee contributions remitted through payroll deduction.	Employee salary reduction contributions and/or employer contributions.	Employee salary reduction contributions and/or employer contributions.	Employer contribution level can be determined year to year.	Primarily employer, may require or permit employee contributions.	Employer contributions only.

Continued

Figure 5.3 (continued)

Options / Features	SEP IRA	Payroll Deduction IRA	SIMPLE IRA	401(k)	Profit Sharing	Defined Benefit	Money Purchase Plan
Maximum Annual Contribution Per Participant	Up to 15% of compensation or a maximum of $35,000; in 2002, up to 25% of compensation or a maximum of $40,000.[1]	$2,000 for 2001; $3,000 for 2002-2004; $4,000 for 2005-2007; $5,000 for 2008.	*Employee:* $6,000 per year, up to $7,000 in 2002 and increasing in $1,000 annual increments until the limit reaches $10,000 in 2005. *Employer:* Either match employee contributions $ for $ up to 3% of compensation (can be reduced to as low as 1% in any 2 out of 5 yrs.) or contribute 2% of each eligible employee's compensation, up to $3,200[2]	*Employee:* $10,500 in 2001; $11,000 in 2002 with $1,000 annual increments until the limit reaches $15,000 in 2006. *Employer/ Employee combined:* Up to a maximum of 15% of compensation or a maximum of $35,000; in 2002, up to a maximum of 25% of compensation or a maximum of $40,000.[1]	Up to a maximum of 15% of salary or a maximum of $35,000; in 2002, up to a maximum of 25% of salary or a maximum of $40,000.[1]	Per plan terms, employer may permit or require employee contribution.	Up to a maximum of 25% of salary or a maximum of $35,000; in 2002, up to a maximum of 100% of salary or a maximum of $40,000.[1]
Minimum Employee Coverage Requirements	Must be offered to all employees who are at least 21 years of age, employed by the business for 3 of last 5 years and earned at least $450 in a year.	Should be made available to all employees.	Must be offered to all employees who have earned at least $5,000 in previous 2 years.	Must be offered to all employees at least 21 years of age who worked at least 1,000 hours in previous year.	Must be offered to all employees at least 21 years of age who worked at least 1,000 hours in previous year.	Must be offered to all employees at least 21 years of age who worked at least 1,000 hours in previous year.	Must be offered to all employees at least 21 years of age who worked at least 1,000 hours in previous year.
Withdrawals, Loans & Payments	Withdrawals at anytime; subject to current federal income taxes and a possible 10% penalty if the participant is under age 59½.	Withdrawals at anytime; subject to current federal income taxes and a possible 10% penalty if the participant is under age 59½.	Withdrawals at any time. If employee is under age 59½, may be subject to a 25% penalty if taken within the first 2 years of participation and a possible 10% penalty if taken afterwards.	Cannot take withdrawals until a specified event, such as reaching 59½, death, separation from service or other event as identified in plan. May permit loans and hardship withdrawals. Withdrawals may be subject to a possible 10% penalty if participant is under age 59½.	May permit loans and hardship withdrawals. Hardship withdrawals may be subject to a possible 10% penalty if participant is under age 59½. Payment of benefits generally at retirement.	Payment of benefits generally at retirement, may offer participant loans.	Payment of benefits generally at retirement, may offer participant loans.

Figure 5.3   (continued)

Options \ Features	SEP IRA	Payroll Deduction IRA	SIMPLE IRA	401(k)	Profit Sharing	Defined Benefit	Money Purchase Plan
Vesting	Immediate 100%	Immediate 100%	Employee and employer contributions vested 100% immediately.	Employee contributions vested immediately. Employer contributions may vest over time according to plan terms.	May vest over time according to plan terms.	May vest over time according to plan terms.	May vest over time according to plan terms.
Contributor's Options	Employer can decide whether or not to make contribution year to year.	Employee can decide how much to contribute at any time.	Employee can decide how much to contribute. Employer must make matching contributions or contribute 2% of each employee's salary up to the set maximum.	Employee makes contribution as set by plan option. The employer may match.	Employer makes contribution as set by plan terms.	Employer makes contribution as set by plan terms.	Employer makes contribution as set by plan terms.

[1] Maximum compensation on which 1997 contributions can be based is $160,000. For plan years beginning on or after January 1, 1998, maximum compensation on which contributions can be based is $160,000.

[2] Maximum compensation on which 1998 employer 2% non-elective contributions can be based is $160,000.

Source: Pension & Welfare Benefits Administration.

2. Your choice to make either reduced matching contributions or non-elective contributions
3. A summary description and the location of the plan, which the financial institution should provide
4. Written notice that the employee's balance can be transferred without cost or penalty if you use a designated financial institution

SHOPPING WISELY

This is one time you won't be able to do everything yourself. Get good advice up front. Turn to your accountant, lawyer, advisors, financial planner, and business peers for recommendations. If you choose a mutual fund family, ask if it has local representatives available to come to you, educate your staff, and be there to guide you through the process, especially if you are without a human resources department. Some companies turn to a professional employer organization (PEO) to handle their retirement programs. Advantages of a PEO are a wide variety of investment choices and the possibility of more advantageous fees and costs because of their volume. PEOs also assume the administrative burdens. Whichever route you take, get help. If you don't keep up on recordkeeping and your plan is disqualified, the company can incur penalties and employees' money might be returned. You need guidance because the laws are constantly changing and you have a business to run, so it's difficult to keep up with all of your legal obligations.

When you're shopping, find out what all your costs will be: not only what you'll pay into the plan but also the cost to manage and maintain the accounts and the costs associated with the investment that employees pay. Over the long term, management fees of even as little as one-half of a percent will significantly eat into employees' returns. You may find that costs are not as exorbitant as you think. They vary depending on factors like total plan assets, number of participants, and plan type; you may pay about $2,000 to $5,000 per year.

Avoid the temptation to take the shoestring approach. There's no point in trying to create a nifty recruitment and retention tool if you don't get a bang for your buck. Realize that a 401(k) without a matching or profit-sharing component lacks a certain pizzazz. It's like building a house and spending a lot of money on the sheet rock, plumbing, and electrical work but then choosing cheap paint—it spoils the house.

Consider your range of choices carefully. Investment flexibility is crucial. You want your employees to have access to a healthy number of fund types and fund families. Many small employers are criticized by their employees for offering too little choice. There should be a mix of conservative, moderate, and riskier investments.

Revisit your plan over the years. Many things can impact the effectiveness of your retirement plan: the size of your business, your labor force, the investment markets, and the law, to name a few. Evaluate your plan every couple of years to see how well it is performing. Assess whether changes need to be made. It's a mistake to think once the plan is set up and running that your monitoring job is over.

RULES, RULES, AND MORE RULES: HOW TO STAY OUT OF TROUBLE

You may have the best intentions in setting up a retirement plan for yourself and your employees, but making a few wrong moves could be like stepping on a land mine. Abide by the rules and regulations so you don't wind up facing hefty penalties, fines, and increased costs.

New Law Nets Other Perks

The 2001 tax law not only raised contribution limits, but it created a new financial incentive for small business owners to jump on the retirement savings bandwagon. As of 2002, certain small employers are able to receive a tax credit for the expenses involved in establishing a retirement plan. The credit applies to 50 percent of the set-up costs and for the first three years a new employer-sponsored plan is established in addition to 50 percent of administrative and retirement education expenses, with a maximum credit of $500 deductible annually. Generally, these provisions apply to companies with 100 or fewer employees. However, no deduction is allowed for the amount claimed as a general business credit.

Don't take reporting requirements lightly. You must file an annual report with the IRS or penalties can be $1,000 a day for every day you're late, up to $50,000. Reporting is the responsibility of the plan administrator, whether the business owner or the company. Third-party administrators are merely recordkeepers, who don't assume the responsibility for filing even though they may compile the report.

Then there are disclosure requirements. Employees should receive an annual summary plan description. In the case of a 401(k), where employees self-direct their investments, the plan administrator is responsible for educating employees and explaining options through seminars and workshops. The big mutual fund families typically do this for you.

Make sure all eligible employees are participating and that new workers are enrolled properly. And if you are the plan trustee, you have to offer a range of prudent investment choices—some conservative and some risky but not too speculative. Keep in mind, too, that the IRS has rules for highly compensated and non–highly compensated employees you must comply with.

Be ready to explain how you chose investment options, and have an investment policy because lawsuits are a real possibility. Because employees, former and present, may try to hold you responsible for lackluster returns, you may be stuck trying to explain why your plan earned returns of 6 to 7 percent or even lost money when the market was roaring along with 20 percent returns. Smart employers are increasingly looking to remove their liability by moving to employee-directed plans.

Perhaps the biggest surprise in our foray into retirement plans is the complexity of *compliance,* the myriad laws and IRS rules. Strict guidelines govern many aspects of a retirement plan, so know your responsibilities as a trustee and fiduciary. Talk to your advisors. Navigate these waters without their help and you just might drown.

Coming up with a good retirement plan that meets your needs as well as those of your employees is a big task but one that ultimately impacts the bottom line. You'll benefit in saving for your own retirement and you'll boost employee morale by rewarding employees. This should help tie employees to your company, but, most important, you'll help them take care of themselves.

RESOURCES

Books, Booklets, and Pamphlets:

Ernst & Young's Retirement Planning Guide (John Wiley & Sons, 1 Wiley Dr., Somerset, NJ 08875; 800-225-5945; www.wiley.com). A comprehensive guide with extensive sections on investment strategy, choosing financial advisors, and maximizing 401(k)s, IRAs, and Keogh plans.

Fidelity Investments Retirement Publications (P.O. Box 500, Merrimack, NH 03051; 800-544-8888, www.fidelity.com). A wide range of free publications on retirement planning and investment strategy as well as an extensive retirement section on the Web site.

Retirement Plans for Small Business (SEP, SIMPLE, and Qualified Plans), IRS Publication 560 (www.irs.gov; 800-829-3676). Explains the rules, regulations, and requirements of these plan types.

Retirement Plans for Small Businesses (The Vanguard Group, P.O. Box 1106, Valley Forge, PA 19482-1106; 800-823-7412; www.vanguard.com). Explains small business owner's retirement plan options and helps with the decision-making process.

The Small Business Decision Guide (T. Rowe Price, P.O. Box 89000, Baltimore, MD 21289-9999; 800-492-7670; www.troweprice.com). A free guide designed to walk employers through the decision-making process for choosing a retirement plan.

Government Agency

U.S. Department of Labor's Pension and Welfare Benefits Adminstration (200 Constitution Ave., N.W., Washington, DC 20210; 202-219-8771; www.dol.gov/dol/pwba). Offers many publications covering retirement issues, SIMPLE and SEP plans, and other topics.

Trade Association

American Savings Education Council (2121 K St., N.W., Suite 600, Washington, DC 20037; 202-775-9130; www.asec.org). The Web site has a small business retirement quiz and a brief true/false quiz for small business owners to test basic knowledge on costs and cosponsorship of a 401(k) retirement plan.

Web Sites

ADP Retirement Services <www.adp401k.com>. Provides retirement plan services to businesses; offers a resource for information about 401(k)s, deferred compensation plans, and SIMPLE IRAs that includes a plan selection tool for business owners.

Invesmart <www.invesmart.com>. Provides retirement services for employers and their employees; information on SIMPLE IRAs, 401(k)s, defined benefit plans, SEPs, profit-sharing plans, and the like.

Quicken.com <www.quicken.com>. The retirement section has a Guide to Pensions that explores the basics of SIMPLE IRAs, Keoghs, and other retirement plans.

Selectaretirementplan.org <www.selectaretirementplan.org>. Sponsored by the U.S. Chamber of Commerce, U.S. Department of Labor, U.S. Small Business Administration, and Merrill Lynch, this site helps business owners choose and implement the right retirement plan.

CHAPTER 6

Individual Retirement Accounts

E ven if you have a defined benefit or defined contribution plan through your employer or you have a Keogh or SEP plan if you are self-employed, you can also establish an IRA as a tax-sheltered vehicle to save for retirement. Determining whether you qualify for a deduction for your IRA contribution can be quite complex. But in any case, the funds inside the IRA grow tax deferred and grow tax free in the case of a Roth IRA. Many people who formerly contributed to IRAs don't any longer because of the complexities of the law and the possibility that they won't be able to deduct their contributions. That is a big mistake, particularly because of the attractiveness of Roth IRAs. Funding your IRA must be accomplished totally on your own initiative because no employer will offer you one. But this flexible account, allowing you to manage your money however you want and offering an enormous range of investment options, is well worth the extra effort.

WHEN CONTRIBUTIONS ARE DEDUCTIBLE

Depending on your employment status and level of income, the contribution you make to an IRA may or may not be deductible. If you are *not* eligible to participate in any qualified retirement plan, which includes the defined benefit and defined contribution plans discussed in Chapters 3 and 4, your IRA contribution currently of up to $3,000 a year and $3,000 for a nonworking spouse is tax deductible, no matter what your income. Thanks to the Economic Growth and Tax Relief Reconciliation Act of 2001, the limits increase in coming years. From 2002 through 2004, you can contribute $3,000; from 2005 through 2007, $4,000; and in 2008, $5,000. In future years the limit is indexed for inflation annually in $500 increments, and, as elsewhere in the law, there is a catch-up provision. Those 50 and older can contribute an additional $500 in years 2002 through 2005 and an additional $1,000 in 2006 through 2010. (See Figures 6.1 and 6.2.)

In addition, if you earn less than $30,000 in adjusted gross income (AGI) as a single filer or $50,000 as a couple filing jointly, you can deduct your IRA contribution, even if you are eligible for a qualified retirement plan. If you need a further incentive, there is now a tax credit for those who meet a certain age (typically over 18) and income requirement ($25,000 or less for single filers and $50,000 or less for joint filers) for contributions to traditional and Roth IRAs. The credit is in addition to any deduction or exclusion that may otherwise apply and varies from 10 to 50 percent of the first $2,000 of your contribution, depending on your income and filing status.

If you participate in your employer's plan, however, the portion of your IRA contribution that you can deduct depends on your adjusted gross income for each year. The deduction phases out between the income levels stated in Figure 6.3.

If your spouse participates in an employer plan but you don't, you can make a fully deductible IRA contribution if your joint AGI is below $150,000. The deduction is phased out between $150,000 and $160,000 in AGI.

Figure 6.1   Traditional and Roth IRA Annual Contribution Limits

Year	Limit
2002–2004	$3,000
2005–2007	4,000
2008	5,000
2009–2010	Indexed to inflation

Figure 6.2   Traditional and Roth IRA Catch-up Annual Contribution Limits for Those 50 and Older

Year	Limit
2002–2005	$ 500
2006–2010	1,000

Figure 6.3   Adjusted Gross Income Phase-Out Range

Year	Joint Return	Single Return
2001	$53,000–$63,000	$33,000–$43,000
2002	54,000–64,000	34,000–44,000
2003	60,000–70,000	40,000–50,000
2004	65,000–75,000	45,000–55,000
2005	70,000–80,000	50,000–60,000
2006	75,000–85,000	50,000–60,000
2007	80,000–100,000	50,000–60,000

NONDEDUCTIBLE IRAS

If you earn more than the maximum level and are eligible for a qualified plan, you can still make a nondeductible contribution to an IRA. You and your spouse can each invest $3,000 a year from earnings, though that amount has changed under the new law (see the previous section). If your spouse does not work, you can contribute $3,000 (again new limits apply) for him or her in a spousal IRA. When you add a nondeductible contribution to your IRA, you must file IRS Form 8606 because the tax treatment of those funds will be different from the treatment of deductible contributions when you withdraw the money at retirement. When you make an after-tax, nondeductible contribution, you will not be taxed on any distributions of your original capital, though you will be taxed on your accumulated earnings.

Even though a nondeductible IRA is certainly not as financially rewarding up front as a deductible IRA, it can still be a potent long-term tax shelter in which to accumulate a retirement nest egg. Because all dividends and capital gains are tax deferred until you are 59½, you gain the advantage of tax-sheltered compounding. In the long run, that shelter can be worth far more than the one-time tax reduction resulting from a deductible IRA contribution.

You can open an IRA account until the April 15 tax deadline and, if you are eligible, deduct your contribution on the previous year's tax return. However, don't wait until the last minute to invest your money because you lose valuable time for your earnings to compound tax deferred. It is far better to make your IRA deposit soon after January 1 of the year you will claim the deduction, so you have the full year of tax shelter. For example, it would have been better to contribute $3,000 on January 3, 2002, for the 2002 tax year than to wait until April 15, 2003, because you will gain more than 15 months of additional tax-deferred compounding. You continue to contribute to your IRA until you reach age 70½, at which point you must start withdrawing capital according to an IRS schedule.

Don't put off opening an IRA. The sooner the better. The table below illustrates the advantages of starting early—the way your IRA can grow if you saved $3,000 each year and your money earned 7 percent annually.

At 5 years you would have:	$ 18,459
At 15 years:	80,664
At 25 years:	203,029
At 35 years:	443,740

Roth IRAs

In addition to traditional IRAs, which permit your investments to compound tax deferred, the Taxpayer Relief Act of 1997 created a new breed of IRA called the Roth IRA, which allows your capital to accumulate tax free if you follow certain rules. It is named after Delaware Senator William V. Roth, Jr., who championed the idea of expanded IRAs. You and your spouse can each put up to $3,000 a year into a Roth IRA, even after you reach age 70½. (Though new limits started in 2002 as noted above.) You can withdraw all the principal and earnings totally tax free after 59½ so long as the assets have remained in the IRA for at least five years after the first contribution. The assets can also be withdrawn tax free if you suffer a major disability. If you die before you start withdrawing from a Roth, the proceeds go to your beneficiaries tax free.

Unlike regular IRAs, you don't have to take distributions from a Roth IRA starting at age 70½. In fact, you don't have to take distributions at all in your lifetime if you prefer, allowing you to pass the assets in the Roth to your beneficiaries free from income tax. You don't receive a deduction for contributing to a Roth IRA unlike some other kinds of IRAs. But the value of completely tax-free withdrawals should far exceed the tax break from an up-front deduction.

Unlike regular IRAs, Roth IRA rules permit you to withdraw assets without the usual 10 percent early withdrawal penalty if you use the money for the purchase of a first home (withdrawals are limited to $10,000), for college expenses, or if you become disabled.

Certain limitations, however, do govern who can open Roth IRAs. You can contribute the full $3,000 (or more, according to new rules) if you are a married couple with an adjusted gross income of $150,000 or less, or a single with an adjusted gross income of $95,000 or less. The amount you can contribute is phased out for incomes between $150,000 and $160,000 for couples filing jointly and between $95,000 and $110,000 for singles. If your income is over those limits in a particular tax year, you are not allowed to make a Roth contribution.

You can roll over assets from a traditional IRA into a Roth IRA under certain circumstances. If your adjusted gross income is $100,000 or less, you can roll over existing nondeductible and deductible IRA balances into a Roth without owing the 10 percent prepayment penalty. However, when you undertake such a rollover, you must pay income tax on all previously untaxed contributions and earnings. Figure out where you will get the money to pay this potentially large tax bill before you initiate such a transaction. The two most likely sources for paying these taxes are your regular earnings or other savings. You should try to avoid selling a large part of your non-IRA portfolio and incurring capital gains taxes to raise the money to pay the taxes generated by a Roth rollover. This would not only decimate your portfolio, but it could also put you in a higher tax bracket in the year you do it. If you don't pay the taxes from IRA proceeds, it is preferable to preserve the maximum tax advantage of the Roth. The rollover is fully taxable in the year it is completed.

Whether it makes sense to roll over money into a Roth from a traditional IRA depends on several factors. In general, the more you have accumulated in a traditional IRA, the more tax you will pay when you roll over a Roth and the more time you will need to recover those taxes from tax-free withdrawals. It probably doesn't make sense to roll over money into a Roth if you expect to be in a lower tax bracket when you retire, because you will pay lower taxes when you make withdrawals than you will when you roll over the funds during your working years. If you are young and haven't accumulated very much in a traditional IRA, it may make more sense to roll over your balances to a Roth than if you have amassed a large sum that would generate a huge tax when rolled over. Many mutual funds and brokerage funds, including Fidelity, T. Rowe Price, Vanguard, Merrill Lynch, and Salomon Smith Barney, offer customers free or low-cost software programs and sections on their Web sites allowing them to figure out whether a rollover to a Roth makes sense in their situation. The best way to take advantage of the Roth is to set one up when you are in your 20s, contribute the maximum allowed every year, invest the money for maximum capital gains, and withdraw huge sums totally tax free as needed in retirement.

TRANSFERRING IRA FUNDS

Once you build a substantial amount of capital in your IRA, you may want to transfer the funds from one institution to another. Your broker may have moved to a different brokerage house, for example, or you may want to relocate your money to a mutual fund company that has performed better than the one holding your money now.

Be extremely careful when transferring IRA assets. Your funds should go directly from one institution to another without your ever touching the money. The same applies to rollovers of funds from pension and profit-sharing accounts into your IRA. These transfers can often take a long time and may get caught in administrative gridlock. Therefore, make sure that they are handled correctly, or you will end up with only 80 percent of the money you deserve when the funds finally arrive at the new custodian's institution.

It is a good idea to deposit all your IRA assets with one custodian. You don't want to drown in the sea of paperwork that could result from filing IRS forms with many custodians. In addition, you will pay fewer fees if you keep all your assets in one place. The best custodian is one that offers a wide array of options so you can shift assets into whatever security or mutual fund suits your needs.

THE NEW ROLLOVERS UNDER CHANGES IN THE LAW

Ed Slott, a certified public accountant and editor of *Ed Slott's IRA Advisor* newsletter, highlights the many changes from the Economic Growth and Tax Relief Reconciliation Act of 2001. Beginning in 2002, company plans including 401(k)s, 403(b)s, and government 457s can be rolled over to IRAs or to other 401(k)s, 403(b)s, or 457 plans. Under previous law, these rollovers were limited; 403(b) tax-sheltered annuities, for example, could be rolled over to an IRA but not to a qualified plan, such as a 401(k). Now, the entire balance in a company plan that is an eligible rollover distribution (ERD) can be rolled over to another plan or an IRA. ERDs are taxable distributions from company plans that are allowed to be rolled over to another plan or an IRA.

Before the 2001 law was enacted, only taxable plan funds (the pretax funds) could be rolled over, and 457 plan balances could not be rolled over at all. The after-tax funds that were not rolled over were simply withdrawn tax free as the tax was already paid on this money.

After-tax funds (the nontaxable amounts) still cannot be rolled over to 403(b) plans as they could under prior law; and 457 plans do not accept after-tax contributions, so no after-tax money can be rolled into or out of a 457. If after-tax funds are rolled from one 401(k) plan to another 401(k) plan, the transfer must be a direct trustee-to-trustee transfer, and the receiving plan must agree to keep a separate accounting of both the taxable and the after-tax funds and the income earned on those funds. IRAs are not required to keep a separate accounting of after-tax funds rolled into them as that is done by the IRA owner and reported to the IRS on Form 8606. For more on what can be rolled where and the rules and regulations governing rollovers, review Figure 4.5 in Chapter 4.

Rolling over after-tax money to an IRA presents an opportunity to keep the after-tax plan money growing tax deferred in the IRA. But it also poses challenges if you need to tap this after-tax money in the near future. Know that once you roll over after-tax plan money to an IRA, you must keep a separate accounting of these funds, because it represents the basis in your IRA. Think of it in much the same way you would if you made a nondeductible contribution to your IRA. You would have to keep track of the nondeductible contributions (your basis) so that when you withdraw funds from your IRA, you know how much of the withdrawal will be nontaxable.

One caveat when rolling over after-tax money to an IRA: You cannot simply withdraw the money tax free from the IRA. Suppose you roll $20,000 of after-tax money from your 401(k) to your IRA; you cannot then withdraw the $20,000 tax free from your IRA. Why? Once that money is in your IRA, it's handled the same as nondeductible IRA contributions.

If you need access to some or all of the after-tax money, then don't roll it over to an IRA because you'll not be able to withdraw it tax free unless you withdraw the entire IRA balance. If you have no need for the money and plan to leave it in the IRA intact for your beneficiaries, then it pays to roll over the after-tax money to your IRA, where it can continue to grow tax deferred. You must still take your annual required distributions when you turn 70½.

WHY YOU CAN'T BEAT AN IRA

Even though new liberalized rollover rules have expanded rollover possibilities from IRAs to plans and from plans to other plans, when all is said and done, an IRA is usually the place you want your retirement assets to be. Think twice before rolling over an IRA into a company plan. Your best distribution and investment options are in your IRA.

On the distribution side, naming your child or any other individual as your IRA beneficiary guarantees that beneficiary the ability to extend distributions over his or her lifetime, a concept known as "Stretch IRA." Most plans don't allow distributions to a beneficiary to be stretched for life. In addition, you have a wider universe of investment choices in your IRA that are generally not available from your plan.

Another reason to keep funds in your IRA is the Roth conversion. You cannot convert plan money to a Roth IRA; that can be done only from a traditional IRA. Once you roll IRA money to a company plan, you become subject to company plan rules that often include restrictions on withdrawals and investments. If you need to withdraw funds from an IRA, you are free to do that at any time. If you are under age 59½, you may be subject to the 10 percent penalty, but you still have unlimited access to your IRA money, which is not necessarily true of your company plan.

Also, if you roll over IRA funds to a company plan, those funds become subject to federal law, which generally requires married plan participants to name their spouse as beneficiary or have the spouse file a special waiver that would allow you to name a different beneficiary. With an IRA, there are no such federal rules; you can name anyone you wish as your IRA beneficiary.

It's not all one-sided, though. Some reasons to roll over a plan's assets might be for postponing required plan distributions (if you're still working), for federal creditor protection, and for the ability to borrow from the plan. You cannot borrow from an IRA, and an IRA is not creditor protected under federal law, though many states do protect IRAs.

Take great care in making your decision.

IRA WITHDRAWAL RULES

To maximize an IRA tax shelter, keep your money in it as long as possible. You are allowed to withdraw from the account without penalty starting at age 59½, and you *must* begin distributions by age 70½. If you take out money before 59½, you will owe a 10 percent early withdrawal penalty, and you must pay income taxes on your distribution in the year you receive it. (Unlike salary reduction plans, IRAs do not allow you to borrow against your IRA assets under any circumstances.) However, a few exceptions to this penalty rule exist. IRA distributions can be made without penalty before age 59½ under the following conditions:

- You die and the IRA proceeds are distributed to your beneficiary or estate.
- You become permanently disabled.
- The amount distributed is paid out as an annuity over your lifetime or your life expectancy.

If you have made maximum use of your IRA tax shelter and didn't touch your proceeds by the time you turned 70½, you have to begin withdrawing at least a minimum amount of money each year thereafter. You must receive the first payment by April 1 of the year after you turn 70½. (*Note:* Your second distribution must be taken by December 31 of that same year you turn 70½.) The IRS requires you to withdraw a certain amount of your account each year based on a uniform actuarial table. In 2001, the IRS greatly simplified what had previously been very complex calculations on how much money you had to take out of the account every year. The life expectancy tables governing required minimum distributions were lengthened, allowing you to leave more money in your account growing tax deferred for many more years than under previous rules. Financial institutions like banks, mutual fund companies, and brokerages must report to the IRS each year how much money you are taking out in distributions, so it easy for the IRS to enforce these rules. If you don't take out enough, the IRS will impose a whopping penalty of 50 percent of the difference between what you withdrew and what you should have withdrawn.

The rules also make it easier for you to select and change the beneficiary of your IRA account. You can even select a new beneficiary after payouts have begun, and your heirs can even change the beneficiary after you have died. This is important because the payout rate is based on the beneficiary's life expectancy. So if the beneficiary is changed to a much younger person, like a grandchild, the payout can take place over many more years and allow the account to grow tax deferred for many more years than if the beneficiary were middle aged.

Another way to draw on your IRA is to take the entire balance in a lump sum. However, this subjects you to an enormous tax, which leaves less money for you to reinvest to generate the income on which you'll need to live during retirement. You may also use the proceeds of your IRA to buy an *annuity*. An annuity makes monthly payments to you for the rest of your life or, if you choose a joint and survivor payout option, for the rest of your life and that of your spouse. To learn more about the different options you have in rolling over assets into an IRA from your company retirement plan, get a copy of the free booklet published by T. Rowe Price: *Managing Your Retirement Distribution Rollover Kit* (available by calling 800-541-7894).

As with any other asset, when you open an IRA, designate a beneficiary who will receive the account's proceeds when you die. If you are married, most likely you will name your spouse as beneficiary. Once you die, your spouse will roll your IRA assets into his or her IRA. However, if you name someone who is not a spouse to receive your IRA proceeds, you must spell out in the plan to whom you want the money distributed.

INVESTING IRA FUNDS

When you understand the rules of contribution and withdrawal, learn to maximize your investment options. IRAs offer many investment vehicles, including individual stocks, bonds, mutual funds, unit investment trusts

(UITs), limited partnerships, futures funds, CDs, options, gold and silver coins minted by the U.S. government such as the American Eagle, and platinum and palladium.

The two classes of investments in which your IRA cannot invest are collectibles and physical real estate that you control. *Collectibles* are defined as artwork, stamps, numismatic coins, gems, antiques, or gold or silver coins minted outside the United States. *Physical real estate* includes both your own home and rental real estate you own as an investment. Although it is legal to invest in municipal bonds with an IRA, it doesn't make sense because you don't need tax-exempt income in a tax-sheltered account.

Two philosophies exist regarding the best way to take advantage of the tax-deferred feature of IRAs. Some investment advisors favor growth and maintain that you want investments with the most growth potential possible, such as aggressive growth stocks or futures funds, because an IRA is a long-term vehicle that allows you to accumulate a significant amount of assets by retirement. You can trade in and out of stocks, bonds, and options without caring about the tax consequences of your actions because all gains are tax deferred for years.

Other investment advisors believe that you should stuff your IRA with the highest-yielding investments available, such as high-yield stocks, bonds, mortgage-backed securities, income mutual funds, CDs, and UITs. They reason that because all IRA income compounds tax deferred, you want to earn the highest income possible. Therefore, if interest rates are high, probably the best IRA investment is a zero-coupon bond, which automatically locks in that high rate of reinvestment until the bond matures. You also know exactly how much capital you will have accumulated as many as 30 years in the future. No other investment guarantees that.

Both ways of thinking are valid. You can decide to go with one strategy or the other, or you can mix the two. However you allocate your IRA funds, though, integrate your IRA into your total investment portfolio to achieve a proper balance. For instance, if your salary reduction plan is invested in conservative guaranteed income contracts (GICs) or bonds, put your IRA funds in more aggressive growth stocks. On the other hand, if you own many growth stocks in your personal portfolio, as well as growth mutual funds in your 401(k), be more conservative with your IRA money and select high-quality bonds or a bond fund.

However you allocate your money, the importance of starting early and contributing each year cannot be overemphasized. The capital that grows in your IRA could make the difference between a comfortable retirement and a meager retirement.

CHOOSING A CUSTODIAN

You'll need a caretaker for your account who is responsible for holding the assets, reporting the account activity, and generally making sure that the basic rules are followed. On the other hand, the custodian isn't expected to steer you away from income tax penalties or incorrect distributions; it's your responsibility to know the income tax rules and how they apply to you. Four types of institutions qualify as IRA custodians: brokerage houses, mutual fund companies, insurance companies, and banks. Depending on the type of IRA you choose, each has its advantages.

Here are a few pointers to help you make a choice.

If you need investment advice, consider a full-service broker or a bank trust department. You'll not only get guidance but a broad range of investment alternatives. However, if you're a savvy investor, go it alone. A discount broker or mutual fund company is probably your best choice.

You can separate the choices by the investment alternatives they offer. If you have a small IRA that you would like to diversify, a mutual fund family is a good option. If you're looking only for a fixed-rate CD, a bank is probably your best choice.

Insurance companies typically offer an IRA through tax-deferred annuity vehicles or through a variable annuity. A tax-deferred annuity, similar to a certificate of deposit, typically pays a stated rate of interest for a period of time. A variable annuity has a group of mutual funds under the IRA/annuity umbrella. Know that your return will be as good or as bad as the performance of the funds in the contract. Note, too, that insurance annuity contracts are guaranteed by the company that issues them. So by all means you'll want to do a little due diligence and check out the quality of the firm. If the company goes out of business, you could be left with an empty bag.

Generally, shop around. Thoroughly investigate all the charges and fees before signing on the dotted line with any custodian. The easiest way to find an annuity is to consult the *Annuity Shopper* (8 Talmadge Dr., Monroe TWP, NJ 08831; 800-872-6684; 732-521-5110; www.annuityshopper.com).

The new contribution limits make the IRA even more attractive. Why wouldn't you want to take advantage of the tax savings while gaining an additional weapon in your retirement arsenal?

RESOURCES

Books, Booklets, and Pamphlets

Individual Retirement Arrangements (IRAs) Including Roth IRAs and Education IRAs, Publication 590, Department of the Treasury, Internal Revenue Service (800-

829-3676; www.irs.gov). Explains the rules, regulations, and requirements covering traditional, Roth, Education, SEP, and SIMPLE IRAs.

IRA Investing Made Easy: A Beginner's Guide to Successful IRA Investment Strategies, by Anna M. Hutchison (Globe Pequot Press, 246 Goose Ln., Suite 200, P.O. Box 480, Guilford, CT 06437; 203-458-4500; 888-249-7586; www.globepequotpress. com). Explains how IRAs can be invested, how they affect your income taxes, and how to deal with financial brokers in addition to everything about self-directed IRAs and SEP IRAs.

The Lump Sum Handbook: Investment and Tax Strategies for a Secure Retirement, by Anthony Gallea (Prentice Hall, 1 Lake St., Upper Saddle River, NJ 07458; 201-236-7156; 800-382-3419; www.prenticehall.com). Explores investment strategies covering bonds, stocks, mutual funds, real estate, and precious metals in IRAs.

Maximize Your IRA: Make the New Rules Work for You, Choose the Right Plan, Discover New Ways to Use Your IRA, by Neil Downing (Dearborn Trade, 155 N. Wacker Dr., Chicago, IL 60606; 312-836-4400; 800-245-2665; www.dearborntrade. com). The complete guide to the many individual retirement choices you now have available; covers the Roth IRA, traditional tax-deferred IRAs, and all the rules surrounding them.

Real Estate in IRAs and Keoghs: A Guide, by Hubert Franz-Josef Bromma (Entrust Administration, 180 Grand St., Suite 1030, Oakland, CA 94612; 800-392-9653; www.entrustadmin.com). Provides on CD-Rom a comprehensive guide to diversifying IRA and Keogh investments to include real estate, notes, mobile homes, and tax lien certificates in addition to stocks, bonds, mutual funds, and the like.

The Retirement Bible, by Lynn O'Shaughnessy (Hungry Minds, 909 Third Ave., New York, NY 10022; 800-762-2974; www.hungryminds.com). A one-stop source for information about retirement planning with two chapters devoted especially to IRAs.

Retire Rich: The Baby Boomer's Guide to a Secure Future, by Bambi Holzer and Elaine Floyd (John Wiley & Sons, 1 Wiley Dr., Somerset, NJ 08875-1272; 212-850-6000; 800-225-5945; www.wiley.com). Through illustrations and a series of questions and worksheets, helps readers determine the amount they must put away to meet their individual future needs.

The Roth IRA Made Simple, by Gary R. Trock, E.A. (Conquest Publishing, P.O. Box 543, Griffith, IN 46319; 800-507-2665). Explains the basics and benefits of the Roth, points out useful strategies for maximizing Roth IRAs, and details factors to be considered before deciding to contribute or convert to a Roth.

Understanding IRAs: 35-Question Multiple-Choice Examination, by Dearborn Trade (Dearborn Trade, 155 N. Wacker Dr., Chicago, IL 60606; 312-836-4400; 800-245-2665; www.dearborntrade.com). Includes information on IRAs: the advantages, variations, traditional IRAs, contributions and deductions, taking money out of a traditional IRA, and Roth IRAs.

You're Retired, Now What? Money Skills for a Comfortable Retirement, by Ronald M. Yolles and Murray Yolles (John Wiley & Sons, 1 Wiley Dr., Somerset, NJ

08875-1272; 212-850-6000; 800-225-5945; www.wiley.com). Covers maximizing IRA distributions, planning cash flow over the years and the best investment strategies for retirees (includes worksheets, case studies, and sample forms).

Newsletter

Ed Slott's IRA Advisor (100 Merrick Rd., Rockville Centre, NY 11570; 800-663-1340; www.irahelp.com). A wealth of information about IRAs, taxes, and estate planning.

Web Sites

Brentmark.com <www.brentmark.com>. The Web site of Brentmark Software (3505 Lake Lynda Dr., Suite 212, Orlando, FL 32817-8327; 800-379-6665; 407-306-6160) focuses on Roth IRA issues, pension planning, and estate taxes; includes a pension distribution calculator, minimum distribution calculators, and a pension and Roth IRA analyzer.

Entrustadmin.com <www.entrustadmin.com>. The Web site of Entrust Administration (180 Grand St., Suite 1030, Oakland, CA 94612; 800-392-9653) offers articles on IRAs, an IRA resource library, investment options for your IRA, and more.

Ernst & Young <www.ey.com/pfc>. The accounting and financial consulting firm's Web site contains information on IRAs, including pension and IRA changes resulting from the Economic Growth and Tax Relief and Reconciliation Act of 2001.

Rothira.com <www.rothira.com>. A vast resource for information about Roth IRAs, including articles, the latest news about IRAs, and links for calculators, seminars, books, tapes, and software.

Rothira911.com <www.rothira911.com>. Explains financial and investment basics and strategies for retirement, including a Roth IRA quiz and much you need to know about Roth IRAs.

CHAPTER 7

Where You Should Invest beyond Tax-Sheltered Accounts

Y ou have Social Security, pensions, and IRAs, but depending on how much you receive from these sources, you'll probably still need anywhere from 30 to 50 percent from other savings and investments to fund your retirement dreams. The truth is that you have to look beyond tax-sheltered accounts to fill the void. You'll need stocks, bonds, mutual funds, annuities, CDs, and other investments to make up the difference.

Let's look at some of your options.

STOCKS

Before you buy any stocks, remember they are vehicles that can enable you to reach your financial goals. When you hear an exciting story about a hot growth stock, you may be tempted to put your life savings in it so you can become a quick millionaire. Resist the temptation. There are different techniques you can use to pick winning stocks without relying on hot tips. A few general suggestions that should help you make profitable decisions are listed in the following paragraphs.

Plan to invest for the long term. Despite endless predictions by market gurus that stocks are about to soar or plunge, no one really knows what will happen to stock prices over the short term. So for the most part, you should ignore most of the prognostications. The same advice holds for the economy, which is just as unpredictable as the stock market.

Your emotions will get the best of you if you do a great deal of short-term trading. When prices are rising, you'll tend to get caught up in the enthusiasm and buy more. When prices are falling, you'll probably get depressed and sell out. Besides, excessive trading activity will generate hefty commissions for your broker and taxes on capital gains for Uncle Sam. Instead of trading for the short term, buy stocks that have good market positions, are financially strong, and offer products and services that seem sensible. If you can't explain what a company does in about two sentences, you probably shouldn't invest in it.

Buy stocks systematically. Instead of putting all your money into a stock in one lump sum, buy a fixed dollar amount of shares on a regular basis, whether monthly, quarterly, or annually. If you buy the same dollar amount of a stock, say $100 a month, you will automatically buy fewer shares when the price is high and more shares when the price is low, thereby assuring yourself of a low average price over time. This is *dollar cost averaging,* which is a lot safer and easier than trying to determine when a stock has hit its low or high point.

Invest in stocks that you know well. Use your professional knowledge to spot companies that seem to be up and coming. For example, if you are a doctor, what new drugs seem to be particularly effective, and who manufactured the new medical equipment that your hospital just installed? If you are a car mechanic, what company is making the best components for new cars? Or if you are a homemaker, what new stores seem to be crowded, and what new products seem to be hot sellers at the supermarket? You may have many stock tips at your disposal. Use them for profit.

Research your choices carefully. For some reason, people will spend weeks investigating every feature of a new car costing $15,000, but when it comes to stocks, they will spend $15,000 based on a hot tip, a broker's recommendation, or a mention in a newspaper story. Before you invest any money, know exactly what business the company is in, how profitable it is, whether it has much debt, who it competes with, and more. Most of all, look at who is running the company. Firms can have great plans, but they need top-quality management to transform those plans into profitable reality. The best way to judge management is by looking at its track record. If the management team has succeeded in the past, chances are that the team can do it again. You can find out a lot about a company simply by surfing the Internet and finding its Web site. Companies often post quarterly and annual reports along with financial and other vital information. You can also go to places like Hoovers.com; Edgar-online <www.edgar-online.com>, a one-stop shop for SEC filings; <corporateinformation.com>; <bloomberg.com>; Yahoo!Finance <http://finance.yahoo.com>; MSN's MoneyCentral <http://moneycentral.msn.com>; and other financial sites.

Key Financial Ratios

Price-earnings ratio (PE): A stock's latest price divided by its earnings for the last four quarters; a way to compare how investors value one stock against another.

Price-to-book value ratio (P/BV): A stock's price divided by the book value (the worth of the company's assets) per share.

Measures of Profitability

Return on equity (ROE): A company's earnings divided by total shareholders' equity; generally, a ROE of more than 15 is excellent.

Net profit: Net income divided by net sales. This figure shows a company's overall success not only in managing operations but in terms of borrowing money at a favorable rate, investing cash wisely, and taking advantage of tax benefits.

Measure of Debt

Debt-to-equity ratio: A company's total liabilities divided by total shareholders' equity, a measure of indebtedness; generally, a ratio of more than 50 percent is a high level of debt.

Measure of Dividend Stability

Dividend payout ratio: Percentage of earnings paid back in dividends; the dividends per share divided by the earnings per share. Generally, the more established a company, the higher its payout ratio.

Monitor the company after you've bought shares. Keep up on the quarterly and annual reports to see whether projections are coming to pass. Was the new product line successful? Did the company pay down its debt as you thought it would? Keep an eye on the company's stock price. You don't need to check it daily—once a week or monthly should suffice. Don't own so many individual stocks that you don't have the time to track them all.

Don't be pressured to buy or sell because everyone else is. In fact, if everyone else is doing it, it's probably the wrong time to be joining in. It takes courage, but you will most likely make the majority of your money by buying stocks when they are down and everyone dislikes them and by selling them when they are rising and every taxicab driver lets you in on this latest "hot" tip.

Don't worry about missing out on a good stock. The best ones rise in value for years at a time, so you have plenty of opportunity to get in on them.

If you had bought Wal-Mart shares any time in the early 1970s, you would have made more than 30 times your money if you had held until the 1990s. Just because a good stock moves up a few dollars, it's not too late to invest.

Have a selling target price in mind when you buy a stock. If the stock reaches that price, either you can sell some of it or you can reconsider your position based on the company's position at that time. You should also know the price at which you would sell the stock at a loss. This might be between 25 percent and 50 percent less than you paid for it.

Consider transaction costs before you buy. If you have only enough money to buy a few shares, the commission you pay might not be worth the investment. Determine in advance whether you will buy the stock through a full-service broker, who offers advice, or through a discount broker, who only executes your order but at much lower commission rates.

Categories of Stocks

Of the many kinds of stocks, some are more appropriate for you than others, depending on your tolerance for risk and your financial goals. Here'a brief look at five categories: cyclical, growth, income, out-of-favor, and value.

Cyclical stocks. Cyclical stocks are so named because they ride the economic cycle; certain companies' fortunes are very closely tied to the ups and downs of the economy. If you time purchases and sales of such company stocks well, you can profit handsomely. Cyclical stocks are typically found in such heavy industries as auto manufacturing, paper, chemical, steel, and aluminum. Companies in these industries all have relatively large fixed costs to run their factories, and as a result, if the volume of product they sell is high and prices they receive are rising because of strong demand, they stand to cover those costs easily and earn enormous profits. However, when demand is weak and prices are falling, they are still burdened by the same costs, so their earnings plummet.

Cyclical stock prices are even more volatile than the companies' earnings. Investors are constantly trying to determine whether the cycle is turning up or down because of its tremendous impact on a company's bottom line. All stock prices reflect investors' expectations of future profits, but cyclical stocks are even more sensitive to perceptions about the future.

The best time to buy cyclical stocks, as hard as it may be to do, is when the companies are still losing money in the bottom of a recession but their situation is no longer deteriorating. The moment that investors sense a turnaround, the stock prices shoot up. Conversely, the time to sell is when the company is earning record profits and everything seems to be going well, because investors are anticipating the downturn.

Growth stocks. Earnings of a true growth stock will compound at 15 percent or more no matter what the overall economy is doing. In choosing growth stocks, look at the *earnings growth rate,* or the rate at which profits grow from year to year. In general, the higher the growth rate, the higher the stock's PE. The ideal growth rate is one selling at a PE below its growth rate; for example, if Go-Go Computer's profits are growing at 30 percent a year, its stock would be considered a bargain if it were selling for a PE of 20. Consistent growth is highly prized; a company whose profits are up 40 percent one year and down 20 percent the next won't earn as high a PE as one that grows 20 percent year after year.

Avoid one of the biggest mistakes people make when buying growth stocks: getting too excited by their prospects and paying too much for the stocks. An easy way to judge whether you're overpaying is to look at the stock's PE; the higher the PE, the more enthusiastic investors are about your company. Compare the PE of your stock with that of similar companies in the same industry; if the PE of your company's stock is much higher, you could be paying too much.

Income stocks. Stocks are not only a way to achieve capital appreciation, but they can also provide steady income, which is especially important during retirement when you'll need to tap that stream. Companies that pay high dividends usually are well-established, profitable firms. Some industries in which you typically find high-paying stocks include banking firms; real estate investment trusts; and electric, gas, telephone, and water utilities. Unlike faster-growing, younger companies, which reinvest profits in their businesses, such firms traditionally pay out at least half their profits to shareholders in the form of dividends.

These stocks are greatly influenced by the direction of interest rates. When rates of Treasury bonds fall, prices of high-yield stocks tend to rise because these stocks' dividends are more competitive with bonds. Conversely, when interest rates rise, high-yield stocks look less attractive, and their prices tend to drop.

To make sure an income stock you like will continue to raise its dividend, look at the company's financial health; debt that is more than 50 percent of the company's equity may be a sign of trouble. Check the stock's rating with a reputable credit rating agency, such as Standard & Poor's Stock Guide or the S&P Web site at <www.standardandpoors.com>. Any rating over B+ means that the company is financially solid. Another key is the payout ratio, or percentage of earnings paid out in dividends. A payout ratio below 60 percent means the company has a sizable cushion to fall back on before it has to cut its dividend.

Out-of-favor stocks. If the age-old way to make money in stocks is to buy low and sell high, then buying stocks when they are out of favor is a good way to buy low. The easiest way to spot neglected stocks is by looking for low PEs. A PE of less than 10 signals that investors don't have much hope for the future of the company, which may, in fact, be an incorrect perception of the situation. The moment the company reports better-than-expected results, perceptions can change and the stock price can shoot up. Do your homework. Don't buy just any stock with a low PE; in some cases, that lowly valuation is in order.

Look for a stock with a fair chance at a turnaround. You may see light at the end of the tunnel if sales and earnings are no longer deteriorating or if the company has a new product or service that has potential. Are company executives buying the stock themselves and are they increasing capital expenditures? If those who know the company best are investing in it heavily, that could be a tip-off that recovery is at hand.

Value stocks. If you could buy a stock worth $10 a share for $8, would you do it? Most people would because they know they are buying something for less than it is worth. In the stock market, this style of choosing stocks is known as *value investing.*

The key to value investing is the ability to perceive when the current price of a company's stock does not fully reflect the value of the company's assets. Those assets might include real estate, brand names, and oil reserves, among other things. Value investors make money by buying when a company's assets are worth more than its stock's price reflects and selling when the value of the assets have been realized.

Trying to determine the true value of assets is tricky and subjective. One way to sort it out is to compare the stock's price to so-called net working capital. That is the amount of cash a company could raise in a hurry if it were liquidated today. To calculate net working capital, subtract short-term and long-term debts from such current assets as cash, securities, receivables, and inventory. If the net working capital of the company you are looking at is 25 percent or more than the current price of the stock, you have found an undervalued stock.

Hot Tip: Growth and value investing are the two broadest kinds of stock-choosing styles. Growth investing refers to selecting stocks with ever-rising earnings; value investing means buying stocks temporarily out of favor that the manager expects will become popular again.

BONDS

When you invest in a bond, you are loaning the issuer of that bond your money in return for a fixed rate of interest for a specified amount of time. Normally, you receive interest payments every six months, and when the bond matures you receive your original principal, no matter how much the price of the bond fluctuated since it was issued. Bonds hold little mystery. You lock in a set rate of income for a long period of time, which can give your retirement stash a rock-solid foundation. In addition, if you want to trade bonds actively, you can earn capital gains by buying them when their prices fall and selling them when their prices rise, just as you can do with stocks.

A few basics about bonds. The yield you receive from a bond is typically higher than a stock dividend yield because bondholders must be compensated for reduced purchasing power in the future because of inflation. Bonds are normally quoted on a price scale of 0 to 200, with 100 being the price at which the bond was issued, or what is known as *par*. Because bonds are sold in minimum denominations of $1,000, a price of 100 means that the bond is trading at $1,000 per bond. If the bond's price rises to 110, your holdings are now worth $1,100.

Unlike stock transactions, bond buy-sell transactions normally occur without a separate commission charge. Instead, a broker makes money from a transaction by taking a piece of the spread between the buying and selling prices.

How Bond Prices Move

When you consider investing in bonds, you should understand one cardinal rule about the movement of bond prices: *Bond prices move in the opposite direction to interest rates.* Normally, you might think that rising interest rates would be good for your bond, but nothing could be further from the truth. Even though it may sound illogical at first, it is true that when interest rates rise, bond prices fall. When interest rates fall, bond prices rise. The following example explains why.

Say you buy a bond yielding 10 percent at a price of 100 (the par price). If interest rates plummet to 5 percent over the next several years, your 10 percent bond would become very valuable, indeed. Its price would soar—maybe to a dollar value of 150—because people would be willing to pay a big premium to get their hands on a 10 percent bond in an environment where bonds pay only 5 percent. Notice that as interest rates fell, your bond's value rose.

Now let's take the opposite situation. You buy your 10 percent bond at 100, and instead of dropping, interest rates soar to 15 percent. Your bond won't be popular now because people would rather buy a new bond paying 15 percent than your old bond paying 10 percent. Therefore, if you want to sell your bond to buy a newer one at the higher current rate, you would suffer a loss. The price of your bond might drop to half, from 100 to 50.

Bond prices move seemingly so perversely because bonds are a fixed-rate instrument. Because the bond's rate is locked in at whatever level it was when the bond was first issued, the bond becomes more or less valuable as interest rates rise or fall. Figure 7.1 may help you better understand the inverse relationship between interest rates and bond prices.

The longer the maturity of your bond, the more its price will react to the ups and downs of interest rates. A bond that locks in a high interest rate for 20 or 30 years is much more valuable to investors if interest rates have fallen than a bond that matures in a year or two. Conversely, if interest rates have risen, investors would rather get their money back quickly so they can reinvest at higher rates.

When calculating the effect of interest rates on an investor's holdings, analysts usually look at the total return—that is, the price change of the bond added to the income it is paying. Figure 7.2 shows how an interest rate increase of from one to four percentage points over one year would affect the total returns of several bond maturities from 6 years to 30 years. This table assumes that 6-year bonds yield 6 percent, 10-year and 20-year bonds yield 7 percent, and 30-year bonds yield 8 percent. Notice that the longer the bond maturity, the more the bond loses value as rates rise.

Figure 7.3 shows how much the total returns on different bond maturities rise as interest rates fall over one year. This bond volatility should always be factored into your decision to buy bonds.

Figure 7.1   Relationship between Bond Prices and Interest Rates

When interest rates move up or down, the price of a bond usually moves in the opposite direction.

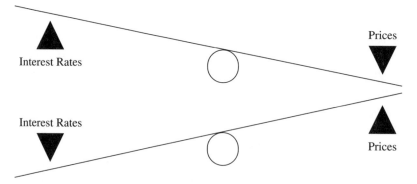

Short-term bonds (bonds that are close to maturity) are usually less affected by changes in interest rates than are long-term bonds.

Figure 7.2   Percentage Points Rate Increase in a Year

Maturity	Unchanged	+1%	+2%	+3%	+4%
6 years	+6%	+2%	−2%	−5%	−9%
10 years	+7	+1	−5	−10	−15
20 years	+7	+1	−7	−13	−19
30 years	+8	−3	−11	−19	−25

Source: Reprinted by permission of The Leuthold Group, an investment advisory firm in Minneapolis, Minnesota.

Figure 7.3   Percentage Points Rate Decrease in a Year

Maturity	Unchanged	−1%	−2%	−3%	−4%
6 years	+6%	+10%	+15%	+20%	+25%
10 years	+7	+13	+20	+28	+37
20 years	+7	+18	+28	+42	+57
30 years	+8	+20	+35	+51	+69

Source: Reprinted by permission of The Leuthold Group, an investment advisory firm in Minneapolis, Minnesota.

The Meaning of Yield

Whereas a bond has only one interest rate, there are four ways to calculate its yield—that is, your return on the bond's current price. They are as follows:

1. **Coupon rate.** This is the interest the bond pays. It may equal the bond's yield when it is trading at its issue price of 100, or its $1,000 face value. A bond with a 10 percent coupon, therefore, would pay $100 a year in interest.
2. **Current yield.** This yield adjusts the bond's coupon rate for the bond's current price to determine the percentage you would receive if you bought the bond at its current price. In the example above, if the bond dropped in price from 100 to 90, for instance, the bond's value would fall from $1,000 to $900; at that price, the current yield would rise to 11.1 percent. Remember that rising interest rates produce falling bond prices. Therefore, in the example, if the bond's price rose from 100 to 110, the bond's value would rise from $1,000 to $1,100. Don't worry about calculating the yield of every bond you consider buying. Current yields are displayed on your broker's computer screen and also in any newspaper's bond listings.

3. **Yield to maturity.** This yield takes into account the bond's coupon rate, its current price, and the years remaining until the bond matures. It is a more complicated calculation, but your broker should be able to tell you the yield to maturity on any bond you are considering. You can also consult a book with yield-to-maturity tables or figure it out using a programmable calculator.

4. **Yield to call.** This is the yield up to the first potential date at which the issuer can call, or redeem, the bond—usually several years before the bond is scheduled to mature. You calculate the yield to call exactly the same way you calculate the yield to maturity, except that you re-place the number of years to maturity with the number of years to the first call date.

   You should always assume that a corporation or municipality will put its shareholders' or constituents' interests ahead of bondholders' interests. Therefore, if interest rates have fallen sharply from the time the bond was issued to the first date that the bond may be called, you should assume the bond will be redeemed. The yield to call is the most realistic yield you can calculate for a bond because you can never assume the bond will remain outstanding between its first call date and its stated maturity.

Hot Tip: A bond can be redeemed before it is scheduled to mature. That sounds illegal, but it isn't—as long as the issuer's ability to re-deem the bond is written in a thick legal document that accompanies the original bond issue. In that document, called the indenture, *bond-holders are guaranteed a certain number of years before which the bond cannot be redeemed. This can be as few as 5 years or as many as 15 to 20 years, although a 10-year call protection is more typical.*

Types of Bonds: Choosing the Best for You

Treasury bonds. Bonds issued by the U.S. government are considered the safest around because Uncle Sam has a weapon to back these bonds that no other entity has: the printing press. If the government doesn't have enough funds to honor its debt, it can always print more money.

From an investor's point of view, Treasury bonds, or Treasuries, trade as though they are free from the risk of default. And because they are consid-ered immune from default, they are the benchmark against which all other bonds are compared. They are issued in minimum denominations of $1,000 and also in $5,000, $10,000, $100,000, and $1 million sizes. To invest in Treasury bonds, you put up your $1,000 (or more) and receive interest checks every six months. Under a program called Treasury Direct, you can have your interest checks deposited electronically in any bank or financial institution you choose.

Treasuries have another feature unique in the bond world: almost all Treasury bonds are noncallable. That means the Treasury cannot redeem them before maturity. Also, all interest you earn is exempt from state and local taxes. What's the downside? In return for the safety, liquidity, and tax advantages, you receive a lower yield than is available from other bonds. How much lower depends on the current market conditions and the bonds with which you compare Treasuries. But for conservative income-oriented investors, there's no match for Treasuries.

U.S. savings bonds. Though savings bonds are another form of Treasury security and share benefits of other Treasuries, here are just some of the ways they are unique:

- *They are available in much smaller denominations.* They start as little as $25 and come in denominations of $50, $75, $100, $200, $500, $1,000, $5,000, and $10,000. The government limits you to investing a maximum of $15,000 a year in savings bonds.
- *Series EE savings bonds are issued at half their face value.* When you buy a $50 bond, for example, you pay $25 for it. They have no set maturity date and pay no current interest, but you can redeem them any time—from within six months of purchase to as long as 30 years later, according to a redemption schedule published by the Treasury Department.
- *Yields on U.S. savings bonds are not fixed.* Instead, bonds issued May 1997 or later earn interest based on 90 percent of the average yields of five-year Treasury securities for the preceding six months. These bonds increase in value every month, and interest is compounded semiannually.
- *The government no longer guarantees a minimum yield.* For many years, the Treasury guaranteed that you would earn at least 6 percent if you held a savings bond for at least five years. In 1995 the minimum was dropped.
- *I Bonds protect the purchasing power of their investment and earn a guaranteed real rate of return.* Interest is added monthly and paid when the bond is cashed. Interest is compounded semiannually. I Bonds are sold at face value and grow in value with inflation-indexed earnings for up to 30 years.

Government Agency Securities

One notch riskier than Treasuries and savings bonds are the securities issued by a plethora of federal government–backed agencies. Though they don't have the full faith and credit of the U.S. government behind them, you can be certain Congress would find a way to make sure these agencies don't default on their debt. They pay slightly higher yields than Treasury securities, but like Treasuries, interest from agency securities is usually taxable at the federal level but exempt from state and local taxes. These bonds, unlike Treasuries, are not auctioned directly to the public but are sold by a network of bond dealers and banks. They're easy to buy. Agencies that issue these securities include groups like the Asian Development Bank, the Federal Housing Administration, the Small Business Administration, and the Federal National Mortgage Association.

Whether a federal agency bond is right for you depends on its current yield and whether you feel comfortable with the slightly higher risk involved in owning one. If you can, it can be a fine choice.

Mortgage-Backed Securities

A mortgage-backed security works as follows: Soon after a bank or savings and loan issues a mortgage to a homeowner, the loan is sold along with thousands of other loans to a federal agency, which repackages it in the form of a mortgage-backed security. The federal agency guarantees it will pay investors interest and principal as they come due, even if a homeowner is late with his or her mortgage payment or defaults on the mortgage. These securities provide regular monthly interest as they are paid by homeowners. In addition, each month a certain amount of the mortgage principal is repaid and that money is passed through to the investor.

These aren't for everyone. The minimum denomination is $25,000, though some older issues trading at lower prices may require less than that. Second, the timing of interest and principal payments is not fully predictable. This is the biggest difference between a mortgage-backed security and a Treasury bond, which pays interest every six months and is not callable for years. The interest and principal repayment schedule is uncertain because the homeowners making the payments can be unpredictable. If mortage rates fall enough to make it worthwhile, they will refinance their higher interest mortgages. On the other hand, if mortgage rates rise, homeowners will hold onto their mortgages for dear life.

Municipal Bonds

Though riskier than Treasuries or agency securities, municipal bonds *(munis)* are extremely popular. These bonds, issued by states, cities, counties, towns, villages, and taxing authorities of many types, have one feature that separates them from all other securities: The interest they pay is totally free from federal taxes. In most cases, bondholders who are also residents of the states issuing the bonds do not have to pay state or local taxes on the interest either. Bonds not taxable by the resident state are called *double-tax-free bonds,* and those also not taxable by a locality are called *triple-tax-free issues.*

The fact that the interest from municipal bonds is federally tax free allows issuers to float bonds with yields that are lower than taxable government and corporate bond issuers must pay. Investors are satisfied to earn 4 percent tax free compared with 6 percent on a Treasury, on which federal taxes are due. The higher the investor's federal, state, and local tax bracket, the more attractive munis become because they permit the investor to escape more taxes. At the same time, the lower yields that municipalities pay make it affordable for them to build roads, schools, sewer systems, and hospitals among other facilities.

Muni bonds are usually issued in minimum demoninations of $5,000, though some can be had for as little as $1,000; brokers often require a minimum order of $5,000. When buying a muni bond, ask how many years of protection against early redemption you will receive.

If you would rather not worry at all about safety, a conservative alternative called *municipal bond insurance* is available on about half of all newly issued bonds today. You cannot buy insurance on your bonds individually, but you can purchase bonds that already have insurance attached to them. The municipal bond insurers guarantee that you will receive timely payments of interest and principal for the life of the bond if the issuer defaults. Insured bonds usually trade as though they have an AAA rating because no risk of default exists. However, because the cost of the insurance is passed on to the investor, insured bonds usually yield a little less than similar noninsured bonds.

Clearly, if you are in a high enough tax bracket, it could be worthwhile to investigate municipal bonds. They are not only safe but their after-tax yields often beat any other taxable alternative.

Corporate Bonds

The next rung down the ladder of bond risk are bonds issued by corporations. Unlike the government and its agencies, for example, corporations can vanish suddenly; thousands of companies, in fact, go bankrupt each year. Because corporations, no matter how solid financially, are thus perceived as vulnerable to changes in the business environment, the bonds they issue are considered riskier than government issues and therefore always pay a rate higher than government issues of the same maturity. Still, only a tiny percentage of corporate bonds—typically less than 1 percent—ever default. Even in the worst-case scenario of a company going bankrupt, bondholders' claims are settled before stockholders receive any compensation.

Depending on the financial creditworthiness of the issuing company, a corporate bond can yield from two to six percentage points more than Treasuries of the same maturity.

Corporate bond prices react to general fluctuations in interest rates as well as to the financial fortunes (or misfortunes) of the issuing companies. For example, a bond's price will rise if the company's finances improve because investors anticipate that the bond's safety rating from agencies like Standard & Poor's might be upgraded. On the other hand, a series of financial setbacks will sink the bond's price.

Corporate bonds are typically issued in denominations of $1,000 and quoted in units of $100 as Treasury bonds are. Most bond dealers don't like trading in lots of fewer than five bonds, or less than $5,000.

As with municipal bonds, research your protection against premature calls carefully. Many corporate bonds offer ten years guaranteed against early redemption, though call protection varies widely.

Zero-Coupon Bonds

These bonds—called *zeros* for short—can, paradoxically, be the safest of all investments or the riskiest. It depends on how you use them.

A zero-coupon bond gets its name from the fact that the bond is issued with a zero percent coupon rate. Instead of making regular interest payments, a zero is issued at a deep discount from its face value of 100 or $5,000. The return on a zero comes from the gradual increase in the bond's price from the discount to face value, which it reaches at maturity.

You benefit from zeros in three ways:

1. You know exactly how much money you will receive when the bond matures.
2. You know exactly when you will receive that money.
3. You don't have to worry about reinvesting the small amounts of interest that regular full-coupon bonds pay.

Very few investments can guarantee you will receive a specific dollar amount years from now. Because zeros have a specific schedule of appreciation, you can use a zero as an integral part of a financial plan to fund specific expenses years in advance.

When you contact a broker about buying a zero, you will usually be quoted the current price of a bond that will mature at a face value of $1,000 a number of years in the future (one advantage is that you can buy almost any amount, not a minimum of $5,000), and the broker will tell you what yield you are locking in at that price. The quote will include the broker's markup so you don't have an additional commission. Because markups can vary widely from broker to broker, shop around.

Once you have the data for various zeros, choose the bond selling for the lowest price and boasting the highest yield to maturity for the date you want. The further into the future you want your money returned, the fewer dollars you must pay now, because you are allowing more time for the zero to compound.

Another attraction of a zero is that your interest is reinvested automatically at the zero's yield, which can be particularly significant if you lock in a high interest rate. There is, however, a risky side to zeros. Because they lock in a fixed reinvestment rate of interest for a long time, their prices react to fluctuations in interest rates far more than does any other type of bond. (See Figure 7.4.)

As a result of zeros' volatility, they are the favorite vehicle for speculators who want to bet that interest rates will fall. This is a game for serious investors, however, because if interest rates rise instead of fall, speculators can lose big. For most investors, though, zeros are far from a speculative investment.

Convertible Bonds

Convertible bonds are hybrids—one part bond and the other part stock. In their role as bonds, they offer regular fixed income, though usually at a yield lower than that of straight bonds of the same issuer. In their role as stocks, convertibles offer significant appreciation potential and a way to benefit from the issuing companies' financial success.

However, you won't benefit as much as common shareholders if the companies' fortunes soar. To some investors, convertibles offer the best of both worlds: high income and appreciation potential. To others, they are the worst of both worlds: lower income than bond yields and less appreciation potential than common stocks. That said, they can make a solid contribution to your portfolio.

Figure 7.4   5-, 10-, 20-, and 30-Year Zeros Responding to Rate Changes

	Percentage Point Change in a Year								
	+4	+3	+2	+1	Unchanged	−1	−2	−3	−4
30-year zero	−64%	−53%	−38%	−18%	+8%	+43%	+89%	+139%	+220%
20-year zero	−47	−37	−25	−10	+8	+30	+56	+88	+117
10-year zero	−23	−16	−9	0	+8	+18	+29	+40	+53
5-year zero	−7	−4	0	+4	+8	+12	+17	+21	+26

Source: Courtesy of Ryan Labs, Inc., New York, New York.

Convertibles come in two forms: *debentures,* which are unsecured bonds, and *preferred stock.* Both pay a fixed rate of interest and are convertible to the common stock of the issuer when the common stock reaches a certain price, known as the common stock's *conversion price.* The conversion price is always set at a level higher than the common stock's price at the time the convertible is first issued; it can be as low as 15 percent above the common stock's price or as high as 50 percent above it.

Like all bonds, convertibles are interest-rate sensitive; the market evaluates them as straight fixed-income securities (which gives them their investment value) and based on their underlying common stock (which gives them their conversion value). When the market takes a dim view of an underlying company, the convertible's investment value is more important than it would be otherwise. If the underlying company is a hot growth stock, however, it will trade more on its conversion value because investors expect the common stock price to rise, and the convertible will eventually be converted into common shares. Convertibles offer no special tax breaks. All interest paid is fully taxable at the federal, state, and local level. Although no taxes are due when you convert from a bond to a common stock, you must pay all the normal taxes on the stock dividends. Convertibles are usually sold in denominations of $1,000, and most brokers like to trade in lots of ten bonds, or $10,000.

Before you buy a convertible, decide whether you want to own the issuer's common stock. If the company's future looks bright, the convertible is an excellent choice. If you're merely looking for income and you wouldn't want to own the underlying stock, move on to another option.

If you're curious about convertibles, a good resource is the newsletter *Value Line Convertibles* (220 E. 42nd St., New York, NY 10017; 800-535-8760).

Junk Bonds

If you have an appetite for risk, *high-yield bonds,* better known as junk bonds, are right up your alley. Junk bonds are issued by corporations that have less than an investment-grade rating from the ratings gurus like Standard & Poor's and Moody's. The corporations are either on their way up or their way down, financially speaking. The new companies may be so new that they don't have enough of a track record to merit a top rating, but they aren't necessarily bad companies. On the other hand, the "fallen angels" are another story; they've had the top grades before but have fallen on hard times for any number of reasons.

So why would you want a junk bond? The company's bonds pay a substantially higher yield than do securities issued by blue chip corporations. How much more depends on the issuer, but decent-quality junk bonds can yield between two and ten percentage points more than investment-grade issues. And that can translate into yields of 9 to 18 percent; lower-quality junk issues can pay up to 20 percent. You can assume with that kind of payoff, the risks are huge too. They are. The company can default, the bonds can be downgraded further, the liquidity of junk bond trading can dry up—you get the picture.

That said, though, junk bonds can provide very high returns if they are chosen well. Look for companies with improving finances rather than those whose financial picture only seems to get darker and that, despite all your wishing, may never turn around.

Most junk bonds are sold in lots of $1,000, but if they're really in the tank, they may go for much less. Brokers like to deal with lots of five, or $5,000. The interest you receive is fully taxable on all levels. If you sell the bonds for a gain, Uncle Sam will look for his share; and if you sell at a loss, you can write it off against other capital gains and $3,000 of ordinary income, as you can with any other investment.

MUTUAL FUNDS

If the process of selecting individual stocks or bonds seems a bit overwhelming, one alternative offers the benefits of stock ownership without the headache of choosing them: mutual funds that invest in stocks and bonds.

Put simply, a stock or bond mutual fund is a pool of money that a fund manager invests in stocks and bonds to achieve a specific objective. The fund is sponsored by a mutual fund company, which may be an independent firm, such as Fidelity, T. Rowe Price, or Vanguard; an insurance company; a bank; or a division of a brokerage firm such as Merrill Lynch or Salomon Smith Barney.

Load versus No-Load Funds

The two basic kinds of mutual funds are differentiated by how they are sold. When you pay a commission to a salesperson, financial planner, or broker, that fee is called a *load* and the fund is called a *load mutual fund* because you have to pay a commission to buy it. The other kind of fund, called a *no-load fund,* is sold directly by the mutual fund company with no salesperson involved. Both types of funds have their role in the marketplace. It's for you to decide which best suits your needs.

The advantage of a load fund is that you receive professional advice on which fund to choose. This can be particularly important because there are more than 9,000 funds to choose from. Ideally, the salesperson will not only tell you when to buy but when to sell and move into a better fund. The downside is the commission that you pay immediately reduces the amount of money you have at work for you in the fund. The load can amount to as much as 8.5 percent of your initial investment, though many funds today charge 3 or 4 percent. Thus, for every dollar you sink into the fund, only 91.5 cents will earn money if you pay the full 8.5 percent load. Clearly, the advantage of the no-load fund is that you have all your money working for you from the moment you open the account. But you're on your own.

Both no-load and load funds, however, charge an annual management fee, which can range from as little as 0.2 percent of your assets to as much as 2 percent. The fees are deducted from the value of the fund automatically, which adds up. If a fund charges a 2 percent management fee and the fund's stock portfolio rose 11 percent over the past year, you earned a 9 percent return.

Those fees may seem worthwhile for a number of reasons. A professional skilled in picking stocks does all the work for you. You get instant diversification from your basket of stocks. A fund exists for every financial goal and level of *risk tolerance.* Transaction costs are much lower than they would be if you bought stocks and bonds on your own. You can get in and out of a mutual fund easily as you can when switching from one fund to another within a fund family, and the fund will reinvest dividends and capital gains automatically.

You do have to do some homework, however. Get the fund's *prospectus* and read it before you plunk down any money. What are you looking for? What is stated as the fund's investment objective? What investment methods does the fund use to achieve its goals? Who is the fund's investment advisor? What amount of risk will the fund assume? What are the tax consequences of holding the fund? What are the fees? What has the fund's performance been for the past five or ten years? These are some of the questions the prospectus will answer.

> ***Hot Tip:*** *A* prospectus *is a formal written offer to sell securities, including mutual fund shares, to the public. Filed with the Securities and Exchange Commission and available to all investors, the prospectus includes a statement of objectives, information on how the fund operates, a history of performance (if it has one), the names of the fund managers, a schedule of fees and charges, and other information.*

Selecting a Fund within a Category

After reading Chapter 4, you have an idea about the types of stock and bond funds you can choose from. But how do you select a fund within a category? What matters most? Performance, convenience, or quality of service?

Performance. You want to choose a fund that has established a solid long-term record of achieving its objectives. It is also preferable if the fund has had the same manager for a long time so that you can be assured the fund's style will remain consistent.

Several independent fund-monitoring organizations rank fund performance. Two of the biggest and best known are Lipper Analytical Services (The Reuters Building, Three Times Square, 17th Floor, New York, NY 10036; 877-955-4773; www.lipperweb.com) and Morningstar (225 W. Wacker Dr., Chicago, IL 60606; 312-696-6000; www.morningstar.com). Results from both are published regularly in the *Wall Street Journal, USA Today,* and *Investor's Business Daily* as well as in *Money* magazine and other reputable personal finance journals. You can also track fund performance in the many newsletters listed among this chapter's resources.

What are you looking for? The best measure of fund performance is called *total return,* a measure that combines all dividends and capital gains distributions with changes in a fund's price. It is a far better yardstick to use when comparing funds than just the change in a fund's price over a period of time. The listing for total return you see from the ratings services and in the media normally shows a fund's results thus far in the current year, over the past 52 weeks, and over the past three, five, and ten years. It also refers to the *average annual return,* which is the averaging of returns over longer periods of time. Any average annual return of more than 15 percent for at least five years is considered exemplary.

In choosing a fund, you should feel comfortable with its style. What exactly is a fund's style? It is the methodology of selecting stocks and bonds that differentiates one fund from another. Some stocks work well at certain points in a stock market cycle, whereas others outperform as the stock market changes. The two broadest kinds of stock-choosing styles are *growth* and *value.* Growth refers to selecting stocks with ever-rising earnings; value means buying stocks temporarily out of favor that the manager expects will become popular again. It is difficult for the average investor, as well as the Wall Street professional, to evaluate whether growth or value stock funds are on the upswing at any particular moment. For that reason, over the long term it's best to diversify among styles. If half of your holdings are in growth and the other half in value, you will perform better over time than if you invest all your money in one style.

Another difference in investment styles is based on whether the fund manager makes decisions about market timing. A fund run by a market timer, even though it is a stock fund, can sell most or all of its stocks if the manager senses the market is about to tumble. This fund is designed to protect shareholders' capital from huge losses. Funds operating under the other style maintain that it is impossible to time the market's ups and downs, so it is best to be nearly fully invested in stocks at all times. These funds will be more volatile than funds that try to time the market. Fully invested funds will rise faster when stocks rise but fall further when they tumble. The managers of such funds leave timing to you.

Convenience. Though you may receive a higher return by having holdings in the top ten funds in ten different fund families, the recordkeeping and headaches in following so many funds are not worth the higher return potential. Find a top-quality fund family or two and keep most of your capital with them. Most families offer consolidated statements, meaning you can see all of your fund holdings on one statement. Also, you will be able to transfer money from one fund to another easily if you keep most of your assets in one place. Several discount brokers like Charles Schwab, Quick and Reilly, and TD Waterhouse allow you to buy almost any mutual fund in any family and keep it in one account.

Quality of service. Good service isn't hard to find, but different fund companies offer different services. Here's what you want access to:

- *Automated phone answering systems.* These should give you prices, yields, and other information about your funds as well as allow you to make transactions 24 hours a day, 7 days a week.
- *Knowledgeable and helpful telephone service representatives.* Remember that phone reps at no-load funds describe funds but won't advise you on which fund to buy. Some large fund companies offer investor help in large walk-in centers, where you can discuss your investing needs with a fund representative in person.
- *Easy-to-read statements.* You should not have to be a lawyer or mutual fund expert to be able to make sense of your statement. It should clearly spell out how many shares you have, how many shares you bought or sold in your latest transactions, the yields on your funds, and other relevant data.

Types of Bond Funds: Choosing the Best for You

Two factors distinguish funds: the kinds of securities they buy and the average maturity of the bonds in their portfolios. In general, the longer the fund's portfolio maturity, the higher its yield and the higher its risk.

Low-risk sector funds include the following:

Government bond funds. These funds invest exclusively in securities issued by the U.S. government or its agencies. No risk of default exists in any of the underlying securities; therefore, these are the safest bonds around. Long-term bond funds do carry substantial risk because of interest rate volatility, however.

Municipal bond funds. These funds invest solely in tax-exempt bonds, so none of the dividends they pay are subject to federal income tax. Depending on your tax bracket, these funds might allow you to keep more interest than you could earn on a higher-yielding, but taxable, bond fund. Three kinds of muni bond funds are available: *national funds,* which buy bonds from municipalities across the country; *state-specific funds,* which are designed by states for residents of those states who want to avoid both federal and state taxation; and *local muni funds,* which buy bonds only from a locality that levies an income tax, such as New York City.

Short-term and intermediate-term bond funds. Such funds, which come in both taxable and tax-free varieties, buy bonds with maturities no longer than ten years and usually as short as five years. Because short-term bonds fluctuate in price far less than long-term bonds during the same interest rate volatility, these funds' prices remain quite stable.

Moderate-risk sector funds include these:

Convertible bond funds. Convertible bond funds buy convertible debentures and convertible preferred stocks. Though convertible yields are lower than those on straight corporate bonds, these funds offer more appreciation potential and provide their highest returns when the stock market is rising.

High-grade corporate bond funds. Such funds buy bonds issued by investment-grade corporations—that is, those with ratings of BBB or higher. The funds' yields are one or two percentage points higher than those of government funds of similar maturities. Yet they remain quite safe because they buy top-quality bonds and diversify widely among hundreds of issues.

Mortgage-backed security funds. These funds invest in mortgage securities issued by quasi-government agencies. The securities are guaranteed against default by those agencies but not against price fluctuations caused by interest rate movements. Mortgage-backed security funds tend to pay yields of one to three percentage points higher than Treasury funds with similar maturities.

The apex of high-risk funds include the following:

Global bond funds. Global bond funds purchase bonds issued by governments and corporations from around the world. When interest rates are higher in countries other than the United States, these funds can pay yields two or three percentage points higher than similar domestic funds. What makes them higher risk is that currency fluctuations can create huge swings in the value of the shares.

High-yield junk bond funds. Junk bond funds buy bonds of corporations that are below investment grade, meaning they have ratings of less than BBB. Junk bond funds can pay yields four to six percentage points higher than government or high-grade corporate bond funds with similar maturities. High-yield fund prices are much more volatile than more conservative bond funds because of rapidly changing values of the bonds they hold. In general, junk bond funds perform well when the stock market rises because junk bonds mirror the performance of their issuers' stocks.

Zero-coupon bond funds. Such funds buy portfolios of zero-coupon bonds, which are issued at a deep discount to face value and mature at a specific time in the future. These funds should be considered very conservative if they are held until they liquidate, which occurs when the bond matures. However, because zero-coupon bonds are the most volatile of all bonds, these funds fluctuate more dramatically than any other kind of bond fund while the bonds are outstanding.

Closed-End Mutual Funds

Like open-end funds, closed-end funds offer the advantages of professional management, diversification, convenience, and automatic reinvestment of dividends and capital gains.

The difference between the types is in the way they sell shares. Open-end funds create new shares continually, as more money is invested in them, or liquidate shares as shares are redeemed. When cash is taken out of the fund, the number of outstanding shares shrinks. The portfolio manager therefore is faced with an ever-changing pool of assets that can be small one month and huge the next. This can make it difficult to manage the fund because millions of dollars usually pour into the fund after it has had a hot record and stock prices are high, and millions leave the fund when it has underperformed the market and stock prices are falling. This volatile cash flow can severely harm the fund's performance because the manager is forced to buy stocks when prices are high and sell them when prices are low.

Closed-end funds are designed to avoid this problem. Instead of constantly creating and redeeming shares, these funds issue a limited number of shares, which trade on the New York or American Stock Exchange or on the Nasdaq National Market System. Instead of dealing with a fund company directly when you buy or sell shares as you do with open-end funds, you trade closed-end shares with other investors just as you do with any publicly traded stock. You pay standard brokerage commissions to buy and sell them, and you can look up the fund's price in the stock tables of the newspaper every day.

The closed-end fund manger has no need to worry about huge flows of cash into and out of the fund. He or she knows how much money must be invested and selects stocks or bonds based on the fund's investment objectives. This allows the manager to concentrate on meeting long-term objectives because he or she doesn't have to keep a stash of cash around to meet redemptions.

Two factors must be considered when buying a closed-end fund. The first is the fund manager's record in choosing winning stocks or bonds that allows the fund to achieve its investment objective. The second is whether you are buying the fund at a *premium* or a *discount*. A premium is when the fund's share price is higher than the value of the securities in the portfolio, whereas a discount occurs when the share price is below the value of the portfolio. Some investors' entire strategy with closed-end funds is to buy them at a discount and wait for them to rise in premium, at which point they sell.

CERTIFICATES OF DEPOSIT (CDS)

CDs are bank, savings and loan, or credit union instruments that allow you to lock in an interest rate for a specific period. If you withdraw your money from a CD before it matures, you face an early-withdrawal penalty set by the institution—often three months' interest. The most popular CDs mature in three months, six months, and one year, although banks offer CDs with maturies as long as five years. Some banks even offer so-called designer CDs, for which you decide the maturity and the bank quotes you a yield. Generally, the longer you commit your money, the higher your CD's yield will be. Banks usually set some minimum amount for CDs, which can be as low as $100 or as much as $1,000, but they never charge a fee to buy a certificate.

Banks pay interest in several ways. In many cases, it is not paid until the CD matures. For longer-term CDs, banks mail checks every three or six months, or they deposit the money directly into your bank account; most banks allow you to reinvest your interest in the CD if you wish. Interest from CDs is taxable at all government levels in the year it is received, even if the interest is reinvested. Remember to calculate the effect of those taxes when you compare your potential CD returns against other alternatives, such as tax-free money funds or municipal bonds.

An attractive feature of CDs is their safety. They are insured by the Federal Deposit Insurance Corporation (FDIC) for up to $100,000. This guarantee means you get back your principal and all interest due, though it does not guarantee that you will be able to withdraw your money at will if a bank is seized. You may have to give the bank up to 30 days' advance notice if you want to take the money out of your account. Because you won't be insured for more than $100,000 per account, if you have more than $100,000 in cash or CDs at any time, spread it among various accounts at several banks.

You don't have to restrict your search for high yields to your neighborhood or even your state. Many banks accept out-of-state deposits by wire or mail, and the highest yields across the country are publicized constantly in major financial newspapers such as the *Wall Street Journal* and *USA Today.* You can also look up the highest yields on Web sites such as <www. bankrate.com>. Or you can subscribe to the newsletter *100 Highest Yields* (Bank Rate, Inc., 11811 U.S. Highway 1, North Palm Beach, FL 33408; 800-327-7717), which surveys banks every week to uncover those with the top yields. In the 1980s, yields on CDs stayed in the double digits for several years, then fell sharply along with all interest rates. By the 2000s, CD yields settled in the 2 percent to 4 percent range.

Institutions use different methods of compounding interest. Some use simple interest, whereas others compound daily, weekly, monthly, quarterly, semiannually, or annually. This effects what banks advertise as the "effective yield" on a CD, which in fact is mythical because it is unlikely that you'll be able to capture exactly the same rate when the CD comes due in three or six months.

Check with your bank to see what happens when your CD matures; it is not required to notify you when a CD is about to mature. Some banks automatically reinvest the money in a new CD at the prevailing rate, which may or may not be what you want. Others will mail you a check for the full amount, and still others will put the money in a low-yielding savings account.

To protect yourself against the ups and downs of interest rates, you might try the CD laddering strategy. Instead of putting all your money in one CD with one maturity, spread it among several CDs maturing every few months or years. That way, CDs will constantly mature, which gives you the chance to reinvest at higher rates if rates have risen. If they have fallen, you still have several CDs locked in at higher rates.

Some banks have added wrinkles to the simple CD in recent years. The rising-rate CD, for example, guarantees that if interest rates rise, your CD's yield will increase as well every six months. Then there's the expandable CD that permits you to add more money to an existing CD at the same rate, which would be advantageous if rates have fallen since you first bought the CD. Other banks allow you to switch to a higher rate for your CD during its lifetime if interest rates have risen.

Whether you invest in a traditional CD or a fancier version, it might have just the combination of high yields, convenience, and safety that is right for you.

ANNUITIES

Insurance companies sell more than insurance; they also sell annuities. Annuities pay a regular stream of income while you live, usually after you retire, in contrast with life insurance, which pays your beneficiaries a lump sum when you die. Annuities also provide the advantage of tax-deferred compounding on the investment portion of the account.

Two basic kinds of annuities exist: immediate and deferred. *Immediate annuities* are purchased with a lump sum (and begin to generate an income stream immediately). Typically, they are purchased by people in retirement to provide a guaranteed stream of income. The lump sum might come from a distribution by a pension plan, a salary reduction plan, an IRA, a Keogh plan, or investments that you have built up over the years. Different insurance companies offer varying levels of monthly income, depending on how long you will receive payments.

Deferred annuities are bought by younger people who want to save on a tax-deferred basis for many years, then convert to a payout schedule once they retire. You can purchase a flexible premium retirement annuity through regular monthly, or annual, deposits of as little as $25. You are not required to pay a premium every year, but the more you invest, the greater your annuity's value grows. You can also buy an annuity with one lump sum; this is called a *single-premium deferred annuity* (SPDA). Most companies require at least $2,500, though they prefer $10,000 or more. Annuities also have a life insurance component because your beneficiaries receive the entire accumulated value of your annuity (what you paid in plus the interest earned) if you die before receiving annuity payments.

Fixed versus Variable Annuities

You have options for how your money is invested. The more conservative is a *fixed-dollar annuity,* which the insurance company invests in bonds and mortgages. Each year, the company announces the *fixed return* for the next year, depending on the current investment portfolio; the fixed return is the rate the company will credit to your annuity. In the mid-1980s, double-digit annual returns were routinely promised, but by the 2000s, rates had dropped to the 5 to 7 percent range. The insurance company usually offers some level of guaranteed minimum return, however—usually about 4 percent. Don't be lured by a high first-year rate, which often drops dramatically in subsequent years. To protect yourself, make sure your policy offers a *bailout provision,* which gives you the right to liquidate all or part of your annuity without cost if your renewal rate is ever less than 1 percent of the previously offered rate. Usually, you must notify the insurance company within 30 days of receiving notice of the renewal rate that you plan to bail out. Nevertheless, do not rely on the bailout clause if you opt for a fixed annuity. Choose a company that has paid a consistently above-average return; chances are that streak will continue.

Then there is the *variable annuity,* which offers the potential for higher returns, though at greater risk. The variable annuity contract gives you a choice among several stock, bond, and money market portfolios. Within the stock category, you will normally be offered a selection of sector, aggressive growth, growth, growth and income, international, and balanced funds. With bonds, you may shift between corporate, government, high-yield, and international fixed-income portfolios. You can allocate your money among stock and bond options any way you like and transfer the funds as market conditions change. As the stock and bond markets swing in value over the years, your annuity's value also rises and falls.

If you select a company with a proven investment performance, you can probably do better in the long term with a variable annuity than with a fixed-dollar annuity. The key is to purchase a contract with top-notch investment managers. The easiest way to find such an annuity is to consult a recent issue of *Variable Annuity Research & Data Service Large Report* (4343 Shallowford Rd., Marietta, GA 30062; 770-998-5186); *Comparative Annuity Reports* (P.O. Box 1268, Fair Oaks, CA 95628; 916-487-7863; www. annuitycomparativedata.com); or *Annuity Shopper* (8 Talmadge Dr., Monroe TWP, NJ 08831; 800-872-6684; 732-521-5110; www.annuityshopper.com). Because it is difficult and expensive to switch from one company's variable annuity to another's, research your decision carefully.

Payout Options

Once you reach retirement age, annuities offer many different payout options. In general, the longer you obligate the company to pay benefits, the lower your monthly check. Whether you think that you will live a short or long time determines your regular payment. Each company determines its payout scale by estimating life expectancy rates and the company's expected earnings on investments. The duration of annuity payments can be based on a life expectancy, a certain period of time, or on a combination of the two. The following are usual choices that you will be offered.

Ten-year term certain annuity. If you think that you will live ten years or less after retirement, you can choose an annuity that will pay you or your heirs for only ten years. This option provides the highest monthly benefit. However, if you live more than ten years, you're out of luck. This is a very risky strategy—unless you are in very poor health when you retire—because the average life expectancy is well into the 80s, or more than 20 years from the usual retirement age of 65.

Life annuity with ten-year term certain. This annuity will pay a fixed monthly amount for the rest of your life. However, if you die before the annuity has paid you benefits for ten years, your beneficiary (usually your spouse) will receive your payments only for the remainder of the original ten years. This form of annuity pays less than the ten-year term certain. It is also significantly riskier for your spouse, who would not receive payments after ten years from the date of your retirement, assuming that you have died. If you select this option, make sure your spouse has enough other sources of income to fall back on to cover the shortfall.

Life annuity. This plan would cut your monthly payout from the ten-year term certain significantly but would assure you of an income for life. After you die, your beneficiary receives no payments.

Refund life annuity. A refund life annuity is a hedge against the possibility of early death. Under the refund life annuity settlement option, the insurance company will pay a monthly benefit for the life of the annuitant. At the annuitant's death, if the amount that was applied to the annuitization of the contract is more than the total of the installment payments received by the annuitant during his or her lifetime, the difference is paid in a lump sum to the beneficiaries. Simply put, the annuitant receives a lifetime income while protecting his or her heirs from losing the unused value of the amount annuitized. However, the monthly income is less because of the higher risk to the insurance company of returning all funds not paid out during annuitization.

Joint and survivor annuity. If you are married or if someone depends on your income, you may want to select this option, which pays a fixed amount until both you and your spouse or dependent die. When you die your spouse or dependent receives qualified joint and survivor annuity (QJSA) payments until he or she dies. These payments are usually less than the amount you received, but by law they cannot be less than 50 percent of your payment. Because both you and your spouse or dependent may live a long time, the joint and survivor plan offers the lowest monthly payment of the options discussed here. However, it is also the safest plan because it ensures that your spouse or dependent will receive a monthly income after you're gone.

If you are married and want to receive your benefits in the life annuity option or assign a survivor benefit to someone other than your spouse, you must obtain written spousal consent confirming that your spouse knows what he or she is relinquishing and that he or she does so willingly. (If you are asked to sign such a consent form, don't unless you fully understand the financial impact of the alternative election or are so wealthy that you can't envision ever needing the money.)

Once you start receiving payouts, you must pay income taxes on a portion of those payouts. Each payment is considered part investment earnings and part return of your original principal. You must pay taxes on the investment earnings but not on the return of capital. The insurance company informs you how much of each payment constitutes earnings and principal.

Unless you're in dire straits, don't touch your annuity money before retirement. If you take distributions before age 59½, you not only pay income tax on the earnings, but you also owe the IRS a stiff 10 percent early-withdrawal penalty. The only ways around this penalty before age 59½ are if you suffer a disability or you die and the annuity proceeds are distributed to your beneficiaries.

Annuity Fees and Expenses

Pay attention to the many fees attached to every annuity contract. Most companies don't explicitly charge an up-front commission, or load. Instead, they levy a hefty surrender charge of as much as 10 percent of your principal if you want to transfer your annuity to another company within the first five or ten years of the contract. After that time, the surrender charge may disappear. However, many annuities offer a free withdrawal provision after the first year and for every year thereafter that surrender charges apply. This allows the contract holder to withdraw a certain percent (usually 10 percent) of the accumulated account value. (Before to age 59½, these partial withdrawals would be subject to the 10 percent early-withdrawal penalty.)

In addition, most annuity marketers charge annual maintenance fees of $25 to $50 to cover the administrative costs of maintaining an account. For variable annuity contracts, annual asset management fees of 0.25 percent to 2 percent are also assessed, just as they are in regular stock and bond mutual funds. All of these fees are automatically deducted from your investment account.

Many annuity charges do not apply to immediate annuities because once you have purchased such a contract, you cannot surrender it; therefore, no surrender, sales, maintenance, or asset management fees are imposed.

GETTING THE MIX RIGHT

All of these vehicles can go a long way toward revving up your retirement nest egg. As discussed in Chapter 4, how you divvy up the pot through asset allocation counts for a great deal. You wouldn't want solely stocks, bonds, or CDs but rather a combination of these to get the most bang for your buck and to protect yourself from the ups and downs of the market. *Diversification* is the name of the game. Figuring out the right mix is a very personal matter. How many years do you have until retirement? How old are you? How much money will you need apart from your tax-sheltered accounts? What is your risk tolerance? In much of the previous discussion, the emphasis hasn't been on risk. It's time to take a good look in the mirror.

Unfortunately for many people, the word *risk,* like the word *budgeting,* has a negative connotation. "Why would I want to risk my hard-earned money?" you ask. "I'm very conservative."

The answer: If you take no risks with your assets, you will be unlikely to earn a high enough return to achieve the retirement lifestyle you're shooting for. To alter the universal saying seen in gyms everywhere for the money world, "No pain, no gain" becomes "No risk, no return."

Not that you should go crazy, and truth be told, every risky investment won't earn you a high return. If it did, it wouldn't be risky. By diversifying your assets among high-risk, medium-risk, and low-risk investments, you're sure to wind up with a larger pool of assets over time than if you keep all your money in low-risk, low-return choices.

In general, the further in the future a return is expected, the greater the risk. It is tricky enough to predict what is going to happen over the next few months let alone what will happen years from now.

As you determine your risk, you should understand several types of risks you are likely to face. Here's a look at some of them.

Currency risk. Although most of your assets will probably be in dollar-denominated investments, you should be aware of the risk of currency movements if you own stocks or bonds in other currencies. When you buy an individual stock or bond in another country, or a mutual fund that invests in foreign securities, the value of your investment fluctuates based on how many dollars it takes to buy a unit of the foreign currency. In effect, when you own a British stock, for example, your money has been converted to pounds. If the value of the pound falls against the U.S. dollar, your British shares will be worth less if you were to sell the stock and translate the pounds back into dollars. It works the other way, too. Currency movements, which swing day to day based on each country's economic and political conditions, can therefore hand you substantial gains or losses.

Deflation risk. If prices are falling sharply because of a severe economic contraction, you face the risk that the value of your assets will drop just as sharply. The key to sidestepping deflation risk is to make sure you don't have too much of your wealth in assets that could get hit by a deflationary wave. Treasury bonds provide a good haven from deflation, for example, because it is safe to assume the government will always honor its obligation to bondholders.

Lack-of-diversification risk. This is commonly known as the risk of keeping all your eggs in one basket. If all your assets are in one kind of investment, such as stocks or CDs, you aren't protected if that asset falls sharply in value. Even more dangerous is to keep most of your money in just one stock, bond, or CD, because if something happens to it, you have no alternate assets to fall back on. The way to lower the risk in this realm is to spread your holdings among different kinds of assets as well as among several individual investments within each kind of asset. As mentioned before, that's a big advantage of mutual funds.

Inflation risk. Even if prices are rising at about 5 percent a year, the value of your dollars is steadily eroding over time. If inflation is galloping at more than 10 percent, your purchasing power disappears much faster.

Interest rate risk. Over the past two decades, interest rates on bonds, money market accounts, mortgages, and all other types of interest-sensitive financial instruments have been extremely volatile. In the early 1980s, the prime rate reached as high as 21.5 percent, and rates on bonds, CDs, and mortgages also soared into double digits. By the 1990s and 2000s, rates had plunged to the low single digits, and savers who had become accustomed to 14 percent CDs were crying, "Bring back the good old days of double-digit yields!" Interest rate risk can therefore cut both ways. If you lock into a fixed-rate instrument like a bond or CD when rates are low and then rates rise sharply, the value of your investment will plunge if you have to resell it. On the other hand, if you set your lifestyle according to the high yields you can earn in an environment of soaring interest rates, you'll endure a painful shock when rates fall and your lifestyle suffers.

Lack-of-liquidity risk. There are times when you need to sell something, but the market for it has dried up temporarily. That leaves you with two options: You can hang on to what you had wanted to sell, or you can sell it anyway even if you must accept an artificially low price. In general, the more aggressive an investment is, the more subject it is to the risk of holding an illiquid asset. Stocks of small companies and junk bonds, for example, are relatively easy to buy and sell under normal circumstances. But when bad news hits these markets or investors become nervous, the ability to sell at a fair price temporarily disappears.

Playing-it-too-safe risk. As mentioned earlier, if you keep all your money in supersafe CDs or money market funds, you run the risk of outliving your assets because your return has not kept you current with inflation. This risk is frequently not recognized, but it is probably the biggest risk people take. By the time you've figured out that you've been too conservative, it's usually too late to recoup.

Political risk. If you invest in countries where the political structure is not as stable as that in the United States, you run the risk of a change in government, which will dramatically devalue the worth of your holdings. On the home front, the risk stems from changes in government policy that favor one industry over another. Such changes can be accomplished by legislation, tax policy, tariffs, subsidies, or many other means.

Repayment risk. Of the two kinds of repayment risk, the most common, also known as *credit risk,* is the chance that you won't be repaid what you're owed when it's due. The second kind is the opposite: you are repaid before you want or expect to get your money back. You are taking credit risk whenever you buy a bond, because your ability to collect on that obligation is only as good as the issuer's ability to repay it.

The other kind of repayment risk entails getting your money back faster than you had expected. You may not think this is a big problem, but in two circumstances it is. First, suppose you lock in a 10 percent yield on a bond, and the level of interest rates drops to 6 percent. If the bond's issuer has the right to redeem the bond before maturity, it will do so to save on interest costs. Because rates have dropped, you won't be able to replace that bond with a new one at the same yield. The other troublesome scenario involves mortgage-backed securities. Known in the trade by names like Ginnie Mae, Fannie Mae, or Freddie Mac, mortgage-backed securities are actually pools of individual mortgages that have been packaged for sale. The repayment problem occurs when mortgage rates fall sharply and homeowners rush to refinance their loans. While it is great for them, the holders of mortgage-backed securities lose because the securities repay most of their principal quickly. Because interest rates have fallen, holders of mortgage-backed securities have the same problem as owners of called bonds: they can't replicate the high rates they thought they had locked in for years.

Volatility risk. This risk occurs when an investment swings wildly in value from a very low price to a high one in a short period. Of course, volatility gives you a greater chance to profit if you buy when the price is low and sell when it's high. But that's easier said than done. Often, your emotions drive you to buy into a volatile investment when its price has been rising because you assume the price will continue to soar. The opposite usually holds true: you are most tempted to sell when the price has plummeted because you fear it will plunge even further. Just because an investment is volatile in the short run doesn't mean you should avoid it altogether. But you should realize what you've bought and feel psychologically able to ride out sudden air pockets when they strike, keeping in mind that you entered into the investment in the hope of long-term gain.

THE INVESTMENT RISK PYRAMID

In putting together a portfolio that both achieves your financial goals and still allows you to sleep comfortably at night, think of your entire mix of assets in the form of an investment risk pyramid as shown in Figure 7.5.

At the top of your pyramid are the riskiest assets, which offer the greatest potential for high returns as well as big losses. The high-risk apex includes collectibles, foreign investments, futures contracts, junk corporate and municipal bonds, new stock issues, oil and gas limited partnerships, options, raw land, small growth stocks, tax shelters, unfinished real estate construction, venture capital, and warrants.

The next tier of the pyramid, the moderate-risk sector, includes stock and bond mutual funds, income-oriented limited partnerships, mortgage-backed securities, individual growth stocks, corporate bonds, and rental real estate.

The third tier of the pyramid, the low-risk sector, consists of annuities, blue chip stocks, Treasury bonds, life insurance contracts, municipal bonds with high credit ratings, short-term bond funds, utility stocks, and zero-coupon bonds.

The base of the pyramid is composed of investments in which you have almost no chance of losing your principal. These include bank CDs, cash,

Figure 7.5   Investment Risk Pyramid

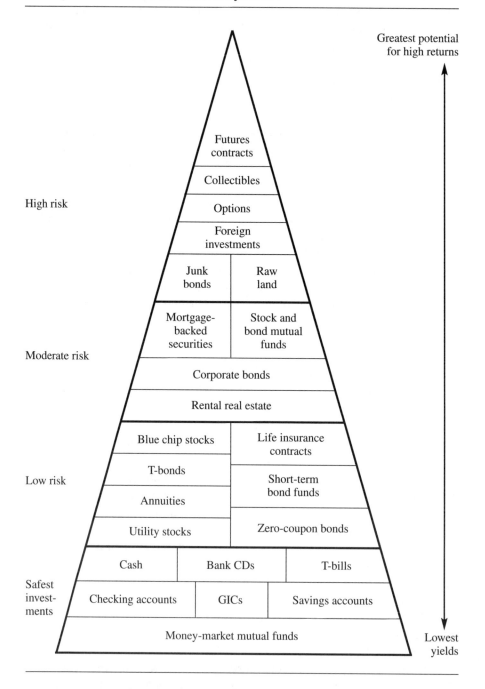

checking accounts, money market mutual funds, and guaranteed investment contracts (GICs) found in salary reduction plans, savings accounts, and Treasury bills.

No matter what your age or situation, you should probably have some of your assets in each of the four sectors of the pyramid at all times. What should change over time is how much you invest in each sector. You may be young and able to take more risk, so more of your money should be in the high-risk apex. Or you may be retired and need to live off of your investments; more of your money should then be in low-risk and base investments. But the young person should still have a cash reserve, and the retiree should still have some money in apex investments, so they both can stay ahead of inflation.

RESOURCES: STOCKS

Books, Booklets, and Pamphlets

All about Stocks: The Easy Way to Get Started, by Esme E. Faerber (McGraw-Hill, P.O. Box 543, Blacklick, OH 43004; 800-634-3961; www.mcgraw-hill.com). Covers stock market basics for newcomers with concise and understandable answers to today's most frequently asked stock market questions.

Beating the Street, by Peter Lynch (Simon & Schuster, 100 Front St., Riverside, NJ 08075; 212-698-7000; 800-223-2348; www.simonsays.com). Explanation by the legendary manager of the Fidelity Magellan Fund of how he picked stocks, how he first heard about companies, and where he found the information so critical to deciding whether to invest in companies.

Benjamin Graham on Value Investing: Lesson from the Dean of Wall Street, by Janet Lowe (Penguin Putnam, 405 Murray Hill Pkwy., East Rutherford, NJ 07073; 800-788-6262; www.penguinputnam.com). A book about famous investor Benjamin Graham that includes his successful value investment philosophy and his investment record.

Buying Stocks without a Broker, by Charles B. Carlson (McGraw-Hill, P.O. Box 543, Blacklick, OH 43004; 800-634-3961; www.mcgraw-hill.com). Shows how individual investors can avoid paying brokers' commissions by buying stock directly from issuing companies.

Common Sense Global Investing: How to Successfully Navigate the International Marketplace, by Maurice K. Thompson (Dearborn Trade, 155 N. Wacker Dr., Chicago, IL 60606; 312-836-4400; 800-245-2665; www.dearborntrade.com). Helps the investor diversify and profit from today's volatile international markets and shows how to invest in the best countries for stability and profits.

The Complete Idiot's Guide to Online Investing, by Douglas Gerlach (Pearson Education, 1 Lake St., Upper Saddle River, NJ 07458; 800-428-5331; www.mcp.

com). Provides users with an easy-to-understand book on the basics of investing and computing, researching options, and using the Internet for portfolio management.

Contrarian Investing: Buy and Sell When Others Won't and Make Money Doing It, by Anthony M. Gallea and William Patalon III (New York Institute of Finance, 1330 Sixth Ave., New York, NY 10019; 212-390-5000; 800-227-6943; www.nyif. com). Describes contrarian strategy and shows the best percentage of a portfolio to have in contrarian stocks.

The Craft of Investing: Growth and Value Stocks, Emerging Markets, Market Timing, Mutual Funds, Alternative Investments, Retirement and Estate Planning, Tax Savings, by John Train (HarperBusiness, P.O. Box 588, Dunmore, PA 18512; 800-331-3761; www.harpercollins.com). Addresses everything from the psychology of the market to practical portfolio management tips and explains growth investing, value investing, when to buy, and when to sell.

The Dictionary of Finance and Investment Terms, by John Downes and Jordan E. Goodman (Barron's Educational Series, 250 Wireless Blvd., Hauppauge, NY 11788; 631-434-3311; 800-645-3476; www.barronseduc.com). The standard reference work of finance and investment that defines more than 5,000 terms in simple language.

Getting Started in Stocks, by Alvin Hall (John Wiley & Sons, 1 Wiley Dr., Somerset, NJ 08875-1272; 212-850-6000; 800-225-5945; www.wiley.com). A primer on the basics of stock investing.

How to Buy Stocks the Smart Way, by Stephen Littauer (Dearborn Trade, 155 N. Wacker Dr., Chicago, IL 60606; 312-836-4400; 800-245-2665; www.dearborntrade. com). A guide to reducing risk, spotting rising stocks, and getting the most from investments.

If You're Clueless about the Stock Market and Want to Know More, by Seth Godin (Dearborn Trade, 155 N. Wacker Dr., Chicago, IL 60606; 312-836-4400; 800-245-2665; www.dearborntrade.com). The title says it all.

The Neatest Little Guide to Stock Market Investing, by Jason Kelly (Penguin Putnam, 405 Murray Hill Pkwy., East Rutherford, NJ 07073; 800-788-6262; www. penguinputnam.com). Provides friendly guidance, sound financial expertise, and all the information needed to make smart stock choices.

The 100 Best Stocks to Own in America, by Gene Walden (Dearborn Trade, 155 N. Wacker Dr., Chicago, IL 60606; 312-836-4400; 800-245-2665; www.dearborntrade. com). Profiles 100 top-quality growth companies and reveals the shareholders' perks each company offers.

Stock Picking: The 11 Best Tactics for Beating the Market, by Richard Maturi (McGraw-Hill, P.O. Box 543, Blacklick, OH 43004, 800-634-3961; www.mcgraw-hill. com). Simple, time-tested techniques for choosing winning stocks in any market environment.

The Unofficial Guide to Investing, by Lynn O'Shaughnessy (IDG Books/Hungry Minds, 10475 Crosspoint Blvd., Indianapolis, IN 46526; 800-434-3422; www.

hungryminds.com). Demystifies the range of investment options available today and provides practical tools that will help readers make financially sound decisions.

Magazines, Newspapers, and Television Stations

Barron's National Business and Financial Weekly (P.O. Box 240, Chicopee, MA 01021; 800-544-0422). Tabloid that features incisive articles on stocks and the stock market, and the best array of statistics around.

CNBC (2200 Fletcher Ave., Ft. Lee, NJ 07024; 201-585-2622; www.cnbc.com). A round-the-clock cable channel devoted to business and financial news for most of the day; market ticker crawls at the bottom of the TV screen during the trading day. Features interviews with prominent market analysts, fund managers, economists, and other stock gurus.

CNNMoney, formerly called CNNfn (5 Penn Plaza, New York, NY 10001; 212-714-7848; www.cnn.com). Airs business news shows in the morning and one called *Moneyline* in the evening; updates what is happening on the stock market every hour while the market is open.

Forbes (60 Fifth Ave., New York, NY 10003; 212-620-2200; 800-888-9896; www.forbes.com). Known for its acerbic and witty style, the magazine uncovers good stocks and exposes stocks it considers overpriced.

Investor's Business Daily (12655 Beatrice St., Los Angeles, CA 90066; 310-448-6000; 800-831-2525; www.investors.com). Daily paper with many short articles about individual companies as well as many pages of statistics, graphs, and charts.

Money (Time and Life Building, Rockefeller Center, New York, NY 10020; 212-522-1212, 800-633-9970; www.cnnmoney.com). A popular magazine that publishes several articles each month on individual stocks and mutual funds; also covers all other areas of personal finance, including banking, taxes, real estate, and retirement.

The New York Times, "Business Day" section (229 W. 43rd St., New York, NY 10036; 212-556-1234; 800-631-2580; www.nytimes.com). Covers corporate news and features columns about individual stocks.

USA Today, "Money" section (7950 Jones Branch Dr., McLean, VA 22108; 703-854-3400; 800-872-8632; www.usatoday.com). A Gannett paper with many short articles on individual stocks and the stock market; also carries a wide range of statistics on stock market activity.

Value Line Investment Survey (220 E. 42nd St., New York, NY 10017; 800-634-3583; www.valueline.com). Monthly, weekly, or quarterly subscription to computer CD-ROMs with data on all the companies followed by *Value Line.* Allows you to screen stocks on the basis of many different criteria.

The Wall Street Journal (100 Avenue of the Americas, Third Floor, New York, NY 10013; 212-416-2000; 800-228-3880; www.wsj.com). Influential daily newspaper that covers the stock market, particularly in the paper's third section, "Money & Investing."

Trade Association

American Association of Individual Investors (625 N. Michigan Ave., Chicago, IL 60611; 312-280-0170; 800-428-2244; www.aaii.org). A nonprofit group that educates individual investors about the stock market through publications, conferences, seminars, and its Web site.

Web Sites

Bloomberg.com <www.bloomberg.com>. Comprehensive site offering current stock quotes, financial news, stock market updates, after-hours trading data, one-year history of stocks, and an S&P snapshot.

MultexInvestor <www.multexinvestor.com>. Allows investors to order copies of reports from a range of brokerage houses and independent research firms over the Internet. Some of the reports are free, but most are available on a pay-per-view basis.

SmartMoney.com <www.smartmoney.com>. Offers hourly stock updates, market news, and stock screen and will track your portfolio; includes tools, calendar, and asset allocator. Offers access to Smart Money University, which has one of the best investor primers available.

RESOURCES: BONDS

Books, Booklets, and Pamphlets

All about Bonds from the Inside Out, by Esme Faerber (McGraw-Hill, P.O. Box 543, Blacklick, OH 43004; 800-634-3961; www.mcgraw-hill.com). Explains the basics of bonds, including the different types, levels of risk, how to spot undervalued and overvalued bonds, how to read yield curves, and calculations for interest rates and return.

The Bond Book, by Annette Thau (McGraw-Hill, P.O. Box 543, Blacklick, OH 43004; 800-634-3961; www.mcgraw-hill.com). Explains how to assess the risks and opportunities of individual bonds; shows investors where to get good information on the bond market.

Bond Market Rules: 50 Investing Axioms to Master Bonds for Income or Trading, by Michael D. Sheimo (McGraw-Hill, P.O. Box 543, Blacklick, OH 43004; 800-634-3961; www.mcgraw-hill.com). Covers the basic nature and structure of bonds, how bond investing functions, the importance of interest rates and risk, and risk analysis.

Bond Markets, by Patrick J. Brown and Patrick J. Ryan (AMACON, 1601 Broadway, New York, NY 10019; 212-586-8100; 800-262-9699; www.amanet.org). Addresses how different bond instruments are normally quoted, how much accrued interest is payable by the buyer in addition to traded price, the cost of a bond if quoted on a yield basis, normal settlement periods, and how yields are quoted and calculated. Not for a beginner.

Fundamentals of Municipal Bonds (Bond Market Association Publications Dept., 40 Broad St., New York, NY 10004; 212-440-9430; www.bondmarkets.com). Excellent overview of everything you need to know about municipal bonds.

How the Bond Market Works, by Robert Zipf (Prentice Hall Press, One Lake St., Upper Saddle River, NJ 07458; 201-236-7156; 800-382-3419; www.prenticehall. com). An explanation of the ins and outs of the bond market.

Getting Started in Bonds, by Sharon Saltzgiver Wright (John Wiley & Sons, 1 Wiley Dr., Somerset, NJ 08875-1272; 212-860-6000; 800-225-5945; www. wiley.com). Guide for the novice bond investor covering basic concepts as well as explaining the broader factors that affect bond prices; well organized with solid fundamental bond information.

The Mortgage-Backed Securities Workbook: Hands-on Analysis, Valuation, and Strategies for Investment Decision Making, by Andrew S. Davidson and Michael D. Herskovitz (McGraw-Hill, P.O. Box 543, Blacklick, OH 43004; 800-634-3961; www.mcgraw-hill.com). Explains the complex world of mortgage-backed securities, including how to calculate prepayment risk and find the highest yields with the least risk.

Mortgage Securities: The High-Yield Alternative to CDs, the Low-Risk Alternative to Stocks, by Daniel R. Amerman (McGraw-Hill, P.O. Box 543, Blacklick, OH 43004; 800-634-3961; www.mcgraw-hill.com). Explains how to invest in mortgage securities, which are the highest-yielding of all government-issued securities.

Magazines, Newspapers, and Newsletters

The Bond Buyer (One State Street Plaza, 27th Floor, New York, NY 10004; 800-982-0633; www.bondbuyer.com). A trade newspaper that covers the municipal bond business. Also available online.

Bondweek (Institutional Investor, 488 Madison Ave., 12th Floor, New York, NY 10022; 212-224-3800; www.bondweek.com). Covers the bond market and is aimed at professional bond investors and bond dealers.

Lynch Municipal Bond Advisory (P.O. Box 20476, New York, NY 10025; 212-663-5552). Aimed at individual investors wanting to select high-quality municipal bonds or bond funds.

Standard & Poor's (55 Water St., New York, NY 10041; 212-438-2000; www.standardandpoors.com). Publishes several newsletters about the bond market, including *Blue List* (upcoming municipal bond offerings), *Bond Guide* (corporate bonds), and *Creditweek* (overall bond market as well as specific bond issues).

Trade Associations

Association of Financial Guaranty Insurors (139 Lancaster St., Albany, NY 12210; 518-449-4698; www.afgi.org). The trade group representing the insurance companies that insure municipal bonds against default makes articles about municipal bonds available on its Web site.

The Bond Market Association (40 Broad St., 12th Floor, New York, NY 10004-2373; 212-440-9400; www.bondmarkets.com and investinginbonds.com). The industry group representing brokerage firms, dealers, and banks that trade government, municipal, and mortgage-backed securities.

Income Securities Advisors (6175 N.W. 153rd St., Suite 201, Miami Lakes, FL 33014; 305-557-1832; www.incomesecurities.com). A nonprofit group that educates the public about bonds and keeps statistics on defaulted bonds. Offers subscriptions to these newsletters: *Income Securities Investor Newsletter* and *Defaulted Bonds Newsletter.*

Web Sites

BondResources <www.bondresources.com>. Education about bonds, lots of expert opinion about bonds and the bond market, and a database of more than 20,000 types of bonds. The site also has links to brokers.

BondsOnline <www.bondsonline.com>. Lots of bond news and views. Connections to the best bond information available covering all types of bonds. Real-time prices for over 15,000 current bond offerings available.

Convertbond.com <www.convertbond.com>. Offers terms, analysis, news, and pricing relating to about 800 convertible securities that can be found in the U.S. convertible market.

Fitch Ratings <www.fitchratings.com>. A Web site for looking up the credit ratings of most corporate debt.

Investing in Bonds <www.investingbonds.com>. Contains information about all kinds of bonds and allows you to calculate your personal taxable-equivalent muni yields.

Moodys.com <www.moodys.com>. Over 68,000 ratings on 16,000 municipal bond issuers, including the general obligations of governments, revenue bonds, and other municipal instruments.

RESOURCES: MUTUAL FUNDS

Books, Booklets, and Pamphlets

The Art of Astute Investing: Building Wealth with No-Load Mutual Funds, by C. Todd Conover (AMACON, 1601 Broadway, New York, NY 10019; 212-586-8100, 800-262-9699; amanet.org). A step-by-step commonsense book that teaches readers how to use their investment dollars to best advantage with no-load mutual funds.

Bogle on Mutual Funds: New Perspectives for the Intelligent Investor, by John C. Bogle (McGraw-Hill, P.O. Box 543, Blacklick, OH 43004; 800-634-3961; www.

mcgraw-hill.com). The founder and chairman of the Vanguard mutual funds group gives sage advice on setting up a portfolio of funds to meet investment objectives, spotting excessive fees and false advertising claims, and interpreting mutual fund data.

Building Wealth with Mutual Funds, by John H. Taylor (Windsor Books, 141 John St., Babylon, NY 11702; 631-321-7830; 800-321-5934; www.windsorpublishing .com). Offers a step-by-step approach to investing in mutual funds. Covers, among other topics, international investing, index funds, variable annuity funds, and socially responsible investing.

But Which Mutual Funds? How to Pick the Right Ones to Achieve Your Financial Dreams, by Steven T. Goldberg (Kiplinger Washington Editors, 1729 H Street., Washington, DC 20006; 800-280-7165; www.kiplinger.com). Walks readers through the basics of mutual funds, helping them decide how much they'll need to invest, for how long, and at what level of risk.

Buying Mutual Funds for Free, by Kirk Kazanjian (Dearborn Trade, 155 N. Wacker Dr., Chicago, IL 60606; 312-836-4400; 800-245-2665; www.dearborntrade. com). How to put together a diversified portfolio of the world's finest funds by opening an account at one of the discount brokers and selecting from the list of no-load, no-transaction-fee offerings.

The Complete Guide to Managing a Portfolio of Mutual Funds, by Ronald K. Rutherford (McGraw-Hill, P.O. Box 543, Blacklick, OH 43004; 800-634-3961; www.mcgraw-hill.com). Explains investment philosophy development techniques, explores all asset classes of mutual funds, and covers statistical and nonstatistical issues of a balanced portfolio of mutual funds.

Getting Started in Mutual Funds, by Alvin D. Hall (John Wiley & Sons, 1 Wiley Dr., Somerset, NJ 08875-1272; 212-860-6000; 800-225-5945; www.wiley.com). Easy-to-follow commonsense guide for successful mutual fund investing suitable for novices; provides everything they need to know about mutual funds.

The Handbook for No-Load Fund Investors, by Sheldon Jacobs (McGraw-Hill, P.O. Box 543, Blacklick, OH 43004; 800-634-3961; www.mcgraw-hill.com). The definitive guide to mutual funds that do not levy sales commissions.

How to Buy Mutual Funds the Smart Way, by Stephen Littauer (Dearborn Trade, 155 N. Wacker Dr., Chicago, IL 60606; 312-836-4400; 800-245-2665; www. dearborntrade.com). A thorough introduction to mutual funds for the financial do-it-yourselfer who likes to be in control, reduce costs, and rely on his or her own judgment.

Investing in Closed-End Funds: Finding Value and Building Wealth, by Albert Freedman and George Cole Scott (Prentice Hall Press, One Lake St., Upper Saddle River, NJ 07458; 201-236-7156; 800-382-3419; www.prenticehall.com). A more sophisticated overview of strategies for buying and selling closed-end funds.

Kurt Brouwer's Guide to Mutual Funds: How to Invest with the Pros, by Kurt Brouwer (John Wiley & Sons, 1 Wiley Dr., Somerset, NJ 08875-1272; 212-860-6000; 800-225-5945; www.wiley.com). A good book explaining how mutual funds work and the best strategies for buying and selling them.

Mutual Funds for Dummies, by Eric Tyson and James C. Collins (IDG Books/Hungry Minds, 10475 Crosspoint Blvd., Indianapolis, IN 46526; 800-434-3422; www.hungryminds.com). Contains all new market data and analysis about the ever-changing world of mutual funds.

Smart Money Moves: Mutual Fund Investing from Scratch, by James Lowell (Penguin Putnam, 405 Murray Hill Pkwy., East Rutherford, NJ 07073; 800-788-6262; www.penguinputnam.com). Mutual fund investing guide with strategies and information for investing online.

Straight Talk about Mutual Funds, by Dian Vujovich (McGraw-Hill, P.O. Box 543, Blacklick, OH 43004; 800-634-3961; www.mcgraw-hill.com). A primer on the basics of mutual funds.

Newsletters

Fund Advice (1200 Westlake Ave., N., Suite 700, Seattle, WA 98109; 800-423-4893; www.paulmerriman.com).

FundNet Insight (Mutual Fund Investors Association, 20 William St., Wellesley Hills, MA 02481; 617-369-2500; 800-444-6342; www.kobren.com).

Mutual Fund Guide (CCH Inc., 4025 W. Peterson Ave., Chicago, IL 60646; 800-835-5224; www.cch.com).

No-Load Fund Investor (410 Sawmill River Rd., Suite 2060, Ardsley, NY 10502; 914-693-7420; 800-252-2042; www.sheldonjacobs.com).

Trade Association

Investment Company Institute (1401 H St., N.W., Suite 1200, Washington, DC 20005; 202-326-5800; www.ici.org). The trade group for lobbying and public education on mutual fund issues.

Web Sites

CBS Marketwatch: SuperStar Funds <http://cbs.marketwatch.com/funds>. Features articles, news headlines, top fund performers, quotes and charts, and a research directory.

FundAlarm <www.fundalarm.com>. Updated monthly, offers information and commentary to help you decide when to sell a mutual fund.

Fund Spot <www.fundspot.com/main.html>. Links to mutual fund companies and investment sites and includes a weekly list of links to the best mutual fund articles on the Web.

ICI Mutual Fund Connection <www.ici.org>. Sponsored by the Investment Company Institute, this site offers information on mutual funds, closed-end funds, and unit investment trusts.

InvestorGuide: Mutual Funds <www.investorguide.com>. Full explanation about mutual funds and how they work. Multiple links to other mutual fund sites, including Morningstar.

Morningstar.com <www.morningstar.com>. Vast resource for everything you need to know about mutual funds, including rankings, charts, analysts' reports, an online university, articles, and Retirement Center.

Mutual Fund Investor's Center <www.mfea.com>. Sponsored by the Mutual Fund Education Alliance, a group of no-load fund families, site designed to teach how to invest in mutual funds.

Mutual Funds Central <www.wrsn.com>. Rates mutual funds with their performance numbers and lists the top 100 mutual funds with links to their Web sites.

Mutual Funds Magazine <www.mutual-funds.com>. Provides access to current and back issues of *Mutual Funds Magazine.*

Researchmag.com <www.researchmag.com>. Information on 10,000 stocks and 5,000 mutual funds; includes quotes and charts. Registration required.

RESOURCES: CDS AND ANNUITIES

Books, Booklets, and Pamphlets

All about Annuities: Safe Investment Havens for High-Profit Returns, by Gordon K. Williamson (John Wiley & Sons, 1 Wiley Dr., Somerset, NJ 08875-1272; 212-860-6000; 800-225-5945; www.wiley.com). Details the advantages and disadvantages of annuities and compares fixed-rate annuities to CDs, variable annuities, and mutual funds.

Building Your Future with Annuities: A Consumer's Guide (Consumer Information Center, P.O. Box 100, Pueblo, CO 81002; 888-878-3256; www.pueblo. gsa.gov). A free brochure by Fidelity Investments that explains various types of annuities and how they should be used. Can also be obtained directly from Fidelity (800-544-2442).

The Complete Idiot's Guide to Buying Insurance and Annuities, by Brian H. Breuel (Pearson Education, One Lake St., Upper Saddle River, NJ 07458; 800-428-5331; www.mcp.com). Provides simple explanations and illustrations to help the reader understand insurance jargon and includes tips to advise the reader on insurance and annuity matters.

Magazines and Newsletters

Annuity Shopper (8 Talmadge Dr., Monroe TWP, NJ 08831; 800-872-6684; 732-521-5110; www.annuityshopper.com). Provides updated performance on immediate, deferred, fixed, and variable annuities.

Comparative Annuity Reports (P.O. Box 1268, Fair Oaks, CA 95628; 916-487-7863; www.annuitycomparativedata.com). Tracks the rates paid by insurance companies on their fixed annuities in its monthly *CAR* newsletter as well as different payout options offered by insurance companies.

100 Highest Yields (Bank Rate, Inc., 11811 U.S. Highway 1, North Palm Beach, FL 33408; 800-327-7717). Surveys banks every week to uncover those with the top yields for 6-month, 1-year, 2½-year, and 5-year certificates of deposit.

Variable Annuity Research & Data Service Report (4343 Shallowford Rd., Marietta, GA 30062; 770-998-5186). Tracks the investment performance of hundreds of variable annuities sold by insurance companies. Will send, for a fee, a monthly performance report on variable annuities.

Web Sites

Bankrate.com <www.bankrate.com>. Provides information on the highest yields on CDs and other products.

CHAPTER 8

Evaluating an Early Retirement Offer

From a purely financial point of view, the later you retire, the more generous your benefits. That applies to Social Security and pensions as well as to IRAs, SEPs, and Keoghs, which have more time to compound tax deferred. However, because you may not want to work into your late 60s for health or other reasons, the notion of kissing the 9-to-5 life good-bye sooner rather than later has great appeal to many folks. Or given the economic environment, with companies downsizing and otherwise cutting expenses, your employer might offer you the option of retiring early.

Some people spend years plotting and strategizing so they'll be able to retire early. But let's assume you hadn't really thought about retiring before your 60s. You're in your mid-50s and your employer dangles a proposal in front of you. Do you take the offer and run—assuming you have a choice in the matter? This is likely to be one of the biggest decisions you'll ever make. How do you begin to make such a choice?

TOUGH QUESTIONS TO ASK

OK, so you're tempted. You should have quite a few questions to ask your employer so you can assess your best response to the offer to retire. You need all the details. Here are a few pointers to get the conversation going.

How much is on the table? What you want to know: How much is the employer willing to "incent" you to leave? How much severance will you receive? Get the details about the financial terms in writing. What companies offer is all over the map. You could be offered one week of pay for every year you've been there, a year's pay, two years—it varies by circumstance. Remember, however, that severance is often negotiable. The company prefers that you leave because it will save money, so don't be afraid to ask for more.

Do I have a choice of how my severance package is paid? Some firms offer only a lump sum, whereas others distribute funds through an annuity. Depending on your ability to invest the money wisely, you may be better off taking the lump sum. You'll probably want to roll that money into an IRA, which will allow the capital to grow tax deferred.

What are the components of my package? Some plans add several years to your actual years of service to boost your pension payout. Some let you keep your retirement funds in company savings plans, though they probably won't let you contribute any more.

What benefits can I keep? This is particularly important because it is extremely expensive to buy health care on your own; the best deals will cover you until you qualify for Medicare. Inquire about dental, life, and disability insurance as well. The less appealing packages cover your health care premiums for a set period, perhaps a year or two, and then allow you to pay for your coverage at a group rate. Under the Congressional Omnibus Budget Reconciliation Act (COBRA), you have a right to carry your group health insurance coverage with you for up to 18 months. You receive the group rate, but you must pay the full premium for the coverage. If you need COBRA benefits, fill out the appropriate forms with your employer's benefits department. If you take no action within 60 days of leaving your company, you may be denied continuing coverage.

What happens if I don't take the offer? Depending on whether the offer is made to a few select employees or to a whole division, you can decide whether you are being targeted for elimination. You should be sure that if you turn down the package, you will not be laid off anyway. Also, investigate the situation on your own to assess whether the company has run into serious trouble and is cutting costs every way it can or whether its prospects are bright and it is offering the packages to cut costs and boost profitability.

Can I work out some kind of continuing relationship with the company if I take the package? Many valued employees become freelancers or consultants when they leave. Is that a possibility in your case? After you're clear on these questions, it's time to do some soul-searching. Perhaps the biggest question is whether you intend to take the buyout and hang up your work hat altogether or look for work, perhaps after a short break. If you're thinking maybe it's time to call it a day, then your next task should be taking a long, hard look at whether you can really afford to call it quits.

You need to figure out how much money you will need in retirement and how much you will receive from Social Security, pensions, and other benefits in addition to whatever early retirement money your company offers. Calculate the value of your accumulated savings and investments to determine how much income they might provide. Remember to factor inflation into your expenses as you assess how much capital you'll need to live comfortably in the future.

If you're in your mid-50s, you're still a few years from being able to tap retirement accounts that require you to be 59½ before you can withdraw without being penalized. However, you may not be aware that those accounts really aren't like Fort Knox after all. The IRS has a rule called the 72(t) exemption that allows you to pull out funds from your tax-deferred plans before 59½ without a 10 percent early-withdrawal penalty if you take your money out in *substantially equal periodic payments*. Think annuitization: not that you're buying an annuity but that you will take out the same amount every month according to a preset withdrawal schedule. You'll likely need to roll over your 401(k) into an IRA because most 401(k)s aren't set up for these distributions; and you will still pay taxes on those withdrawals. Be extremely clear about how much you need to live on. Then decide which of three IRS formulas you should use to determine your withdrawals: the life expectancy method, the amortization method, or the annuity factor method. Each is based on dividing your funds equally, taking into account how long the IRS expects you to live. (See Figure 8.1.)

Don't make the decision about withdrawal method alone. Consult with your accountant or financial planner, and have him or her walk you through the process. Much of the decision rests on how much you need the maximum

Figure 8.1   Three Methods for IRA Early Withdrawals

	Life Expectancy	Amortization	Annuity Factor
Optimal retiree age	Age 30 to 50	Age 50 to 59	Age 55 to 59
Size of annual withdrawal	Small	Large	Largest
Recalculate annually?	Yes	No	No
Chance of outliving IRA assets	Small	Large	Largest
Adjust annual withdrawal for changes in IRA asset value	Yes	No	No
Difficulty in making withdrawal calculation	Low	Medium	High

Source: John P. Greaney, RetireEarlyHomePage.com.

monthly payment to be. The easiest method is based on life expectancy, which you can determine by relying on the IRS's mortality tables, and you have to repeat this calculation yearly. This method also provides the smallest withdrawals, which may or may not be a positive. On the upside, you'll keep a larger share of your assets growing, but the payout may be so small that it's not enough to meet your living expenses. The other types of withdrawals let you take a fixed amount every year, which is always more than the amount allowed under the life expectancy method, and both assume that your account will continue to earn solid returns. The annuity method allows you to adjust your annual distribution each year for inflation. Most often, the annuity method provides the biggest payouts.

Be careful in making your choice. Once you've made it, you're stuck with it until you're 59½. Once you begin taking substantially equal periodic payments, federal law requires you to continue receiving them for at least five years or until you're 59½, whichever is longer. (See Figure 8.2.) Check out the Retire Early site at <www.RetireEarlyHomePage.com>, which offers loads of information, calculators, and other advice that could help you make a decision.

Hot Tip: Any change in the payment schedule after you have begun taking withdrawals would subject you to the 10 percent penalty tax applied retroactively to all previous withdrawals. It behooves you to make the right choice the first time. Mistakes are expensive.

Figure 8.2   Substantially Equal Periodic Payments at a Glance

Minimum age to begin	• None
Maximum age to begin	• 59½
Frequency of payments	• At least once a year
Duration of payments	• At least five years or until you reach age 59½, whichever is longer
IRS-approved calculation methods	• Life expectancy
	• Amortization
	• Annuity
Ordinary income tax applies	• Yes*
10% penalty tax applies	• No**

*Ordinary income tax applies upon the withdrawal of any pretax or deductible contributions and of any earnings on pretax, deductible, and nondeductible contributions.
**Failure to meet requirements for any reason other than your death or permanent disability means that all of your SEPPs may be subject to the 10% penalty tax and retroactive interest on this penalty.
Source: The Vanguard Group, Inc. Reprinted with permission.

Even though you have the option of breaking into your piggybank, better ask yourself if you really want to start chipping away at your accounts. Remember that you're going to need the money for even longer than you imagined if you retire sooner than planned. You could definitely run out of money sooner than you expect. Once those paychecks stop coming, you'll have less money to invest for your future. You have to keep in mind that you'll need a hefty cushion to deal with the unexpected, such as caring for an aging parent, your own unreimbursed medical bills, increases in taxes, higher inflation, and investments that don't pan out as you had hoped they would.

Look at your income realistically. You can't tap Social Security until you're 62, and, as discussed before, doing so then reduces the amount you'll receive over the long haul. Also, depending on the deal you get from your employer, you'll lose several years of service that could contribute to a larger pension from your employer as well as sacrifice a larger benefit from Social Security.

If your severance package doesn't cover health insurance, one of your biggest challenges will be finding an affordable plan on your own. Medicare doesn't kick in until you're 65. Depending on your age, that may mean you have to fork out for your own insurance for several years. Individual rates are far more expensive than group rates. You may be able to find less expensive coverage if you belong to a club, association, local chamber of commerce, college alumni group, or other group through which you may be able to get a group rate for medical as well as dental and life insurance.

Scout out any discounts for retirees, such as homeowners and auto insurance; you could qualify for a discount of 10 percent or more. And face the reality that sticking to a budget will no longer be optional. There probably won't be much breathing room for extravagance or missteps.

Don't be discouraged though. There are other ways besides tapping into your retirement kitty to find the money you need to make taking that early retirement package a possibility. Much depends on how far you're willing to go to make it happen.

HOME SWEET HOME

Your lovely home has probably appreciated over the years—it could be a gold mine of sorts. You could take the proceeds if you sell, buy something smaller or even rent, and invest the capital to produce an income stream. You can keep the gains tax free as long as they are under $500,000 (for couples filing jointly; $250,000 for singles). A smaller place usually has lower expenses, such as taxes, maintenance, and utilities; and a rented house or apartment could cost even less.

You could also leave town—go where the living is easy and cheaper. A lot of information is available about the cost of living across the country. One favorite is *Money* magazine's "Best Places to Live" feature <www.cnnmoney.com>, which offers an online calculator as well as information on recreational and cultural activities, medical facilities, climate, and more. You can check mortgage rates, find Realtors, and view home listings nationwide at several places online, such as <www.homestore.com>.

If you're the adventurous type, you could consider a housesitting arrangement. The *Caretaker Gazette* <www.caretaker.org> provides information about such opportunities where you take care of the place and live rent free.

Then, too, you could take advantage of the whole life, variable, variable universal, or universal life insurance policy you own that may have grown quite nicely over the years. You may be able to borrow against the cash value at a low rate and defer repayment; and when you die the loan amount is deducted from the death benefit. You won't have to pay taxes on the loan, but if for whatever reason you later allow the policy to lapse, you'll have to pay taxes on the amount of the loan that exceeds your premium payments. (See Chapter 9 for more on insurance.)

You could simply withdraw a portion of your policy's cash value without affecting your death benefit and you'll pay taxes only on the withdrawals that exceed the amount you've ponied up in premiums. Or if you decide that you can do without the policy, you can annuitize the cash value without triggering income taxes.

MAKING THE CHOICE: IT'S ALL YOURS

So there are ways to make early retirement happen. Do you really want to? On one hand, if you don't take the buyout, you have to wonder what the environment will be like on your job. If the cutbacks are so severe that you and the remaining workers will be overburdened with work, morale could plummet and you'd regret not leaving. However, you can't dismiss the impact of leaving your longtime job. If your job was your main source of self-fulfillment, you may feel a tremendous emotional loss if you give it up. What will you do with all the time on your hands? It's a question that confronts all retirees, but it can be even more challenging for those who are suddenly retiring and haven't had time to think about the possibility of volunteering, going back to school, or finally getting around to writing that book or pursuing some other dream they never had time to chase.

If you receive an early retirement offer, you'll need to spend time and thought exploring your options carefully. Taking the offer could be the best or worst move you ever make.

RESOURCES

Books, Booklets, and Pamphlets

The Complete Idiot's Guide to Retiring Early, by Dee Lee and Jim Flewelling (Pearson Education, 200 Old Tappan Rd., Old Tappan, NJ 07675; 800-428-5331; www.mcp.com). Seeks to provide the tools that demystify retirement planning and walks readers through each step of determining how much they will need to retire early.

How to Retire Early and Live Well with Less Than a Million Dollars, by Gillette Edmunds (Adams Media Corporation, 57 Littlefield St., Avon, MA 02322; 508-427-7100; 800-872-5627; www.adamsmedia.com). The author, a former tax attorney and journalist, retired at the age of 29 and shares what he learned about living off his investments.

Last Minute Retirement Planning, by Steve Rosenberg (Career Press, P.O. Box 687, Franklin Lakes, NJ 07417; 201-848-0310; 800-227-3371; www.careerpress. com). Advice for potential retirees close to retirement. Discusses last-minute strategies to use to make retirement comfortable.

The Late-Start Investor: The Better-Late-Than-Never Guide to Realizing Your Retirement Income, by John F. Wasik (Owl Books, Henry Holt, 115 W. 18th St., New York, NY 10011; 212-886-9200; 888-330-8477; www.henryholt.com). Directed to people 50 years old or older who have very little money saved for retirement.

Moneysense: A Commonsense Road to Financial Security and Early Retirement, by Patrick Bohan (Nova Kroshka Books, a division of Nova Science Publishing, Inc., 227 Main St., Huntington, NY 11743; 631-424-6682). Examines investing issues and other important variables related to daily living that have a direct impact on investing strategies.

Retire Early and Live the Life You Want Now: A 10-Step Plan for Reinventing Your Retirement, by John F. Wasik (Henry Holt, 115 W. 18th St., New York, NY 10011; 212-886-9200; 888-330-8477; www.henryholt.com). A guide for those who would retire early, covering spending, structuring income, and selecting the best investment strategies.

Retirement Places Rated, by David Savageau (Hungry Minds, 909 Third Ave., New York, NY 10022; 800-762-2974; www.hungryminds.com). The lowdown on terrific, affordable places to spend your retirement.

Substantially Equal Periodic Payments (The Vanguard Group, Retirement Resource Center, P.O. Box 2600, Valley Forge, PA 19482-2600; 800-205-6189; www.vanguard.com). A booklet that covers what to consider before withdrawing assets before age 59½ and methods for taking payment.

You Can Retire While You're Still Young Enough to Enjoy It, by Les Abromovitz (Dearborn Trade, 155 N. Wacker Dr., Chicago, IL 60606; 312-836-4400; 800-245-

2665; www.dearborntrade.com). Offers financial planning advice for early retirement and details the author's early retirement experience.

Your Next 50 Years: A Completely New Way to Look at How, When, and If You Should Retire, by Victoria Collins and Ginita Wall (Henry Holt, 115 W. 18th St., New York, NY 10011; 212-886-9200; 888-330-8477; www.henryholt.com). Replete with worksheets, challenges baby boomers who have saved little and seen their pensions cut to look at retirement as a time to renew, refocus, and recharge based on long-range dreams and goals.

Web Site

Retire Early <www.RetireEarlyHomePage.com>. For those looking to quit the 9-to-5 routine early, covers safely withdrawing from your retirement portfolio, top ten reasons to retire early, tips on how to retire early, free downloadable software, retirement reports, and an IRA toolkit.

CHAPTER 9

Getting the Best
Deal on Insurance

Most of your insurance coverage is provided by your employer while you are working; you simply choose from myriad options. Once you leave the security of your job's nest, however, you have to fly solo. For the first time, it's up to you to make critical decisions about insurance, and in retirement your insurance needs change. How much do you need of which types of insurance? What's no longer necessary? How do you find the best deals? This chapter answers some of the many questions you might not have had to face before.

Insurance assumes the risk of bad things happening to policyholders. Fortunately for insurance companies, not everyone becomes ill or dies at the same time. By collecting and investing premiums from millions of policyholders, insurance companies have built up the capital to pay claims as they arise.

The field of insurance is difficult to understand, and as a result, many people pay for more insurance coverage than they actually need. The insurance industry is notorious for using jargon and complex presentations that baffle most people. What you don't know about insurance can hurt you in two ways: (1) You may pay too much for a policy that you could have bought much cheaper had you understood how to compare insurers and policies; and (2) the coverage you purchase may be too much or too little for your needs, or it may duplicate existing coverage in some areas and leave you unprotected in others. You could be ruined financially if you have a large claim that isn't covered.

How do insurers price their policies? Several factors influence premium prices:

- *The risk that you will file a claim.* The greater the chance that you will collect, the higher your premium. For example, if you smoke and have already suffered two heart attacks, you stand a much greater chance of dying than you would if you exercised regularly and had no health problems. Clearly, your premium would be higher if you smoke.
- *The liability to which the insurance company is exposed.* The more losses the insurance policy covers, the more potential claims that exist. And the more potential claims that exist, the higher the premium.
- *The percentage of the loss the insurance company covers.* In some cases, such as life insurance, the company must pay 100 percent of the loss. In other cases, policyholders pay for part of the loss by signing up for a *deductible.* For example, a policy might stipulate that the policyholder pay the first $1,000 in health claims and the insurance company will cover any amount exceeding $1,000. A policy with such a deductible would charge a much lower premium than would a contract on which the insurance company covers claims starting at the first dollar of loss.
- *The insurance company's level of expenses and investment expertise.* The greater an insurance company's expenses for administration and marketing, the higher its premiums tend to be. On the other hand, the better its investment performance, the lower its premiums usually are. A company confident in its ability to invest premium dollars successfully can be profitable with lower premium rates.
- *The general level of competition in a particular line of insurance.* The law of supply and demand rules the insurance industry as much as it does the stock market, for example. If only a few insurance companies take on a specific risk, they can charge higher premiums. On the other hand, if many companies offer standard insurance coverage, premiums tend to be lower because of increased competition.

TYPES OF INSURERS

Though the principles of insurance remain the same no matter what insurer issues a policy, it is important to understand the four types of insurers. Each has its own set of incentives, which affect the quality of policies each offers.

Stock Companies

Insurance companies owned by shareholders are in business to earn a profit for their shareholders and to make their stock price rise over time. As such, they tend to raise premiums or cut dividends on policies to bolster profits. Of course, stock companies can't go too far; otherwise, their policies would be uncompetitive. If a stock company profits significantly, the benefits flow to shareholders, not policyholders. On the other hand, if the company is marginally profitable or sustains losses, policyholders pay higher premiums and earn lower dividends on their policies. Despite all this, don't necessarily avoid buying a policy from a stock company. Firms such as Allstate, Equitable, Metropolitan, Chubb, and American International Group are all extremely strong financially, because they raise capital by selling shares and therefore offer very competitive policies.

Mutual Companies

Insurers organized in mutual form are owned by their policyholders. No shares of a mutual firm's stock are publicly traded. When you buy a policy from a mutual company, you benefit if the company does well, and you lose if the firm performs badly. For example, if you own a life insurance policy from a mutual company that keeps its expenses down, pays few death claims, and enjoys superior investment performance, your policy dividends will rise. Part of your premiums contribute to building the company's financial cushion, called a *surplus.* If you cancel your policy, however, you keep none of the surplus to which you have contributed. Several mutual insurance companies have accumulated enormous surpluses over the years and are therefore extremely strong financially. The biggest mutual insurers include State Farm, Northwestern Mutual, and Penn Mutual.

Cooperatives

These are groups of people or companies that band together to provide insurance for themselves. Cooperatives hire professional managers to perform such administrative duties as collecting premiums and paying claims; but each cooperative is designed to provide insurance protection only to its members, not to earn a profit for shareholders or to build a surplus for policyholders. One form of cooperative, known as a *producer's cooperative,* is formed by service providers to make it easier for people to afford their services. The best example of such a cooperative is the Blue Cross/Blue Shield system, which was established by doctors, hospitals, and the health care industry to give patients access to medical care and to ensure payments to doctors and other health care providers.

Government Entities

A panoply of federal and state government programs provide insurance for millions of people. In many cases, the government supplies insurance that private companies cannot or will not offer. Just a few examples at the federal level include Social Security, Medicare, and the Department of Veterans Affairs (VA) benefits.

INSURANCE RATINGS SYSTEMS

Before you buy a policy from an insurance company or contact one of its sales representatives, you want to have some idea of the firm's financial condition. Several large insurance companies, notably Executive Life based in California and Mutual Benefit Life based in New Jersey, failed in the early 1990s when their investment portfolios soured and thousands of policyholders rushed to redeem their contracts. These dramatic cases underlined the importance of knowing the strength of the company that issues your policy.

Five principal independent firms rate insurance companies' financial strength (addresses, phone numbers, and descriptions of their publications and services appear in the "Resources" section at the end of this chapter). The four traditional agencies are A.M. Best, Fitch IBCA, Moody's Investor Service, and Standard & Poor's (S&P) Corporation. The newest entrant in the field, Weiss Research, is considered a maverick by the insurance industry because it uses a different, and far more conservative, method of assessing insurers' financial condition.

Rating agencies base their grades of insurance companies on a combination of factors. Some of the key determinants of a rating include how widely the company spreads risk; how sufficient its reserves and surplus are; the quality of its management; its profitability, investment returns, mortality experience, expense ratios, and debt levels; the amount of cash it has available to pay claims; the quality of the firm's assets, including whether it holds risky junk bonds or speculative real estate.

Once these factors are analyzed, rating companies assign one of the following grades. Each rating service uses a different combination of letters and symbols to signify the same ranking.

- **Superior:** Companies that have achieved superior overall performance when compared with industry averages. They have a strong ability to meet policyholder obligations over a long period of time and under a variety of economic and underwriting conditions. Best: A++; Fitch: AAA; Moody's: Aaa; S&P: AAA; Weiss: A.
- **Excellent:** Companies that have achieved excellent overall performance when compared with industry averages. They have a strong ability to meet policyholder obligations over a long period of time. Best: A and A–; Fitch: AAA; Moody's: As; S&P: AA+ to AA–; Weiss: A.

- **Very good and good:** Companies that have achieved good overall performance when compared with industry averages. They have adequate ability to meet policyholder obligations, but their financial strength is susceptible to unfavorable changes in underwriting or economic conditions. Best: B++ to B–; Fitch (very strong: AA; strong: A, good: BBB); Moody's: Ba; S&P: A+ to BBB–; Weiss: B.
- **Fair:** Companies that have achieved fair overall performance when compared with industry averages. They have a reasonable ability to meet policyholder obligations, but their financial strength is susceptible to unfavorable changes in underwriting or economic conditions. Best: C++ to C+; Fitch (moderately weak: BB); Moody's: B; S&P: BB+ to BB–; Weiss: C.
- **Marginal:** Companies that have achieved marginal overall performance when compared with industry averages. They have a current ability to meet policyholder obligations, but their financial strength is very vulnerable to unfavorable changes in underwriting or economic conditions. Best: C to C–; Fitch (weak: B); Moody's: Caa; S&P: B+ to B–; Weiss: D.
- **Below minimum standards:** Companies that meet minimum size and experience requirements but not minimum standards for financial strength. Best: D; Moody's: Ca; Fitch (very weak: CCC, CC, C); S&P: CCC; Weiss: E.
- **Under state supervision, in liquidation, or failed:** Companies that are placed under some form of supervision, control, or restraint by a state insurance regulatory authority. Best: E or F; Fitch (distressed: DDD, DD, D); Moody's: C; S&P: R; Weiss: F.

Plenty of insurance companies offer ratings in the A range; therefore, you have little reason to take the risk of a lower-rated company. Because the five rating agencies sometimes differ in their opinions of a particular company's financial condition, you should purchase policies from a company with high ratings in at least three or four rating systems.

In addition to checking commercial ratings, ask your state insurance department whether it knows of any problems with an insurance company you are considering.

DIFFERENT WAYS INSURANCE IS OFFERED

Insurance Agents

These sellers of insurance must be licensed in the state where they do business. The ideal agent assesses your needs and finds the policy that provides the coverage you need for the lowest premium. In return, the agent receives a commission for making the sale and often receives a fee, called a *renewal commission,* every year that you retain the policy.

Two types of agents exist: independent and exclusive. *Independent agents* sell policies for many companies and therefore can shop around among competing firms to get you the best coverage and price. *Exclusive agents,* also called *captive agents,* represent only one company.

No hard-and-fast rule decrees you will do better with an independent or an exclusive agent. Independents, in theory, can obtain a better price for you through comparison shopping. However, independents are not always familiar with the provisions of each company's policies. Also, they may steer you to a contract that pays them the highest commission rather than to one that offers you the lowest premium. On the other hand, a top-producing independent agent may be able to get a discount for you on the price of a policy because he or she sells a large volume of insurance for the company.

Exclusive agents usually know their company's product better than independent agents do because that is all they sell. If they work for a top-notch company, they often incur lower selling costs because they are more careful to offer policies to people unlikely to make a claim. For example, a captive life insurance agent tries to sell policies to people in good health, which lowers his or her company's death benefit expenses. Nevertheless, exclusive agents often must meet certain sales goals set by their company, which means they might use high-pressure tactics to sell you a policy that generates a certain level of commission even though it may not meet your needs exactly.

Insurance Brokers

Brokers are employed by the insurance buyer to find the best policy at the most competitive price. They may buy the policy directly from the insurance company, or they may go through an agent. Because their goal is to please you, the customer, brokers may bargain harder than agents with an insurance company to get you the best deal. Like agents, brokers must be licensed to sell insurance in the state where they practice.

A relatively new kind of insurance broker is the *independent quote service.* Firms like Insurance Quote Services, SelectQuote, and TermQuote (see the "Resources" section for addresses and phone numbers) maintain databases of rates for term life insurance from many companies. When you call the toll-free number of one of these companies, tell the customer service representative your age, your health condition, and how much coverage you need. The company will then send you a printout of the terms of four or five policies with the lowest premiums. If you like one of the offerings, you can buy the policy through the quote service, which receives a commission from the insurance company just as any other broker does.

Insurance Advisors

The latest way to find the best insurance policy is by consulting an independent insurance advisor. Unlike agents or brokers, advisors earn no commissions from policies they sell; rather, they charge a flat fee—which varies depending on the size of the policy you seek—for finding the cheapest policy providing the coverage you need. Because they are not tied to insurance companies, advisors usually recommend insurers paying no—or very low—commissions to salespeople and providing the highest returns. (A list of the top low-load insurance companies appears in the "Resources" section at the end of this chapter.) To find an advisor near you, call the Life Insurance Advisers Association (890 Treasure Island Rd., Mattawan, MI 49071; 800-521-4578). Another source for such advice is INSurance INFOrmation (Cobblestone Court #2, 23 Route 134, South Dennis, MA 02660; 800-472-5800).

Direct Marketing

To reduce the cost of maintaining an expensive sales force, many insurance companies offer coverage directly through the mail or over the telephone. Such coverage can be less expensive than policies sold in person, but you have little, if any, contact with a company's representative. Scrutinize such offers and compare them with policies you could get through an agent or a broker. Direct mail policies are not always as attractive as insurance companies make them sound, but they can be better than the alternatives if you research the contracts carefully.

LIFE INSURANCE

Life insurance is designed to protect the survivors of the insured, which is not to say that a life insurance policy yields no advantages while the insured lives. Nevertheless, the main reason to purchase a policy is for the death benefit, which you hope that your dependents collect far into the future.

If your family or other people depend on your income, you need life insurance to help them live without your support if you pass away. The insurance contract requires that the insurance company pay your beneficiaries a set amount, called the *death benefit,* if you should die for almost any reason (suicide is usually excluded for the first few years of a policy). Your beneficiaries can receive the money in one lump sum free of federal income taxes. The funds should be enough to replace your paycheck, cover the beneficiaries' daily living expenses, and pay your final medical bills and burial costs. In addition, the insurance proceeds should be invested to provide beneficiaries income for long-term needs such as retirement, estate taxes, or college costs.

How Much Is Enough?

That is the key question: How much insurance is really needed? You should figure this out long before you listen to any insurance agent's sometimes confusing pitch or the details of different policies. Unfortunately, assessing how much is enough is not a simple process, because each family is different. No general formula exists. You may want to consult with an independent insurance advisor, your financial advisor, or run through some of the exercises available on software like Microsoft Money or Quicken.

The first step in determining your ideal amount is to examine your current family situation and your potential family situation. If you were to die today, would your family be able to make it? For help with that answer, use the Death Expense Worksheet in Figure 9.1.

Next, determine your family's ongoing future income and expenses if you were to die. The worksheet in Figure 9.2 provides space to record one year's net cash flow, but you must project this amount many years into the future if your family is young. When calculating income, include any benefits from government programs your family may be entitled to as a result of your death, such as Social Security and veterans survivors programs. To

---

Figure 9.1   Death Expense Worksheet

Expense	$ Amount
Federal Estate Taxes	$ _____
State Death Taxes	_____
Probate Costs and Attorney Fees	_____
Funeral Expenses	_____
Unreimbursed Medical Costs (for deceased's last illness)	_____
Other (specify)	
_____	_____
TOTAL IMMEDIATE EXPENSES	$ _____

Figure 9.2   Survivor's Worksheet

Income	Annual $ Amount
Benefits Income	
Life Insurance	$ _____
Pensions	_____
Social Security	_____
Trusts	_____
Veterans	_____
Other	_____
Investment Income	
Annuities	_____
Dividends (from stocks, mutual funds)	_____
Interest (from bank accounts, bonds, mutual funds)	_____
Rent (from owned real estate)	_____
Other	_____
Survivor's Salary	_____
Other Income	_____
TOTAL ANNUAL INCOME	$ _____

Expenses	
Child Care	$ _____
Children's Education	_____
Clothing	_____
Entertainment and Recreation	_____
Food	
At Home	_____
Outside the Home	_____

Figure 9.2   Survivor's Worksheet (continued)

Expenses	Annual $ Amount
Housing	
Mortgage	$ _____
Rent	_____
Utilities	_____
Other	_____
Insurance Premiums	
Auto	_____
Disability	_____
Health	_____
Life	_____
Other	_____
Loan Repayments	_____
Medical and Dental	_____
Taxes	
Federal Income	_____
State Income	_____
Local Income	_____
Property	_____
Other	_____
Transportation	_____
Other Expenses	_____
TOTAL ANNUAL EXPENSES	$ _____
Total Annual Income	$ _____
Minus Total Annual Expenses	$ (_____)
Equals **TOTAL NET CASH FLOW**	$ _____

learn how much these programs pay, call the Social Security Administration and the Department of Veterans Affairs (VA).

After you complete the worksheet, combine your total immediate expenses with your total net cash flow to see how much of a gap exists between your expenses and your income. This gap is what your life insurance should fill; depending on your life situation, you will probably discover that this gap is larger than you thought it would be.

Some simple rules of thumb can give you an idea of how much life insurance you need. At the least, you probably need three times your annual income; at the most, ten times. Many people require at least $100,000 of coverage, and most need several hundred thousand dollars more if they truly want to cover all the immediate and future expenses listed in the Death Expense Worksheet and the Survivor's Worksheet.

TYPES OF LIFE INSURANCE

Now that you have figured out how much insurance you need, consider the pros and cons of the four basic types: *term, whole life, universal life,* and *variable life.* The debates about which type is best will rage forever among insurance professionals. You must decide what is best for you based on how much coverage you need, how much premium you can afford, and whether you want insurance only for its death benefit or also for its savings potential. Term insurance merely pays off if you die; whole life, universal life, and variable life insurance are versions of *cash-value insurance,* which combines a death benefit and an investment fund.

Term Insurance

Term insurance offers financial protection on your life for a specified and finite period, usually 1, 5, 10, or 20 years; the only way your term policy will pay out is if you die during this period. In that case, your beneficiaries will probably be offered a lump sum payout or a series of annuity payments. When the period expires, you can usually renew the policy, though at a higher premium because you are older and statistically more likely to die. If your policy offers a *guaranteed renewability feature,* you don't have to take the medical test or otherwise prove insurability to continue coverage for another term. You can also buy term insurance that provides a *convertibility feature,* which allows you to convert some or all of the coverage into whole life insurance with a medical exam. If you stop paying premiums on a term policy, your coverage ceases.

You can purchase far more protection for your dollar with term insurance than you can with a cash-value policy. Term insurance is therefore ideal if you have a large insurance need for a specific period. For example, you might need coverage for the years before your children become self-supporting, which should be in their mid-20s, you hope!

The chief advantage of term insurance is its low costs. Hundreds of companies offer term, so the market is extremely competitive. You can obtain price quotes on term coverage through any insurance agency, many direct mail insurers, banks, or quote services (such as AccuQuote, BestQuote, INSurance INFOrmation, QuoteSmith, and others listed in the "Resources" section at the end of this chapter). Make sure that the policy you buy is not only low priced but also backed by a financially strong insurance company. Preferably, the carrier should have at least an A rating from two or three of the major rating agencies.

If you're purchasing term insurance on your own, you may be able to obtain a good group term policy through a trade association, an alumni group, or another organization to which you belong.

The disadvantage of term insurance is a premium rise over time if you have an annual renewable policy (with a guaranteed level premium policy you get a set premium). As mentioned earlier, your premium stays the same during the term of a policy but increases each time you renew because your chance of dying becomes greater as you age, and the insurance company needs to collect a higher premium to offset the greater risk of having to pay a claim. Term premiums rise slowly while you are in your 20s and 30s but get much more expensive as you progress through your 40s and 50s. By the time you reach your 60s, term insurance is astronomically expensive and probably should be dropped.

Cash-Value Insurance

Instead of buying term insurance, which offers pure protection, you can choose to purchase one of several varieties of cash-value insurance. All of these policies, which are called *whole life, universal life,* or *variable life,* add a tax-deferred savings feature to the insurance protection component of the policy.

Whole life insurance. Whole life insurance, often called *straight life* or *permanent insurance* by agents, is different from term, in that you start with low premiums that rise over time on renewal and you're provided with investment reserves. Whole life locks in one premium rate for life, part of which is invested for your benefit. However, whole life premiums are much more expensive than term premiums, particularly when you are in your 20s and 30s.

Whole life remains in force as long as you live and pay your premiums. You need not renew it frequently, as you do term. The younger you are when you buy a whole life policy, the lower your lifelong premium rate.

The insurance company uses your premium dollars to cover three expenses: death claims, administrative costs, and investments. Most of your money ends up invested in stocks, bonds, real estate, and other capital assets that can appreciate and produce income over time. The cash value that your whole life policy accumulates results from investments that are paid in the form of policy dividends minus death claims and administrative expenses. All whole life policies, however, make a minimum earnings guarantee, usually about 4 percent.

One big advantage of all forms of cash-value insurance is that your investment dollars compound tax deferred. The insurance industry has fought off numerous attempts to repeal this tax shelter and is likely to do so for a long time. If you ever cancel or surrender your whole life policy, you can withdraw in a lump sum whatever cash value has accumulated, and you'll pay taxes only if your cash value and policy dividends exceed the total amount of premiums you paid during the life of the policy.

You have several other ways to use any accumulated cash value in a whole life policy:

- You can borrow up to the full amount of your cash value. You must pay nondeductible interest that usually floats two or three percentage points above the prime rate, which is far better than the rate you would pay on a credit card. If you die before the loan is repaid (and there is no requirement that the loan must be repaid), your loan balance plus any interest due is deducted from the death benefit paid to your beneficiaries.
- You can tap your cash value to pay some or all of your premiums if you have built up enough value in the policy.
- Once you reach retirement age, you can convert your accumulated cash value into an annuity, which can pay you a guaranteed monthly income for life.

Universal life insurance. Born in the high-interest-rate years of the early 1980s, universal life offered policyholders very high rates of return from investments in money market instruments. When rates dropped by the 1990s and 2000s, universal life became much less popular, although this form of cash-value insurance offers much more flexibility than traditional whole life policies. Universal life policyholders can pay premiums at any time and in any amount as long as certain minimum levels are met. Also, the amount of insurance protection can be increased or decreased easily to meet your current needs. In addition, you always can tell exactly how much of your premium dollar is allocated to insurance protection, administrative expenses, and savings, figures that are never clearly disclosed when you own a whole life policy.

Unlike whole life premiums, which are invested in long-term bonds and mortgages, universal life premiums reflect the current short-term rates available in the money markets. Insurance companies set a rate of return for one year and then readjust the yield up or down depending on the level of interest rates. Nonetheless, universal life policies guarantee a minimum yield of about 4 or 5 percent.

A final advantage of universal life, therefore, is that the returns you earn on your cash value reflect a sharp upturn in interest rates far more quickly than the returns on a traditional whole life policy. However, if rates fall or remain depressed, you may have to settle for lower returns for many years.

Variable life insurance. If you are willing to take higher risks in search of juicier returns, variable life offers the option of investing your cash value in stock, bond, or money market funds managed by the insurance company. As with other cash-value policies, these returns compound tax deferred until you withdraw your principal. A good fund manager operating in a bull market can easily provide double-digit gains and outperform a traditional whole life portfolio. But markets don't always rise, and this year's hero can become next year's goat. You have the option of shifting your money among stocks, bonds, and cash vehicles, but the chances of buying and selling at just the right moment are remote.

Your investment timing affects not only the appreciation or depreciation of your cash value in a variable life policy. The death benefit also rises and falls based on investment performance, although the death benefit will never drop below the original amount of insurance coverage for which you contracted.

Because the stock, bond, and money market funds within variable insurance policies are legally considered securities, the life insurance agent who sells you a policy must be a licensed registered representative of a broker-dealer. He must give you a prospectus, as with any mutual fund, and explain the risks as well as the potential rewards of the plan.

When choosing a variable life policy, study the long-term track record of the funds offered. It is very difficult and expensive to switch out of one variable contract and into another under the management of a new insurance company if performance starts to lag.

Second-to-die insurance. One of the trendiest new forms of cash-value insurance—second-to-die, also called *survivorship life*—is usually acquired in the names of a husband and wife. The policy pays a death benefit intended to cover estate taxes on the demise of the insured who survives longer. Survivorship life premiums can be invested in either traditional whole life vehicles or in universal or variable options. Because the policy is based on the joint life expectancy of both husband and wife, the premiums cost less than they would if traditional cash-value policies were bought on both lives.

Before you obtain this kind of insurance, however, make sure that your estate taxes will be significant enough to warrant the coverage. Ask a financial planner or an estate lawyer if he or she can set up trusts to reduce your estate taxes so you don't have to pay survivorship life premiums.

Accelerated death benefit insurance. Another recent development in life insurance is the introduction of policies that allow you, in particular cases, to access your death benefit while you are still living. These are known as accelerated death benefit insurance or *living benefits policies,* and they usually make payments while you are alive under three circumstances:

1. You need long-term care, either in a nursing home or at home.
2. You are struck by a catstrophic illness or disease that accrues enormous medical bills. The policy lists specific diseases and surgeries covered, most commonly heart attacks, strokes, life-threatening cancers, coronary artery bypass surgeries, renal failures, paralyses, and major organ transplants.
3. You are diagnosed as terminally ill. If your doctor confirms in writing that you have only weeks or months to live, you can tap your death benefit.

Remember, however, that if you withdraw part or all of your death benefit while you are still living, your beneficiaries receive less when you die.

HEALTH INSURANCE

The soaring cost of medical care probably wasn't of great concern when your employer was footing the tab, but in retirement it's suddenly a major issue. Not only is the current health system costly, but it is also extremely complex and constantly changing.

Years ago, health insurance was relatively simple. You went to the doctor of your choice, who billed your insurance carrier directly, or you paid the bill and submitted it for reimbursement. If you worked for a large company, you paid no premiums and your copayments, if any, were minor.

Now you have many more choices to make: a traditional fee-for-service indemnity plan, a health maintenance organization (HMO), or a preferred provider organization (PPO). The alphabet soup can be confusing and the costs a lot to swallow; premiums for individual policies are usually based on your age and your medical history. When you're a party of one, check with professional organizations, your alumni association, chamber of commerce, or other groups to see if you might be able to sign up for a group plan under their umbrella and save yourself a ton of money.

Here's a look at some of the options.

Traditonal Fee-for-Service

The optimal traditional fee-for-service indemnity policy is divided into two plans. The *basic plan* reimburses you for doctors' bills, drugs, outpatient surgical procedures, and other medical expenses up to a certain annual dollar limit. The second plan, *major medical,* covers extended hospital visits and other major medical procedures.

The basic plan usually applies deductibles of $100 to $1,000 or more before your bills are reimbursed. After you pay the deductible out of your pocket, all further bills are usually reimbursed for 80 percent of your cost up to a specified annual limit. Once you have spent more than that limit, you are reimbursed 100 percent.

Needless to say, some basic plans are more generous than others. Depending on the insurance carrier, some expenses may be limited or omitted altogether—such expenses, for example, as home health care, dentist bills, psychiatric care, and drug or alcohol treatment.

Although many fee-for-service plans pay hospital expenses in full, some reimburse at 80 percent. Hospitalization charges usually include room and board, nursing care, drugs, medical devices, food, and fees for specialists, such as surgeons, who work in the hospital. If your surgery can be performed on an outpatient basis, this expense is also usually covered. Most major medical policies have either an annual or a lifetime cap, typically between $250,000 and $1 million. Some medical plans, such as those offered by Blue Cross/Blue Shield, require you to cover the first $2,000 to $5,000 of hospital costs as a deductible before they pay hospital bills directly. This stipulation is often called the *stop-loss clause* because it limits your loss to the deductible. You're responsible for the initial deductible (say $250), after which the insurer pays 80 percent of the covered medical costs and you pay 20 percent. When your total out-of-pocket expenditures reach a certain amount, such as $2,000, the insurer pays 100 percent.

For even more protection, you can buy excess major medical coverage to supplement a regular major medical policy with a low lifetime limit. *Excess major medical policies,* often called *catastrophic policies,* usually have a very high deductible of about $15,000 but can be vital if you need an expensive medical procedure.

The HMO (Health Maintenance Organization) Alternative

Instead of choosing your own doctors and getting reimbursed for expenses under the traditional fee-for-service health insurance plan, you can opt for an HMO. Hundreds of HMOs across the country offer full medical services for a flat annual fee, which you may pay in part on a monthly basis.

Before you join an HMO, ask plenty of questions. Following are a few to explore:

- How competent are the doctors? What percentage are board certified? (The more doctors who are board certified, meaning that they successfully passed a specialty test, the better. The average certification rate is about 70 percent.)
- How long do patients wait for an appointment to see a specialist?
- How are HMO members treated at HMO-affiliated hospitals?
- Is the HMO accredited? (This is not required, but it is certainly better to join an accredited HMO than an unaccredited one. Agencies such as the National Committee for Quality Assurance set the the most stringent standards.)
- Is there a high staff turnover rate at the HMO you are interested in? (A high rate can mean that the patient load is too large and that doctors are unhappy.)
- What is the member retention rate? (A higher rate indicates a better level of member satisfaction. Good HMOs conduct annual patient surveys, so review them to determine member satisfaction.)

When you become an HMO member, you have unlimited access to the organization's medical services. You can visit a doctor for preventive check-ups, minor problems, or emergencies, sometimes for a small fee of $5 to $10 per visit. If the HMO runs a central medical facility, you must go there for all procedures, although if you are out of town, the HMO will reimburse you for visits to approved doctors or hospitals. In a true life-or-death emergency, you can go to any hospital and still be reimbursed.

An HMO offers several advantages, primarily that your out-of-pocket costs are limited to the annual HMO fee plus small charges for special services. Because the HMO charges group rates, the premium will be less than the fee you normally would pay for traditional insurance coverage. In addition, you no longer must deal with deductibles or coverage limits. Nor must you search for a generalist or specialist practitioner, because the HMO employs just about every type of physician you probably will ever need. If you have an extremely rare condition that no one on the HMO's staff can handle, the HMO will locate a specialist for you. You will also receive prescription drugs at very low cost because the HMO buys them at bulk prices directly from manufacturers. Finally, all of your medical records are kept in one place, so your medical history is immediately available to any doctor who treats you.

If HMOs are so great, why doesn't everyone join one? What you gain in financial control you lose in medical choice. You cannot bring your existing doctor to the HMO, so you must choose a new primary care physician from a list provided by the HMO, although these days the networks are wide. It's quite possible that your physician may be in the HMO. If your chosen doctor is not available on the day you visit the clinic, you must see whoever is working; but if your HMO is the Independent Practitioner model, you make the appointment with your doctor in his office. If you need a specialist, you must select one from the HMO's approved list, regardless of whether he or she is the best qualified in town. In addition, many HMO generalists hate to refer patients to specialists because it costs the HMO more, and one of the main goals of HMOs is controlling costs. Some HMOs also have a reputation for discouraging medical tests. In addition, services such as vision, hearing, and dental care and psychiatric treatment are considered basic in some HMO plans but not in all.

The same lack of choice can apply to hospitals. You go where the HMO sends you, not where you prefer. If you seek treatment at a hospital not specifically authorized by your HMO, you probably have to pay the entire bill on your own.

For an evaluation of a managed care plan you are thinking of using, contact the National Committee for Quality Assurance (NCQA) (2000 L St., N.W., Suite 500, Washington, DC 20036; 202-955-3500; 800-236-5903; www.ncqa.org). NCQA is a private, not-for-profit organization dedicated to assessing and reporting the quality of managed care plans. Its mission is to provide information enabling purchasers and consumers of managed care to distinguish among plans based on quality. NCQA accredits managed care organizations by surveying them and making sure they meet certain standards in both clinical and administrative functions. NCQA's Health Plan Report Card can help you answer questions about health plans that would be difficult or impossible to answer on your own, such as: Does this health plan provide good customer service? Will I have access to the care I need? Does the plan check doctors' qualifications? Because NCQA's Health Plan Report Card covers hundreds of health plans, you can create a customized report card for the health plan or plans you want to know about via NCQA's Web site, or you can call 800-839-6487.

The PPO (Preferred Provider Organization) Alternative

Somewhere between the traditional fee-for-service plan and the HMO is a relatively new form of health coverage: the PPO. Under this type of insurance, you'll have access to generalists, specialists, hospitals, and many other types of health care providers.

Your costs will probably be lower under a PPO than under a traditional plan because the medical professionals and hospitals in the network offer discounts in exchange for a steady flow of patients. As long as you get your care from these providers, they should not require any additional payment unless your plan requires a copayment at the time you receive care, which you have to pay. Like doctors in HMOs, caregivers in PPOs may try to contain costs by discouraging tests and referrals to specialists unless they are absolutely necessary. However, PPOs provide more choice over which doctor you see because you can go to anyone who is part of the network. But if you visit a doctor who doesn't work for the PPO, you will be reimbursed by the health insurance company at a reduced rate. For example, you may be reimbursed 70 percent of the bill instead of 80 percent. When investigating a PPO, ask questions similar to those posed for HMOs.

Whichever route you take, you want to take into consideration the benefits offered, your choice of providers, the quality of care, costs, and location.

Medicare

For those 65 or older, for some under 65 with disabilities, and for people with end-stage renal disease (ESRD), Medicare provides substantial insurance benefits—whether you are retired or still working. Medicare is designed to help cover such medical expenses as hospitalization, surgery, doctor bills, home health care, and medically necessary skilled nursing care.

The original Medicare plan, known as Medicare Fee for Service, has two parts: Part A, Hospital Insurance, and Part B, Medical Insurance. You may go to any doctor, specialist, hospital, or other health care provider that accepts Medicare. Generally, a fee is charged each time you get service, but most people don't have to pay for Medicare Part A. Part B, which is optional, has a monthly fee of $54 that is usually taken out of your monthly Social Security, Railroad Retirement, or Civil Service Retirement payment. If you don't receive a monthly benefit, you are billed quarterly.

Medicare Part A helps to cover:

- *Hospitalization.* After you meet your deductible ($812 per beneficiary per year), Medicare pays all costs from your 1st through 60th day in the hospital. From your 61st through 90th day, Medicare covers your full costs after you meet your coinsurance payments, which are the daily cost of hospitalization that you pay.
- *Skilled-nursing facility care.* Medicare pays 100 percent of approved amounts for your first 20 days of care in a skilled-nursing facility after

What Medicare Won't Cover

Even though the list of services that Medicare covers seems extensive, many medical expenses are excluded. For example, you will not be reimbursed for the following:

- Nursing care beyond 100 days in a skilled-nursing facility; private nursing care; and any care in a center not approved by Medicare
- Custodial and intermediate nursing care
- Prescription drugs not given in a hospital
- Routine physicals, dentistry, acupuncture, immunizations, cosmetic surgery, and foot, eye, and hearing care
- Doctors' charges that exceed approved Medicare levels or that Medicare does not consider medically necessary. Each year, the government publishes a fee schedule listing maximum Medicare payments, which are usually far less than doctors charge regular commercial patients.
- Care in foreign countries, except in certain limited circumstances in Canada and Mexico

you have been in the hospital for at least 3 days. From your 21st through 100th day in the nursing facility, Medicare pays all costs after you meet your coinsurance payments.

- *Home health care.* Medicare pays 100 percent of any approved home health care services as well as 80 percent of approved medical equipment.
- *Hospice care.* Medicare covers all costs, though it sets limits for outpatient drugs and inpatient respite care.
- *Blood.* After the first three pints, Medicare pays for blood you receive in a hospital or skilled-nursing facility during a covered stay.

Medicare Part B helps to cover:

- *Medical services.* After you meet your deductible of $100, Part B pays 80 percent of approved amounts for doctors, surgeons, supplies, and medical equipment.
- *Clinical laboratory services.* Part B pays 100 percent of approved amounts for medical tests, laboratory work, biopsies, and blood work.

- *Home health care.* Part B pays for all costs of approved home health care services with no deductible. In addition, it covers 80 percent of the cost of medical equipment used in the home after a deductible.
- *Outpatient hospital care.* Part B covers 80 percent of any approved procedures performed in a hospital on an outpatient basis.
- *Blood.* The plan pays for 80 percent of the cost of approved amounts of blood after the first three pints.

For more details on the expenses Medicare covers, as well as the cost of deductibles, copayments, and premiums, call 800-MEDICARE or visit its Web site at <www.medicare.gov>. You can order or view the comprehensive, 76-page *Medicare & You* handbook by calling or visiting the Web site.

In addition to the original Medicare plan, you may have, depending on where you live, health plan choices known as Medicare managed care plans and called Medicare + Choice that are offered by private companies. Medicare + Choice plans include Medicare managed care plans and Medicare private fee-for-service plans. Complete information is available on the Web site <www.medicare.gov>.

To be eligible to join a Medicare + Choice plan you must fulfill the following requirements:

- Be entitled to Medicare Part A
- Be enrolled in Medicare Part B
- Live in the plan's geographical service area
- Not have end-stage renal disease
- Agree to provide the necessary information to the plan
- Agree to follow the plan's rules
- Belong to only one plan at a time
- Make the election during the election period

Medicare Supplemental Policies

Because Medicare coverage is limited in so many ways, several plans, called *Medigap* or *MedSup* plans, have been designed to fill the gaps. They pick up where Medicare leaves off, covering Medicare copayments and deductibles. Some supplemental policies also pay for products and services not covered by Medicare, such as outpatient prescription drugs. As long as you enroll in Medicare Part B within six months after enrolling in Medicare Part A, you cannot be rejected when you apply for a Medicare supplemental policy if you are at least 65 years old. Currently, ten standard Medicare supplemental policies, labeled letter A through letter J for easier comparison, are available. Policy A is the most basic and is available to all Medicare recipients. Policies B through J offer increasingly more benefits, and more and more people are excluded from qualification.

All the Medigap policies cover at least the daily coinsurance amount for hospitalization under Medicare Part A. The more inclusive policies pay additional benefits for such services as preventive medical care, coverage in a foreign country, hospice care, prescription drugs, or home visits—none of which Medicare covers. The table in Figure 9.3, provided by courtesy of the National Association of Insurance Commissioners (NAIC), lists the benefits included in each supplemental policy.

A new form of Medicare supplemental insurance, called *Medicare Select,* is being tested in several states. It is a form of private Medigap insurance designed to be less costly to policyholders, because policyholders must use a designated group of health care professionals and facilities. The insurance company selects the providers, which may include HMOs and PPOs. The medical service providers offer discount prices because they are assured a steady flow of patients.

When shopping for a Medigap policy, watch for preexisting-condition clauses that preclude you from receiving benefits if you already have developed an ailment. Also, make sure that your policy is guaranteed renewable, and determine whether your premiums rise as you age. Finally, examine the elimination periods imposed for hospital stays. You may have to be hospitalized several days before benefits kick in, which could mean that you never collect a dime.

The process of choosing a Medigap policy can be quite complex and confusing. Many people are pressured into making quick decisions by commission-hungry salespeople. Instead, take your time, and make sure that you understand exactly what you are buying. Don't make a common mistake and purchase too much insurance; one comprehensive Medigap plan should be all you need. According to federal law, even after you buy a policy, you have 30 days to review it and obtain a full refund for all premiums paid.

Medicaid

Medicaid is a health insurance program for low-income families and individuals. However, Medicaid doesn't provide health care services even for very poor people unless they are in one of the groups designated below. The Medicaid program is funded by both federal and state government. Each state administers the program within broad national guidelines established by federal statutes, regulations, and policies.

Medicaid policies for eligibility and services can be complex and vary among states. A person who is eligible in one state may not be eligible in

Figure 9.3   Benefits Offered by Medicare Supplemental Policies

A	B	C	D	E	F	G	H	I	J
Basic benefits	Basic benefits	Basic benefits	Basic benefits	Basic benefits	Basic benefits	Basic benefits	Basic benefits	Basic benefits	Basic benefits
		Skilled nursing co-insurance	Skilled nursing co-insurance	Skilled nursing co-insurance	Skilled nursing co-insurance	Skilled nursing co-insurance	Skilled nursing co-insurance	Skilled nursing co-insurance	Skilled nursing co-insurance
	Part A deductible	Part A deductible	Part A deductible	Part A deductible	Part A deductible	Part A deductible	Part A deductible	Part A deductible	Part A deductible
		Part B deductible-			Part B deductible-				Part B deductible
					Part B excess (100%)	Part B excess (80%)		Part B excess (100%)	Part B excess (80%)
		Foreign travel emergency	Foreign travel emergency	Foreign travel emergency	Foreign travel emergency	Foreign travel emergency	Foreign travel emergency	Foreign travel emergency	Foreign travel emergency
			At-home recovery			At-home recovery		At-home recovery	At-home recovery
							Basic drugs ($1,250 limit)	Basic drugs ($1,250 limit)	Extended drug benefit ($3,000 limit)
				Preventive care					Preventive care

Source: Used by permission of the National Association of Insurance Commissioners.

another; and Medicaid services in one state may differ from services in another similar or neighboring state.

In addition, you must meet income and resource standards. Resources include cash on hand, bank accounts, IRAs, certificates of deposit, stocks, and bonds. Medicaid does not consider the following a resource: a burial fund and burial space; a home (if it is your primary residence); clothing and personal effects; household furniture; and appliances, for example.

Medicaid pays for most medical costs and in New York State includes hospital care, doctors' visits, prescription drugs, and prenatal care as well as many more services.

Who is eligible for Medicaid? Medicaid is not just for people on public assistance. You may be eligible for Medicaid even though you have too much money to qualify for public assistance.

Generally, you must be an American citizen or legal immigrant (depending on the date of entry to the United States). However, being an American citizen or a legal immigrant and meeting the income and resources standard are not sufficient to qualify for Medicaid. An individual must also fit into a covered eligibility category.

There are three basic categories of low-income people eligible for Medicaid:

1. Parents and children
2. The elderly (age 65 and over)
3. Disabled persons (don't have to be receiving Social Security disability but must meet the same disability criteria used by the Social Security Administration)

How can you apply for Medicaid? You should contact your local department of social services or county welfare office to learn more about the medical assistance programs that may be available to you. You'll find lots of useful information about Medicaid on the Centers for Medicare & Medicare Services Web site <www.cms.hhs.gov>, and you'll find Medicare links at <www.hcfa.gov/medicaid/mcaicnsm.htm>.

DISABILITY INSURANCE

Though you may think it highly unlikely that you will ever become disabled either on the job or outside of work, you are mistaken. According to the American Council of Life Insurers, someone aged 35 is six times more likely to become disabled than die before reaching 65.

If you miss work for a short time, your employer will probably provide short-term sick leave. You might also collect benefits from workers' compensation if you were injured on the job. Other government programs, such as veterans benefits, civil service disability, or black lung insurance for miners, could also kick in. If you were injured in a car accident, your auto insurance pays you a certain amount of cash for a limited period. And if you are a union member, you could be eligible for group disability coverage.

You qualify for Social Security disability benefits if you become severely disabled. How much you receive depends on your salary and the number of years you have been covered by Social Security. Following are the ground rules for receiving Social Security disability payments:

- *You must be disabled for at least five months and expect to be out of commission for a total of at least a year.* Expect the Social Security Administration to take at least three months to process your claim, so file as soon as you think you will be eligible.
- *The amount you receive from Social Security is reduced by other payments you get from other government disability programs.* For example, any money you receive from military, civil service, or government pensions, or from workers' compensation is subtracted from your Social Security benefit. All of these income sources combined cannot exceed 80 percent of your average earnings before you became disabled.
- *You must not be able to perform any job whatsoever, not just the work you did before you were injured.*
- *You qualify for Medicare after receiving Social Security payments for two years.* You must enroll and pay the monthly premium to receive both medical and hospital coverage under Medicare.
- *You must pay federal income tax on your disability benefits if your income exceeds a certain limit.* The most recent limit for adjustable gross income (AGI) plus nontaxable interest income and half of all Social Security benefits is $34,000 for a single person and $44,000 for a couple filing jointly.

Even if you collect from several government programs, you probably won't receive enough money to live comfortably. You could wind up spending your hard-earned retirement savings just to make ends meet. Because you don't want your dreams evaporating, individual long-term disability insurance becomes crucial. If you qualify, you can receive between 50 and 80 percent of your regular salary, depending on the policy, plus cost-of-living adjustments in some policies. Companies don't pay 100 percent of your salary because they want you to have an incentive to go back to work.

Many clauses in disability contracts can be crucial in determining the benefits you receive if you are injured.

Definition of disability. Some policies pay if you are unable to perform your customary job. Others stipulate that you must be unable to do *any* job before they will consider you disabled. Many use a combination of the inability to perform your own job for an initial period (usually the first year of your disability) and then the inability to perform at any job for which you are suited based on your education and experience. Some policies require that you be totally disabled; others pay if you are only partly disabled.

Cause of disability. Some policies provide benefits only if you are injured in an accident; others pay if you become injured or ill. The best policies cover both accidents and illnesses, and they pay no matter how you become disabled.

Exclusions. Insurers usually won't pay disability benefits if an injury is caused by a suicide attempt, drug abuse, a crash in a noncommercial aircraft, or military service, for example.

Residual benefits. Residual benefits are partial benefits. For example, if you are healthy enough to work one day a week or earn 20 percent of your former income by performing less demanding tasks, a policy offering residual benefits will pay you 80 percent of the full benefit. The more you work, the less residual funds you receive.

Payment amount. Your monthly benefit is based on your level of income before you become disabled. You can expect anywhere from 50 to 80 percent of your predisability income from all sources combined. Higher-paid workers tend to receive a smaller percentage of their former pay than do lower-paid workers. If you pay your own premiums on a disability policy, they will cost less if you accept a smaller percentage of your predisability pay. For an extra premium you can add a cost-of-living adjustment clause to your policy that would raise your disability payments based on an index tied to the yearly change in the consumer price index (CPI).

Benefit payment method. Some policies pay weekly but most pay monthly. A policy might also include a provision allowing the insurance company to pay the entire benefit in one lump sum, cutting short any further liability.

Beginning payment date. Some policies begin paying benefits within a month of your disability; others wait six months or even a year. The longer you can go without receiving insurance benefits, the lower your premiums are. Before you choose a longer waiting period, however, make sure you have enough savings and other resources to cover your expenses over that time.

Payment caps. All policies limit the monthly amount of disability benefits paid to recipients. It could be as much as $2,000 or $3,000 or far less, depending on the policy. Try to estimate realistically how much income you would need if you were disabled.

Ending payment date. Disability insurance is designed to replace earned income, so benefits may last from a year to the rest of your life, depending on when you get injured and what other sources of income are available to you. If you agree to receive benefits for a shorter time, your premiums will be lower. Most people buy policies that pay benefits until age 65, when they qualify for various government programs.

Renewability. The last thing you want to happen if you are disabled is for your insurance company to cancel your policy. Make sure that the coverage you buy is guaranteed noncancelable, which means that it is renewable at the original premium price. If your insurance carrier doesn't offer a noncancelable policy, it may offer a guaranteed renewable policy instead, which guarantees that your policy will be renewed no matter what your health condition, though the premium may change.

If you become disabled and you have paid the premiums for disability insurance, any benefits you receive are free of federal, state, and local income taxes. However, if your employer has paid some or all of the premiums, your benefits are partially or totally taxable. Though prices vary widely among disability policies, expect to pay about $1,000 a year for $12,000 worth of annual disability income coverage. Several kinds of insurance companies offer disability coverage, but life insurers specialize in the product and offer the best options at the lowest prices. You most likely will obtain a much better price and more generous benefits if you buy through a group plan—for example, through your union or trade association—if you don't get it through your employer.

Hot Tip: A specialized type of disability insurance—credit disability— covers your loan payments if you become disabled and is sold by banks, finance companies, car dealerships, and other lenders. Mortgage lenders push mortgage disability insurance, which makes your home payments if you have an accident. In general, both credit and mortgage disability insurance policies are poor investments because they are overpriced. You are better served by more comprehensive forms of disability coverage.

The worksheet in Figure 9.4 will help you total your potential sources of disability income. Fill in the monthly amount you would receive from each policy, the waiting period before benefits begin, and the number of years you would receive benefits.

By completing the Disability Income Worksheet when you are not disabled, you will have a better idea of how you might cope if such a tragedy ever occurred. By adding your potential sources of disability income, you can also calculate how much private insurance you need to buy either through your employer or on your own.

LONG-TERM CARE INSURANCE

Long-term care includes a range of nursing, social, and rehabilitative services for people who need ongoing assistance. A disability, injury, or prolonged illness can make even the most routine daily tasks such as bathing, dressing,

Figure 9.4   Disability Income Worksheet

Disability Insurance Program	Monthly $ Amount	Waiting Period (Months)	Benefits for How Long (Years)
Government Programs			
Black Lung	$ _____	_____	_____
Civil Service	_____	_____	_____
Department of Veterans Affairs	_____	_____	_____
Medicaid	_____	_____	_____
Social Security	_____	_____	_____
Workers' Compensation	_____	_____	_____
Group Programs			
Employer	_____	_____	_____
Sick Leave	_____	_____	_____
Union	_____	_____	_____
Individual Programs			
Auto	_____	_____	_____
Credit Disability	_____	_____	_____
Individual Disability	_____	_____	_____
Mortgage Disability	_____	_____	_____
Other (while disabled)			
Savings and Investments	_____		
Spouse's Income	_____		
Other	_____		
TOTAL MONTHLY INCOME (while disabled)	$ _____		

eating, or taking medicine challenging. Although long-term care may conjure up images of a nursing home, in fact most care is provided at home, in an assisted living facility, or in community settings like an adult day care center.

The most important service a policy should cover, according to the American Health Care Association (1201 L St., N.W., Washington, DC 20005; 202-842-4444; www.ahca.org) is custodial or personal care. A good long-term care insurance policy covers all levels of care, especially personal care, and all settings, including facility care, community adult day care, assisted living, and nursing facilities.

What's not covered? The typical exclusions are an illness caused by an act of war, treatment already paid for by Uncle Sam, and alcohol and drug addiction. In some cases, mental and nervous disorders or diseases other than Alzheimer's disease and related dementia may be excluded. Be sure, too, to check with your agent whether the insurance company covers preexisting conditions (which could be excluded for six months).

You're probably thinking that long-term care insurance sounds great, but what's it going to cost me? Well, it depends. Premiums vary greatly, from several hundred to several thousand dollars. They are based on your age at the time of application, your prior and current health conditions, the benefits you select, and the number of years you want a company to pay benefits, for starters, according to the United Seniors Health Cooperative, a nonprofit organization (409 Third St., S.W., Second Floor, Washington, DC 20024; 202-479-6973; 800-637-2604; www.unitedseniorshealth.org). If you buy a policy, be prepared to pay for the rest of your life until you need the benefits; otherwise, if you start and then stop, you're just throwing money down the drain. You're far better off buying a policy in your mid-50s than your mid-60s. If you buy at age 55 a policy that costs $800 a year, you'll continue to pay the same premium, but if you wait until 65, that same policy will cost you around $1,700 a year.

So is it worth the money for most people? If you have less than $75,000 or so in assets, chances are you'll go through your money until you become eligible for Medicaid. Those with substantial assets will probably be able to self-insure and therefore may be better off investing the money they would have plunked down on premiums. For those somewhere in between, the United Seniors Health Council offers some guidelines; long-term care insurance is worth considering under the following conditions:

- You own assets of at least $75,000 (excluding home and car).
- On average, you have an annual retirement income of $25,000 to $35,000 if you're single, or $35,000 to 50,000 if you're a couple.
- You can pay premiums without adversely affecting your lifestyle.

- You can absorb possible increases in premiums without financial difficulty.

What to Look for in a Policy

In trying to assess which policy is best for you, much depends on your personal situation, how much you can afford, your preferences regarding long-term care options, and the level of risk you're willing to assume.

There are, however, a few factors you should keep in mind. Make sure you understand what the policy covers and what it doesn't. What conditions are required to qualify for coverage? What is the daily maximum dollar amount of care the insurer will provide? How long will you need coverage?

For most people coverage of three to five years is cost effective and really all that you will likely need. Be clear when your benefits kick in; typically, they are payable once you are unable to perform a certain number of the routine activities of daily living or you suffer from a cognitive impairment such as Alzheimer's. Are you protected from inflation? You want a policy to keep up with rising costs. The United Seniors Health Cooperative (USHC) recommends policies that automatically increase benefits at the rate of 5 percent annually. Compounded inflation protection is recommended for people applying up to age 70 and simple inflation for those applying after 70. Though this coverage will cost you more, it'll likely pay off in the long run. To be able to afford the extra coverage, you can choose a policy with a shorter benefit length or a less comprehensive policy.

What are the renewal terms? The best policy is one that is guaranteed renewable, which means the insurance company cannot cancel the policy unless, of course, you fail to pay premiums. Then there are tax issues. Tax-qualified policies let you deduct part of your premium from your federal taxes if your medical costs exceed 7.5 percent of your adjusted gross income (AGI). Policy benefit payments paid will not be taxed as income, but premiums for nonqualified plans can't be deducted as a medical expense; and it is unclear if benefits received will or won't be taxable.

As with other types of insurance, you'll want to check on the financial health of the insurer. Do a little digging to find out about the firm's reputation; shop around for price and quality, and you'll probably want professional guidance for this significant decision, perhaps from your existing insurance agent, your financial planner, or other financial advisors.

No one ever said that buying insurance was going to be much fun. Picking your way through the complexities is a chore you probably want to postpone indefinitely. Resist the urge. Once you go through the process of obtaining the proper kind and amount of coverage, you'll have earned a benefit that is hard to put a price on: peace of mind.

RESOURCES

Books, Booklets, and Pamphlets

The Alzheimer's Caregiver: Dealing with the Realities of Dementia, by Harriet Hodgson (John Wiley & Sons, 1 Wiley Dr., Somerset, NJ 08875-1272; 212-850-6000; 800-225-5945; www.wiley.com). Covers the expectations, costs, and difficulties of caring for Alzheimer's patients.

Buying Insurance, by Stuart Schwartz and Craig Conley (Capstone Press, P.O. Box 669, Mankato, MN 56002; 800-747-4992; www.capstone-press.com).

The Complete Guide to Long-Term Care Insurance, by Robert W. Davis (Long-Term Care Quote, 600 W. Ray Rd., Suite D4, Chandler, AZ 85224; 602-899-9983; 800-587-3279; www.searchltc.com). A comprehensive guide to long-term care insurance, including extensive analyses of costs of care in every state.

How to Insure Your Life: A Step-by-Step Guide to Buying the Coverage You Need at Prices You Can Afford, by Reg Wilson and the Silver Lake editors (Silver Lake Publishing, 2025 Hyperion Ave., Los Angeles, CA 90027; 323-663-3084; 888-663-3091). Provides tips and tactics to help people get the best life insurance coverage for their money.

The Insider's Guide to HMOs: How to Navigate the Managed-Care System and Get the Health Care You Deserve, by Alan J. Steinberg (Penguin Putnam, 405 Murray Hill Pkwy., East Rutherford, NJ 07073; 800-788-6262; www.penguinputnam. com). Explains the differences between various health care plans, evaluates the doctors in different systems, and shows how you can pay the best rate for a better HMO.

Legal Rights for Seniors: A Guide to Health Care, Income Benefits, and Senior Legal Services (HALT, An Organization of Americans for Legal Reform, 1612 K St., N.W., Suite 510, Washington, DC 20006; 202-887-8255; 888-367-4258; www. halt.org). A self-help book containing information for seniors on Medicare, Medicaid, Medigap policies, Social Security, estate planning, pensions, life insurance, guardianships, nursing home care, and veterans benefits.

Life Insurance: A Consumer's Handbook, by Joseph M. Belth (Indiana University Press, 601 N. Morton St., Bloomington, IN 47404; 812-855-8817; 800-842-6796; www.indiana.edu/~iupress/). A systematic approach to understanding personal insurable risk and how to transfer that risk to an insurance company.

Life Insurance Boot Camp Buyer's Guide, by William Brownlie (Life Insurance Boot Camp, 87 Parkhurst Dr., P.O. Box 441, Westford, MA 01886; www. lifeinsurancebootcamp.com). Complete coverage of the various types of life insurance and how to decide which policy and which company are right for you.

Managed Care Made Easy: Survival in the HMO Era, by Vikram Khanna (People's Medical Society, 462 Walnut St., Allentown, PA 18102; 610-770-1670). Comprehensive guide to getting the most out of managed health care.

Senior Savvy: How to Make the Most of Your Life Savings Before and After You Retire, by Ken Stern (Career Press, P.O. Box 687, Franklin Lakes, NJ 07417; 201-848-0310; 800-227-3371; www.careerpress.com). Teaches seniors how to survive financial distress; how to withstand government changes in Medicare and Medicaid; and how to avoid the risk of a long illness and protect their assets.

Newsletters

Insurance Forum (P.O. Box 245, Ellettsville, IN 47429; 812-876-6502). Devoted to insurance issues and directed mostly at insurance professionals. Discusses what is being done and what should be done to protect policyholders including explanatory material.

Annuity Shopper (8 Talmadge Dr., Monroe TWP, NJ 08831; 800-872-6684; 732-521-5110; www.annuityshopper.com). Provides updated performance on immediate, deferred, fixed, and variable annuities.

Trade Associations

American Associaton of Health Plans (1129 Twentieth St., N.W., Suite 600, Washington, DC 20036; 202-778-3200; www.aahp.org). A trade group for managed health care plans, including HMOs, PPOs, and point-of-service plans, that upholds strict standards of financial soundness and medical excellence among its members.

American Council of Life Insurers (1001 Pennyslvania Ave., N.W., 5th Floor South, Washington, DC 20004-2599; 202-624-2000; www.acli.com). A trade group of life insurance companies that lobbies on life insurance, long-term care insurance, disability income insurance, and retirement savings matters.

American Insurance Association (1130 Connecticut Ave., N.W., Suite 1000, Washington, DC 20036; 202-828-7100; www.aiadc.org). Property and casualty trade group that provides a forum for the discussion of problems.

Centers for Medicare and Medicare Services (formerly the Health Care Financing Administration) (7500 Security Blvd., Baltimore, MD 21244-1850; 410-786-3000; www.hcfa.gov). The federal agency that oversees the Medicare and Medicaid health insurance systems.

Consumer Federation of America Insurance Group (1424 16th St., N.W., Suite 604, Washington, DC 20036; 202-387-6121; www.consumerfed.org). A consumer-oriented group frequently critical of the insurance industry that will help you (for a $40 fee) evaluate life insurance policy proposals and analyze the projected rates of return on your insurance policies.

Federal Consumer Information Center. Free publications. (www.pueblo.gsa.gov, 888-878-3256). Covers choosing a doctor, choosing a hospital, and choosing treatments for Medicare patients plus a variety of information about Medicare.

Health Insurance Association of America (1201 F St., N.W., Suite 500, Washington, DC 20004-1204; 202-824-1600; www.hiaa.org). The lobbying group for health insurance companies that also educates the public about health insurance.

Independent Insurance Agents of America (127 S. Peyton St., Alexandria, VA 22314; 703-683-4422; 800-221-7917; www.iiaa.org). Association of agents not tied to selling any particular insurance company's products offers several free Consumer Education Guides on various insurance topics available by calling 800-261-4422.

Life and Health Insurance Foundation for Education (2175 K St., N.W., Suite 250, Washington, DC 20037; 202-464-5000; 888-LIFE-777; www.life-line.org). This nonprofit organization is a resource for educational information about life, health, and disability insurance.

Life Insurance Advisers Association (890 Treasure Island Rd., Mattawan, MI 49071; 800-521-4578). A group of independent life insurance consultants who provide advice for a fee but don't sell policies.

Medical Information Bureau (MIB) (160 University Ave., Westwood, MA 02090; 617-426-3660; www.mib.com). Organization of life insurance companies operating a confidential exchange of underwriting information about consumer's medical records.

Medicare Rights Center (1460 Broadway, 11th Floor, New York, NY 10036; 212-869-3850; www.medicarerights.org). Established to provide free counseling services to people with Medicare questions or problems.

National Association of Health Underwriters (2000 N. 14th St., Suite 450, Arlington, VA 22201; 703-276-0220; www.nahu.org). Represents professionals who sell disability income, hospitalization, and major medical health insurance policies.

National Association of Insurance and Financial Advisors (2901 Telestar Ct., Falls Church, VA 22042; 703-770-8100; ww.naifa.org). Group of life and investment advisors representing health, property, and casualty insurance agents.

National Association of Insurance Commissioners (2301 McGee, Suite 800, Kansas City, MO 64108; 816-842-3600; www.naic.org; Washington office: 444 N. Capital St., N.W., Suite 701, Washington, DC 20001-1512; 202-624-7790). A nonprofit association of the chief state insurance regulatory officials in the United States that coordinates the regulation of insurance.

National Committee for Quality Assurance (NCQA) (2000 L St., N.W., Suite 500, Washington, DC 20036; 202-955-3500; 800-236-5903; www.ncqa.org). A private, not-for-profit organization dedicated to assessing and reporting on the quality of managed care plans that accredits managed care organizations.

Society of Financial Service Professionals (270 S. Bryn Mawr Ave., Bryn Mawr, PA 19010-2194; 610-526-2500; 888-243-2258; www.financialpro.org). Chartered life underwriters specializing in life and health insurance, education funding, and estate planning; chartered financial consultants provide overall financial planning.

United Seniors Health Cooperative (409 Third St., S.W., Second Floor, Washington, DC 20024; 202-479-6973; 800-637-2604; www.unitedseniorshealth.org). Dedicated to helping seniors obtain good health care coverage and insurance. Advises seniors on selecting both private Medigap insurance and federal Medicare coverage that best meet their needs.

Web Sites for Health-Related Topics

American Cancer Society <www.cancer.org>. Offers information on all types of cancer and available treatment options.

Best Doctors <bestdoctors.com>. A referral site for the best doctors for the condition you may have; refers you to the best local doctor for $25.

Centerwatch <www.centerwatch.com>. Lists clinical trials by condition and geographic location and invites patients to participate (cash awards sometimes available to participants).

Coalition for Medicare Choices <www.medicarechoices.org>. A group of Medicare beneficiaries concerned that federal government officials are making changes to Medicare that are reducing choices and benefits and raising out-of-pocket costs.

Drugstore.com <www.drugstore.com>. Online drugstore fills prescriptions you mail or faxed from your doctor's office; also responds to doctors' phone calls.

Extendedcare.com <www.extendedcare.com>. Provides links for consumers, hospitals, and extended care providers; has links to about 75,000 providers for seniors or those taking care of seniors.

HealthAllies.com <www.healthallies.com>. Connects members with doctors, hospitals, clinics, and pharmacies in local areas who agree to provide discounted fees and drugs. Intended for people who have no, or limited, health insurance coverage.

HealthGrades.com <www.healthgrades.com>. Rates and grades hospitals, physicians, health plans, nursing homes, home health agencies, hospice programs, chiropractors, dentists, acupuncturists, assisted living programs, and birth centers.

Intelihealth <www.intelihealth.com>. Johns Hopkins University and Aetna U.S. Healthcare's site with questions on common ailments answered by the center's world-class doctors.

The Mayo Clinic <www.mayohealth.org>. The Mayo Clinic Health Oasis offers general information and lets you e-mail questions to clinic doctors.

Medicare <www.medicare.gov>. Contains a lot of information about Medicare; compares qualified HMO plans in your county offered to Medicare participants; and tells who offers Medigap policies in your county.

Medlineplus <www.medlineplus.gov>. Offers comprehensive medical and drug information, including an enormous number of resources.

National Insurance Consumer Helpline (Insurance Information Insitute, 110 William St., New York, NY 10038; 800-942-4242; www.iii.org). A consumer information service sponsored by insurance industry associations. Answers your questions about insurance, refers any complaints to the appropriate sources, and sends informational brochures.

National Institutes of Health <www.nih.gov>. Gateway to the resources of federal agencies, including a list of diseases being studied by various institutions; medical publications and fact sheets online.

National Women's Health Information Center <www.4woman.gov>. Provides comprehensive information in English and Spanish.

OncoLink <www.oncolink.com>. A comprehensive information site about cancer provided by the University of Pennsylvania Cancer Center.

PlanetRx.com <www.planetrx.com>. An online pharmacy and drugstore that fills prescriptions phoned, faxed, or mailed directly from the doctor's office or mailed by the patient.

WebMD Health <www.webmd.com>. Links the newly diagnosed to support groups and information on diseases and conditions, self-care, drugs and herbs, clinical trials, food, and nutrition.

Insurance Quoting Services

The following services quote insurance rates and help evaluate insurance policies based on your age and health condition:

AccuQuote (3180 McArthur Blvd., Northbrook, IL 60062; 847-480-7000; 800-442-9899; www.accuquote.com). An Internet-based service for term policies, whose Web site explains how to figure how much insurance you need, qualify for coverage, and criteria used to rate the financial strength of insurance companies.

Best Quote (3700 Park East Dr., Beachwood, OH 44122; 800-896-8006; 216-292-7900; www.bestquote.com). Offers free quotes on various term insurance policies and is able to sell you the policies that fit your needs.

Choice Quote (887 Oak Grove Ave., Suite 201, Menlo Park, CA 94025; 800-778-2001; 650-327-4571; www.choicequote.com). Quoting service that assesses your needs over the phone and recommends the lowest-cost term life policy you qualify for that will suit your needs.

INSurance INFOrmation (Cobblestone Court #2, 23 Route 134, South Dennis, MA 02660; 800-472-5800). Offers to find the lowest-cost term insurance policy; will suggest a new policy or evaluate a policy you already own. Provides only advice.

Insurance Quote Services (Building C, 3200 N. Dobson Rd., Chandler, AZ 85224; 480-345-7241; 800-972-1104; www.iquote.com). A database with term insurance prices. After asking your age, how much insurance you want, and your health condition, sends an IQ analysis listing the five lowest-cost term insurance policies in the country based on your situation.

Long-Term Care Quote (600 W. Ray Rd., Suite D4, Chandler, AZ 85224; 602-899-9983; 800-587-3279; www.searchltc.com). Promises to find the best long-term care policy and premiums for you or your loved ones.

QuickQuote (9650 Gateway Dr., #201, Reno, NV 89511; 800-867-2404; 775-850-3030; www.quickquote.com). Founded as an Internet-based real-time insurance and annuity quoting service. On the basis of a brief questionnaire on its Web site, helps determine what insurance you qualify for.

Quotesmith (8205 S. Cass St., Suite 102, Darien, IL 60561; 800-556-9393; www.quotesmith.com). Provides prices for term insurance policies from over 140 companies and also provides safety ratings from A.M. Best, Duff & Phelps, Moody's, Standard & Poor's, and Weiss Research on all its quotes.

SelectQuote (595 Market St., 6th Floor, San Francisco, CA 94105; 800-343-1985; www.selectquote.com). Tracks term insurance prices across the country. Quotes the lowest rate for your situation and can sell you the policy.

TermQuote (6768 Loop Rd., Centerville, OH 45459; 937-434-8989; 800-444-8376; www.term-quote.com). Searches its database of about 70 companies to find the lowest-cost insurance policy for your age and health condition. Employs a Certified Financial Planner and Chartered Life Underwriter to help you determine how much insurance you need.

Insurance Ratings Services

The following services rate insurance companies based on financial strength and investment performance:

A.M. Best & Co. (Ambest Rd., Oldwick, NJ 08858; 908-439-2200; www.ambest.com). Provides ratings on life and property/casualty insurance companies. Best's ratings are available online, or call their ratings hotline at 312-368-3158.

Fitch Ratings (One State St., New York, NY 10004; 212-908-0800; www.fitchratings.com). An international ratings agency that covers more than 800 insurance companies.

Moody's Investor Service (99 Church St., New York, NY 10007; 212-553-0300; www. moodys.com). The Moody's Insurance Financial Strength Ratings, from Aaa to Ca, are available for all North American corporate bond, life, private mortgage bond, and property/casualty insurance companies as well as for all major reinsurance companies.

Standard & Poor's Insurance Ratings Service (55 Water St., New York, NY 10041; 212-438-2000; www.standardandpoors.com). Provides publications and extensive ratings of life, health, and property/casualty insurance companies. S&P will provide a free rating for the insurance companies you are interested in when you call.

Weiss Research (4176 Burns Rd., Palm Beach Gardens, FL 33410; 800-289-9222; 561-627-3300; www.weissratings.com). Issues conservative ratings of insurance companies financial stability. For a small charge, you can get a Weiss Verbal Rating over the telephone.

Low-Load and No-Load Insurance Companies

These companies offer various kinds of life insurance, annuities, and auto insurance direct to consumers. Because no salesperson is involved in the sale, you pay little or no sales commission to buy a policy. This allows the savings to be passed on to you in the form of lower premiums and higher cash value buildup than you would receive from a standard load policy. Most of the policies sold by these companies also impose no surrender charge, which is the fee traditional insurance companies assess if you try to get out of your policy within the first few years after purchasing it. Low-load and no-load companies provide service on your policy 24 hours a day over a toll-free phone line.

American Direct Consumer Services (5 Greenway Plaza, #1400, Houston, TX 77046; 713-621-8531; 800-555-4655; www.ameritasdirect.com). For survivorship life (second-to-die) insurance, term insurance, universal insurance, variable annuities, and variable universal insurance.

Ameritas Life Insurance Corp. (5900 O St., Lincoln, NE 68501; 800-745-6665; www.ameritas.com). For survivorship (second-to-die) life, term insurance, universal life, variable annuities, and variable universal life policies.

Charles Schwab (101 Montgomery St., San Francisco, CA 94104; 800-435-4000; www.schwab.com). Universal and variable annuities from Great West Life and Annuity Company.

Fidelity Investments Life Insurance Co. (P.O. Box 1440, Merrimack, NH 03054-9805; for term insurance call: 800-642-6974; for variable annuities call 800-544-2442; www.fidelity.com). For term insurance and variable annuities.

Lincoln Benefit Life (2940 S. 84th, Lincoln, NE 68506; 800-525-9287; www.lbl.com). Offers life insurance, long-term care insurance, and annuities.

USAA Life (9800 Fredericksburg Rd., San Antonio, TX 78288; 800-531-8000; www.usaa.com). For auto insurance, fixed annuities, term insurance, universal insurance, variable universal life, variable annuities, and whole life policies.

Web Sites of Internet Insurance Companies and Brokers

The following are Web sites of Internet insurance companies, brokers, or independent insurance-related sites. You can usually obtain insurance quotes online from these companies, and in many cases you can sign up for the policy and company of your choice. Many of these sites offer basic insurance information and in some cases include calculators. Some of these sites display a number of quotes in order by price from many different insurance companies.

BudgetLife <www.budgetlife.com>. Database of about 175 companies for getting life insurance rates; also works with independent life insurance agents.

DirectQuote <www.directquote.com>. Offers a term life quoting service based on a pool of more than 60 companies ranked in order of price.

eHealthInsurance.com <www.ehealthinsurance.com>. A source for health insurance that covers individuals, small businesses, and seniors.

e-insure <www.e-insure.com>. Offers auto, home, health, life, business, and other insurance from around 400 insurance companies and 300 agents.

ePolicy.com <www.epolicy.com>. Working with a number of major insurance companies, this site will manage your insurance needs, from quotations to downloading the final policy.

InsuranceAgents.com <www.insuranceagents.com>. Matches you with a local insurance agent who can provide the type of insurance you need.

Insure.com <www.insure.com>. Packed with insurance information from explaining the basics of various types of insurance to rating and ranking insurance companies by the number of complaints against them and by financial strength.

Insweb <www.insweb.com>. Using your personal profile, this site will obtain quotes for auto, motorcycle, home, condominium, renters, term life, individual health, small group health, and pet insurance.

Itech Automated Life Insurance Quotation Systems <www.itechusa.com>. Online life insurance broker that will obtain quotes from a number of insurance companies to meet your needs and sign you up to the policy and company of your choice.

LifeInsurance.Net <www.lifeinsurance.net>. Connects you with life insurance agents in your area after you provide certain personal details and preferences.

Quicken.com <www.quicken.com>. Offers quotes from a database of companies for life, auto, and home insurance; also offers long-term care, disability, and small business insurance.

The following are Web sites of major insurance companies. In some cases, you can obtain a quote online and buy insurance directly through the Web site or through a local agent identified on the Web site:

CNA <www.cna.com>. Offers a large range of insurance products, many for commercial organizations; also offers individual life insurance, long-term care and travel insurance, and certain medical insurance products.

The Hartford Group of Companies <www.thehartford.com>. Auto, homeowners, flood, home business, and life insurance. Underwrites AARP, auto, home, RV, and other insurance products.

Liberty Mutual Insurance Group <www.libertymutual.com>. Offers auto, homeowners, and life insurance. Online quotes available for auto insurance only.

MetLife <www.metlife.com>. Information about auto, disability, health, homeowners, life, and long-term care insurance, along with a way to meet with a Metlife representative.

New York Life Insurance Company <www.newyorklife.com>. Contains a wealth of information about life insurance and has links to a customer service representative.

Northwestern Mutual <www.northwesternmutual.com>. Contains many useful calculators that can help you determine how much life and disability insurance you need and how to estimate the value of your 401(k) at retirement.

State Farm Fire & Casualty Insurance Company <www.statefarm.com>. Offers online auto, life, and renters insurance quotes. Insurance products sold through State Farm agents only.

CHAPTER 10

Enjoying Retirement

If you have done everything right and have a reliable stream of retirement income, you still must decide on the lifestyle you want in your golden years. In addition to figuring out how you will spend and continue to invest during retirement and how much or whether you will work during retirement, you must make choices about housing, possibly continuing your education, delving into new hobbies, volunteering, and travel.

INVESTING AND SPENDING DURING RETIREMENT

The first place to start is the money issue. You spent a lifetime building that kitty, but if you don't keep up good habits, the rest of your wish list may remain a wish and never be realized.

Sticking to a budget is no longer optional. It's critical. Remember that working overtime or depending on bonuses to wash away your spending sins is history. Being budget conscious becomes more important then ever. Your need for an emergency fund doesn't vanish; in fact, it increases. You don't want to have to sell long-term investments (especially in a down market) to meet unexpected expenses, which can come from just about anywhere—unreimbursed medical bills or costly repairs for your home or car. Experts recommend a rainy-day fund to cover at least three to six months of expenses or perhaps even as much as a year, particularly if you're heavily dependent on your investments for income.

As for your investments, you may be in your late 60s, 70s, or older, but don't play it too safe, as I pointed out in earlier chapters. Fight the urge to put all your money into bonds or other conservative vehicles in the quest for steady income. If you make it to the centurian club or even to 90, you could regret dearly having gotten out of the equities game too soon. The inflation beast could prove to be quite an eating machine.

If you weren't fastidious about monitoring your investments, you should be now. Sure, your portfolio will have good and bad years, but overall there should be more growth than shrinkage. If you aren't getting the returns that you had hoped for, see what needs adjusting and do a reality check. Are your expectations realistic? By the same token, if in your early years of retirement you do better than anticipated, don't start spending like those double-digit returns will continue for eternity. An important strategy for boosting the longevity of your money is withdrawing conservatively in the early years of retirement.

Perhaps one of your biggest questions: Which nest egg should you crack first? Well, much like all financial scenarios, the answer depends on a number of factors, such as the types of investments you have, your income tax bracket, your age, and your estate planning. But conventional wisdom generally gives the nod to spending assets in taxable accounts first, then deploying assets in tax-deferred accounts. Why? If you delay using tax-deferred retirement plan assets, they'll grow without being taxed for a longer period, meaning you keep more of your investments compounding for you. Another good reason is you'll pay less in taxes when you sell those assets than you will when you withdraw money from a traditional IRA or employer-sponsored plan because you will likely be in a lower tax bracket.

However, beginning the year after you turn 70½, Uncle Sam will come calling. You are required to withdraw some money from your tax-deferred retirement accounts. This is no joking matter, for the penalties for not taking your required distributions are stiff. Make these withdrawals first, and tap other accounts only if necessary.

Until recently, trying to figure out how much to withdraw each year was a major ordeal. In 2001 the rules were simplified and may work to your advantage because they may reduce the amount you are required to withdraw each year, therefore letting your kitty grow longer. All distributions for 2002 and later must follow the new rules, which eliminate the need to choose a calculation method for most people's accounts. There is now a single life expectancy table (see Figure 10.1) that assumes your primary beneficiary is ten years younger than you are. If, in fact, your beneficiary is older than you, or less than ten years younger, then the new rules reduce the amount of your required minimum distribution. However, if your spouse is your primary ben-

Figure 10.1   Figuring Your Minimum Required Distribution

Age	Distribution Period	Age	Distribution Period
70	27.4	93	9.6
71	26.5	94	9.1
72	25.6	95	8.6
73	24.7	96	8.1
74	23.8	97	7.6
75	22.9	98	7.1
76	22.0	99	6.7
77	21.2	100	6.3
78	20.3	101	5.9
79	19.5	102	5.5
80	18.7	103	5.2
81	17.9	104	4.9
82	17.1	105	4.5
83	16.3	106	4.2
84	15.5	107	3.9
85	14.8	108	3.7
86	14.1	109	3.4
87	13.4	110	3.1
88	12.7	111	2.9
89	12.0	112	2.6
90	11.4	113	2.4
91	10.8	114	2.1
92	10.2	115 and older	1.9

eficiary and is more than a decade younger, you may use a separate IRS joint expectancy table, which would generate a lower required minimum distribution than the previous life expectancy table. Also, financial institutions are now required to calculate your required minimum distribution on assets you have under their care and inform you and the IRS of the appropriate minimum amount to be withdrawn from your retirement account.

HOUSING OPTIONS HERE AND ABROAD

Probably the most important decision you must make is where you want to live as you grow older. Most people remain in the homes they lived in while working, but many retirees move to a warmer climate or to a town that imposes less of a tax burden or offers a quieter lifestyle. Although the lure of a warm and possibly faraway place and fresh start may be appealing in theory, think through such a decision carefully. It can be difficult to put down new roots at a stage in your life when you may want to relax. You may also find that moving farther away from your children and close friends means that you see them less, or you'll have to adjust your budget to account for trips back home. You'll also have to replace your entire network of professionals—from doctors and plumbers to financial planners—which took years to assemble. On the other hand, you might make this transition easily and thrive in your new setting.

If you want to move, consider the following factors as you evaluate potential locations:

- Access to high-quality medical care
- Cost of housing as well as the ongoing cost of living
- Crime rate
- Cultural and recreational activities
- Ease of making friends
- Educational opportunities
- Estate tax rules
- Proximity to friends and family
- Quality of shopping
- State and local income taxes
- Weather

To help you choose, consult one of the guidebooks that rate retirement communities, such as Rand McNally's *Places Rated Retirement Guide.* Wherever you pick up to move, it's a good idea to rent in the new place for a few months to make sure you like it before you sell your home and move there. You don't want to go through the ordeal of selling your home of many years and moving all your possessions to a new place, only to discover that you don't like living there after all.

For the most adventurous retirees, a move to a foreign country makes sense. The U.S. dollar often goes much further in other countries than it does at home, and you may be able to find an enclave of retired Americans, which will make you feel almost like you still live in the States. The countries with the largest concentrations of expatriate Americans are Mexico, Canada, Italy, the Philippines, Greece, Germany, Great Britain, and Israel.

If you are thinking of retiring abroad, evaluate the political stability of the country as well as the exchange rate for the dollar. Some developing countries like Mexico and the Philippines offer a lower cost of living, whereas industrialized nations like Great Britain and Germany are far more expensive. Inquire about your tax obligations if you move abroad. As long as you remain a U.S. citizen, you owe U.S. taxes; in some countries, you must pay local income tax as well. Usually, you can claim a foreign tax credit on your U.S. return to off-set those local taxes. Also look into health insurance coverage because it is un-likely that Medicare will cover you if you live abroad.

Check out AARP's Web site <www.aarp.org>, which provides useful in-formation on international living. You'll need a local bank account to sign up for utilities. AARP warns that it's challenging to open a bank account over-seas as an American citizen. You should carry a letter of reference from your U.S. bank showing a solid banking history; and it helps to make a large de-posit to open the account. You should check the requirements and limits for bringing cash and assets into your country of choice by contacting the em-bassy or consulate. And while you may be dreaming of buying that perfect home abroad, the process can be daunting and expensive, given the high cost of real estate transactions and taxes. Some foreign countries don't allow Americans to purchase homes, so if you're really serious about going off-shore, you'll want to be thorough in researching the cost of living, tax rules (some countries will tax your U.S. Social Security benefits, for example), and visa requirements, among other issues. Embassies, consulates, and ex-patriates are good places to start. See the "Resouces" section in this chapter for other leads.

Other Housing Alternatives

As you age, you may find that maintaining your home is becoming too much of a burden. If so, several options offer varying levels of independence combined with help with everyday living. The most common alternatives follow:

Independent living facilities. Such facilities include government-subsidized housing developments designed for retirees in good health who need minimum assistance. They also include private retirement communities with separate housing for each resident.

Manufactured home parks. If you own a mobile home, you can move it to a retirement-oriented park, where you pay rent and a service fee for elec-tricity, water, and recreational facilities. In some cases, retirees band together and run such parks as nonprofit cooperatives, in which each resident owns a share of the corporation that owns the park.

Congregate housing facilities. In such facilities, you live independently in your own apartment and share with other residents common services such as a dining room, social and recreational programs, and housekeeping.

Assisted living facilities. If you are less able to take care of yourself, these facilities offer private or semiprivate rooms, meals, housekeeping, and ongoing medical attention. Help with dressing, grooming, and other personal care is also available.

Continuing care communities. These housing developments are designed for all stages of a retiree's life, including independent living, assisted living, and nursing home care. As your needs change, you move from one facility to another within the community. You usually sign a long-term continuing care contract with the community, which provides that the community's administrators will make sure you receive the level of aid you need as you age. You also must pay an entrance fee plus a monthly charge that covers you for as long as you live in the community. Contact the American Association of Homes and Services for the Aging (2519 Connecticut Ave., N.W., Washington, DC 20008; 202-783-2242; www.aahsa.org) for a list of continuing care communities that are accredited by the association.

Don't rely only on the answers you get from the facility's administrators. Tour the place several times. Talk not only to staff but to as many residents and their families as possible to learn whether they are satisfied with the condition of the physical plant and the level of service provided. If a residents' association or council exists, attend a meeting to get a sense of how well the facility is managed.

Get details, details, and more details. Horror stories abound of people who signed on to assisted living facilities without reading the fine print. They discovered the hard way that assisted living facilities were not equipped to handle severe illness. Be clear what conditions might necessitate someone having to move to a nursing home. You don't want the hassle and the expense of an unplanned move. Make sure you really understand the fee structure; for example, over 80 percent of assisted living residences charge more than $1,000 a month in addition to one-time sign-up fees.

Think long and hard about what matters most to you. If you're not much of a social butterfly, bingo and many assorted activities may be of no interest to you. Once you've decided you've found the place that you'd like to call home, have an elder care attorney look over the agreement you're asked to sign with the facility. You want to be sure what you're getting into.

Nursing Homes

A nursing home is not likely to be your first choice, but sometimes health concerns predominate. Be prepared for sticker shock—nursing home care on average runs around $50,000 a year and can be more than $90,000. You can't expect much help from Uncle Sam either. Medicaid pays for nursing home care only when you are financially eligible, meaning you've exhausted most of your assets before Medicaid takes over. Medicare steps in if you were recently hospitalized and now need skilled care, but it doesn't pay for long nursing home stays.

Picking a Long-Term Care Facility

In order to make a good decision, you'll need to do lots of homework. Ask yourself the following questions:

- *Does the facility offer the services I need now and am likely to need in the future?*
- *Do I like the facility's location?* Does it offer nearby recreational or cultural attractions?
- *What is the track record of the company operating the facility?* Is it financially solid? How long has it been in the business of operating retirement facilities? What is the facility's occupancy level? (An 80 percent occupancy level within a year or two of opening should mean that clients are satisfied.)
- *What kind of contract must I sign?* You may be offered a rental agreement for a few months or years; or you may have to buy the housing unit to live there. Or you may have to pay a life-use fee, which guarantees you the right to live in the facility until you die for a one-time investment of several thousand dollars in addition to a monthly fee. In this case, if you move out, some of your investment may be refunded.
- *What services are available in the facility?* Ask about appliances, parking, utilities, exercise and recreation classes, security, housekeeping, meals, and transportation.
- *What is the quality of medical care provided?* Look into the availability of general practitioners and specialists, dentists, home health care aides, drug dispensaries, physical therapists, and psychiatric care. Ask whether the facility is certified to receive Medicare or Medicaid payments.
- *Does the facility accept Medicare assignments or Medicaid patients?* For example, ask whether the facility accepts Medicare and your Medicare supplement as payment in full. Do you have to pay the difference between the actual charge and Medicare's allowable charge? What other fees do you have to pay? What are optional services that could add to your fees?

You need to do much legwork to find a suitable place. Come up with a list of nursing homes that are close to family and friends; it's important to have a small army of sorts to regularly check up on you. Talk to the local or state long-term care ombudsmen who visits nursing homes and investigates

Staying Put

If it's really important that you stay in your home for as long as is physically possible, be sure to investigate in-home care. The reality is that your family and friends may not have the time to serve as your primary caregiver. You may have to hire someone to help out. The Eldercare Locator (1112 16th St., N.W., Suite 100, Washington, DC 20036; 800-677-1116; www.eldercare.gov) can assist you in locating the nearest area agency on aging as well as providing information on community services that support older adults. Another good resource is the National Association for Home Care (NAHC) (228 Seventh St., N.E., Washington, DC 20003; 202-547-7424; nahc.org), which offers help in choosing a home care provider. These are a few questions you should begin asking:

- *How long has the provider been in the community?*
- *How does the provider select and train its employees?*
- *Is the patient's course of treatment documented?*
- *Are supervisors assigned to oversee the quality of care patients receive in their homes and, if so, how often?*
- *Is the provider equipped to handle emergencies?*
- *Are caregivers available 24 hours daily?*

As much as staying at home has major appeal, particularly cost-wise—costs average about $12,000 a year for service five days a week—costs depend on the level of expertise and skill of the caregiver. There are other considerations. Will you have to make renovations to your home to accommodate your changing needs? Stairs can be problematic and downright dangerous for frail bones. Tally up what it might cost to put in stair lifts, make your home wheelchair accessible, and the like.

complaints. Much like other housing options, you'll want to talk to staff and to residents and their families and to check with the state licensing agency about any violations there.

The American Association of Retired Persons suggests reviewing the state surveys of each nursing home you're interested in. Medicare and Medicaid facilities are required by law to let you see their survey (inspection) reports. When you're making your visits, include one evening and one weekend visit. Eat a few meals there. How do you know a good nursing home when you see it? Does the staff treat residents with respect? Do they answer calls for help promptly? Are residents active? How homelike is it? You want signs that this is a place to live, not to die. Be wary of a place that has unpleasant odors, which could be a sign there is insufficient staff to help residents to the bathroom or to keep residents and the place clean. Look for any signs of restraints. Vests and other devices that tie or otherwise hold people down in their bed and wheelchair are dangerous and humiliating. Good nursing homes seek safe and respectful ways to protect residents from falls and wandering.

THE FUN STUFF

To live a fulfilled life in retirement, you may cultivate activities that you never had time for during your working life. After you've cleaned the house and caught up on your reading, you'll probably want to get involved in something that gives you a sense of satisfaction. The four most common pursuits for active retirees are continuing education, hobbies, volunteering, and traveling.

Continuing Education

Most colleges offer courses aimed at retirees on almost every subject you can imagine. You can take them either for credit toward a degree or on a non-credit basis to expand your knowledge. Some courses take only a few weeks, others a quarter or semester. In addition, many communities offer free or low-tuition programs aimed at seniors and funded by the state or local government. Some universities sponsor *learning-in-retirement institutes* (LIRs), in which members serve as instructors. A few of the better-known LIRs include the Institute for Retired Professionals at the New School for Social Research in New York City; the Academy of Lifelong Learning at the University of Delaware; and the College for Seniors at the University of North Carolina at Asheville.

Aside from contacting local schools and community centers, another way to learn about continuing education programs is through *Elderhostel* (11 Avenue de Lafayette, Boston, MA 02111-1746; www.elderhostel.org). This organization conducts classes in many subjects in about 40 countries. Each course usually lasts a week and is held on a college campus, where you stay in a college dormitory and eat in the college cafeteria. You may also want to look into *Interhostel,* a program combining courses and touring in many countries. It has links with universities and cultural institutions around the world that host the program. Contact Interhostel (University of New Hampshire, 6 Garrison St., Durham, NJ 03824; 603-862-2015; 800-313-5327; www.learn.unh.edu) for more information.

If you don't want to travel for your courses, bring them into your home. For a copy of the National University Continuing Education Association's

Guide to Independent Study, a list of correspondence classes, contact Peterson's Publishing (Princeton Pike Corporate Center, 2000 Lenox Dr., Lawrenceville, NJ 08648; 609-896-1800; www.petersons.com). If you're computer savvy, distance learning provides an opportunity to learn at home via your computer. You can find out about distance learning from the Distance Education and Training Council, formerly called the National Home Study Council (1601 18th St., N.W., Washington, DC 20009; 202-332-1386; www.detc .org). Another resource for distance learning is the Web site <www.college-distancedegree.com>, which has a directory of accredited colleges like Duke, Tulane, and Stanford, where you can earn a degree without going on campus. Peterson's Web site <www.petersons.com> has a distance education link that allows you to search from thousands of programs and courses as well as from articles on distance learning; it also has links for financing options and a tool for assessing whether distance learning is right for you.

Hobbies

Once retired, you'll have more time to pursue a new hobby or develop one you could only dabble in during your working years. Most of the following hobbies are inexpensive, though some can become costly for avid hobbyists. These are just a few of the hobbies you might find interesting:

- *Collecting.* You can collect stamps, coins, antiques, artwork, or anything else that interests you.
- *Crafts.* You can become an expert in many crafts, including quilting, needlework, photography, painting, model building, ceramics, furniture repair, and stained glass.
- *Games.* You might take up bingo, bridge or other card games, checkers, chess, Monopoly, backgammon, dominoes, and many other social games.
- *Group activities.* You can join civic, political, religious, or social clubs that draw on your professional experience.
- *Outdoor activities.* You may enjoy birdwatching, camping, gardening, or hiking.
- *Pets.* You might get satisfaction from raising cats, dogs, horses, ducks, or fish.
- *Reading.* You can join or start a book club or frequent your local library to enrich your knowledge.
- *Sports.* To stay in shape and have fun, you might participate in boating, bicycling, tennis, bowling, fishing, or swimming, to name a few.
- *Theater.* You can join a local theater group to learn acting or attend plays with a group and discuss the performance in a structured way.

Getting into Collectibles: Treasure or Trash?

One man's junk is another man's treasure. With the explosion of eBay and other online auction sites, trinkets are changing hands as quickly as folks can clean out their attics and garages. You may be thinking that getting into collectibles will not only be fun but also a way to make a little cash to add to your income during retirement.

However, the collectibles market is not all fun and games. If you don't know what you're doing, you could end up paying too much for worthless stuff or unloading goodies for a mere pittance when you should have been skipping off to the bank to deposit a bundle of cash. The collectibles craze is intoxicating—but sober up. You don't want to get soaked. If you want to play the game, better bone up on the rules.

Forget about striking it rich. One can no more predict whether what you're picking up today will be highly prized in five or ten years than one can predict where hemlines will be then. Because this is a game with no guaranteed winner, focus on what you love. That way, whether you make a killing doesn't matter. You'll at least have an attic full of things that please you.

But if you're up for taking your chances, take at least a little advice.

Educate yourself. There are volumes of books on collecting just about anything. Get familiar with the collecting terrain. Become a regular at flea markets, and scout out the antique shows. For the truly serious, there's a home study course offered by the Ashford Institute of Antiques <www.ashford.com>. Plug in *"Antiques and Collectibles"* on the Net and you're sure to find many communities, clubs, Web sites, and newsletters devoted to hard-core collecting types. The Maloney's Antiques and Collectibles Resource Directory <www.maloneysonline.com> can help you find experts, appraisers, dealers, clubs, and museums that specialize in any kind of collectible. You can find loads of information and links at <collectorsuniverse.com>; and Krause Publications <www.krause.com> offers more than 40 periodicals, how-to books, and hobby shows on everything from antiques to sewing and hunting.

Get a clue about prices. An overheated market will bear just about any price, but you want to know what's reasonable before you start bidding. One good source is <www.kovels.com>. You'll find guidelines for prices, articles, a directory of sources, and more.

Another is <www.collectingchannel.com>, a portal with a pricing and images database, online appraisals, news, articles, and videos on a wide variety of collectibles. When considering a price, whether you're selling or buying, what counts is the item's authenticity, its rarity, and its condition. Know, too, that if you are fortunate enough to make a substantial profit on something you sell, the tax man will look for his share. Your good luck is a capital gains tax if you've held the asset for more than a year and regular income tax if you've held it for less than a year.

Leave your emotions at home. The bidding process is like war. It's easy to get caught up in the moment and pay too much. Patience is key. One thing about bidding online is that software allows you to bid at the last second, which is called "sniping." If your emotions get the best of you and you spend a princely sum for an item, make sure you take advantage of escrow, which means a third party will hold on to your cash until you've had a chance to look at the item and determine if it's worth the dough.

Once you've found your treasure, treat it as such. When storing it, be mindful of the potential damage caused by light or extreme heat or cold. Keep all your items in their original packages and in mint condition.

Realistically, though, you should look at collectibles trading less as a financial proposition and more as a hunting and seeking adventure to help fill your retirement days.

Whatever you fancy, the Internet is chock full of information; merely type in the word *hobbies* on a search engine like Yahoo! and you'll find sites for everything imaginable. Magazine City.net <www.magazinecity.net> is just one site offering hobby and collectibles magazines at significant discounts. Buzzle.com <www.buzzle.com> has a section for hobbies and special interests—from bird watching and breeding to cake baking, miniature dollhouses, sports collectibles, and photography, to name but a few. The Hobby Industry Association's <www.i-craft.com/seniors/html> consumer section has a Senior Center with tips and project ideas for making candles, pillows, and more.

Volunteering

One of the most rewarding ways to spend your time in retirement is to volunteer to help those who can learn from your experience or benefit from your time. For example, if you operated a business, you can help a struggling entrepreneur turn a profit. If you know art, volunteer to be a museum guide. If you are a member of a church or temple, volunteer your help wherever necessary. And to help those who are less fortunate, volunteer at the Salvation Army or almost any social service organization. The following organizations can help you locate the volunteer opportunity that is best for you:

- AmeriCorps (1201 New York Ave., N.W., Washington, DC 20525; 800-424-8867; www.seniorcorps.org). This is the federal agency that coordinates all volunteer activities. Some of its programs include the Foster Grandparent Program, the Retired Senior Volunteer Program (RSVP), the Senior Companion Program, the Service Corps of Retired Executives (SCORE), and Volunteers in Service to America (VISTA).
- Corporation for National and Community Service (CNS) (1201 New York Ave., N.W., Washington, DC 20525; 800-942-2677; www.cns .gov). This is a nonprofit management consulting group that places top-caliber, retired executives who volunteer their time and expertise to nonprofit organizations in education, the arts, and social services. CNS also operates the Senior Career Planning and Placement Services and the Math-Science Education Program, which places retirees with technical skills in schools.
- National Association of Partners in Education (901 N. Pitt St., Suite 320, Alexandria, VA 22314; 703-836-4880; www.NAPEhq.org). This association will direct you to volunteer programs in schools.
- National Council on the Aging (409 3rd St., S.W., Suite 200, Washington, DC 20024; 202-479-1200; www.ncoa.org). This is an advocacy organization for retired people, which publishes *Innovation in Aging* magazine, covering topics of interest to older Americans.
- Peace Corps (1111 20th St., N.W., Washington, DC 20526; 800-424-8580; www.peacecorps.gov). This agency appeals to hardy retirees who want to make a difference in impoverished parts of the world. You must first go through training and then live under spartan conditions, where you earn a small monthly stipend.

The Internet is a treasure trove of resources for information about organizations that might need your help and has sites that match volunteers, such as <www.volunteermatch.org>; <www.planetvolunteer.com>; and <www.communityservice.org>. The Travel with a Challenge Web site <www .travelwithachallenge.com> showcases well-established and freshly minted alternative travel opportunities throughout the world, including independent and group trips for ecological, educational, cultural, and volunteer vacations suited to those age 50 and over.

Whatever retirement activities you choose, you have myriad opportunities to learn and help others.

Traveling

Another big joy in retirement is the opportunity to travel to places you have always wanted to visit—and to do it at your own pace. Not only do you have the advantage of time, you can also qualify for discounts of as much as 50 percent on tours designed for seniors.

If you travel with a group on a prepackaged tour, you'll receive a better price than if you booked airfare and hotels on your own, and you'll be shown the highlights of the places you visit. The tour operator also takes care of your luggage and other arrangements. Because you may not want to spend your entire trip sightseeing with the group, make sure that any tour you choose leaves enough time for you to explore on your own at your own pace. A convenient way of visiting many locations without constantly packing and unpacking is to board a cruise ship that stops in several ports.

If you want to plan your own itinerary, do plenty of research before you book airlines and hotels. Many good books and Web sites can guide you to the best accommodations at the best prices. Before making reservations, set up a budget that details how much you will spend for transportation, hotels, food, and souvenirs. It's easy to get carried away once you arrive at the destination of your dreams.

Use your senior power to get the biggest discounts possible. Following is just a sampling of the perks available:

- All U.S. national parks are free to any U.S. citizen 62 years or older who has a Golden Age Passport. This passport, which you can apply for in person with proof of age at any National Park or Forest Service Station, allows you to pay half-price for boating, parking, camping, and other park services. Make sure to reserve your spot months in advance.
- Most U.S. airlines offer discounts of as much as 25 percent to seniors who buy airline coupon books. Some airlines provide special frequent-flier clubs for seniors that offer extra discounts.
- Amtrak, Greyhound, and Trailways offer price breaks of 10 to 15 percent for seniors on most of their fares.
- Membership in some senior organizations grants you substantial discounts. You can qualify for discounts at certain hotels if you show that you are a member, for example, of a group like AARP or the National Alliance of Senior Citizens (listed in the "Resources" section of this chapter).
- Membership in some senior organizations grants you substantial discounts. The AARP Privileges (800-424-3410) provides hundreds of dis-

count tour packages. You also qualify for hotel discounts if you prove that you are a member of the National Alliance of Senior Citizens.

For more information on travel for seniors, consult one of the many travel agencies that specialize in arranging travel for seniors, such as Grand Circle Travel in Boston (347 Congress St., Boston, MA 02210; 800-221-2610), whose free booklet is titled *Going Abroad: 101 Tips for Mature Travelers.*

Travel bargains. A little research can reap enormous travel bargains. If you are willing to spend a little time and effort contacting specialized travel sources, you can save a great deal of money on hotels, cruises, dining, and airfare. In the "Resources" section of this chapter, I have listed several hotel services that book rooms in particular cities and that usually offer you a far better rate than you get by calling the hotels directly. Two national services offer the same service in many cities and are also listed in the "Resources" section as are bargains in cruises, restaurants, and airfares.

By using the Web sites sponsored by various airlines, you can save a considerable amount of money on airfares. Most airlines post their available inventory of seats on a regular basis on their site. If you find that space is available for the destination and time that suits your needs, you can book the flight online, often at substantial savings over regular fares. Airlines would rather sell their seats at 50 percent off regular fares than have the seats go empty. So the nearer a flight is to taking off, the larger the discounts become. There is a complete list of all the airline Web sites in the "Resources" section of this chapter.

Stay up late to catch the deals. Airlines usually reload their computers at midnight with the low-cost seats customers reserved but didn't pay for, so come 1 AM or so, you'll find a temporary glut of cheap seats available. Don't fret if you aren't able to book a flight on one of the no-frills airlines. Chances are if you call the bigger airlines and request a flight leaving at the same date and time, you'll find that for competitive reasons the larger carrier has a similar fare.

In retirement you have the luxury of time. Know that Monday morning flights are often overbooked. If you agree to be bounced, you could reap benefits like a free round-trip, cash, or some other substantial perk. Because you're no longer punching a time clock, it behooves you to travel to your destination off-season. Not only will you save money, but you'll avoid big crowds too.

If you're a Hilton Hotel fan, check out the Hilton Senior Honors program. If you're over 60, you and your spouse can pay $50 a year to get discounts of 50 percent at Hilton Hotels throughout the United States and around the world. (You can find out more by calling 800-432-3600.) Single seniors can join the

Travel Companion Exchange (800-392-1256; www.travelcompanions.com) to find a buddy to share the expense of rooms and cars.

Check out parking options before you check out. You know how pricey long-term airport parking can be. Investigate budget hotels near the airport. Ask if you could park your car there while you're away. That freebie could save you a lot if you have a week-long trip.

Help finance your vacation. If you're going to be away for two weeks or more, consider renting out your home while you're away. You'll have someone to water the plants and bring in the papers and mail; and, who knows, you could fetch enough to significantly defray vacation expenses.

Venture out. Realize that the shops and restaurants closest to your hotel are tourist haunts, and the prices will likely be higher. Go even a few blocks away and you'll probably find more affordable prices and higher quality, and possibly more than your everyday standard fare.

For those planning to travel overseas, update your passport and obtain any needed visas. Also check whether the country to which you are headed requires or recommends immunizations. Because health insurance policies, particularly Medicare, often don't cover medical problems when you are out of the United States, it may be worth paying for the Medical Assistance Program, which provides short-term coverage for health problems while traveling in a foreign country. You can obtain it through either your regular health insurer or your travel agent. Make sure to bring plenty of whatever medication you are taking because the drug may be difficult, if not impossible, to find outside the United States. In addition, you might look into buying travel insurance, which covers canceled or delayed trips, lost baggage, accidents, and other mishaps on the road. These maladies are not normally covered by your regular homeowners policy, although they may be included in insurance attached to your credit or American Express card.

The bottom line is that you can have a ball in retirement, and it doesn't have to cost a fortune. Be creative and take advantage of all the perks that come with the senior citizen title. You've earned them.

Resources

Books, Booklets, and Pamphlets

Alzheimer's Disease: Questions and Answers, by Paul S. Eisen, Deborah H. Marin, and Kenneth L. Davis (Merit Publishing International, 8260 N.W. 49th Manor, Pine Grove, Coral Springs, FL 33067; 954-755-4280; www.meritpublishing.com). Includes risk factors, causes, symptoms, management, and treatment with traditional and alternative medicines.

Beat the Nursing Home Trap, by Joseph L. Matthews (Nolo Press, 950 Parker St., Berkeley, CA 94710; 800-992-6656; www.nolo.com). A practical guide to help consumers make the best choices for long-term care.

Comfort Zones: Planning Your Future, by Elwood N. Chapman and Marion Haynes (Crisp Publications, 1200 Hamilton Ct., Menlo Park, CA 94025; 800-442-7477; ww.crisplearning.com). Covers all the basics of the transition from work to retirement with planning tools, case studies, and exercises.

From Work to Retirement, by Marion E. Haynes (Crisp Publications, 1200 Hamilton Ct., Menlo Park, CA 94025; 800-442-7477; ww.crisplearning.com). Deals with the stages from career to retirement, covering four phases—acknowledgment, acceptance, disengagement, and redefinition—and covers the emotions that can accompany the transition.

How to Enjoy Your Retirement: Activities from A to Z, by Tricia Wagner and Barbara Day (VanderWyk & Burnham, P.O. Box 2789-WS, Acton, MA 01720-6789; 617-714-0287; www.vandb.com). Contains 1,000 activity ideas with artwork and quotations. Included are toll-free numbers, Web sites, and snail-mail addresses.

Investing during Retirement (The Vanguard Group, P.O. Box 2600, Valley Forge, PA 19482-2600; 800-662-7447; www.vanguard.com). A booklet that covers creating a realistic budget, evaluating your ongoing income and assessing and managing your investments.

The Prosperous Retirement: Guide to the New Reality, by Michael K. Stein (Emstco Press, 1469 S. Meadow Dr., Boulder, CO 89391; 800-345-6665). Shows how modern retirement is different from the retirements of earlier generations. Discusses the financial and nonfinancial challenges in modern retirement.

Retirement Living: A Guide to Housing Alternatives, by Richard Forrest and Mary Brumby Forrest, L.P.N. (Facts On File, Inc., 132 W. 31st St., New York, NY 10001; 800-322-8755; www.factsonfile.com). A handy guidebook that describes in simple terms the costs, living conditions, and accessibility for the disabled.

World's Top Retirement Havens: How to Relocate, Retire, and Increase Your Standard of Living, by Margaret J. Goldstein (Avalon Travel Publishing, 5855 Beaudry St., Emeryville, CA 94608; 510-595-3664, www.travelmatters.com). A comprehensive guide for finding the most suitable place to live during your sunset years.

Magazines and Newsletters

Condé Nast Traveler (Condé Nast Publications, 4 Times Square, New York, NY 10036; 212-286-2860; www.cntraveler.com). This sophisticated, stylish magazine lets you know the best islands, cities, spas, castles, and cruises.

Guides to Living Abroad (32 Nassau St., Princeton, NJ 08542; 609-924-9302; www.livingabroad.com). Offers how-to-live, relocation, and other vital information, such as visas, housing, insurance, and health insurance, for more than 90 countries.

Kiplinger's Retirement Report (1729 H St., N.W., Washington, DC 20006-3938; 888-419-0424; www.kiplinger.com/retreport). The monthly newsletter provides advice and guidance on managing your retirement finances, protecting your assets, Medicare and long-term care insurance, and estate planning.

Modern Maturity (601 E. St., N.W., Washington, DC 20049; 800-424-3410; www .aarp.org). The official magazine of AARP covers legislative issues facing retirees and provides inspirational stories and informative features to help people achieve more fulfilled retirement years. AARP also publishes *My Generation* magazine.

New Choices: Living Even Better After 50 (Retirement Living Publishing Co., Reader's Digest Rd., Pleasantville, NY 10570; 800-388-6111; www.newchoices. com). Dedicated to helping readers enjoy retirement.

Retirement Letter (Phillips Publishing, 7811 Montrose Rd., Potomac, MD 20854; 301-340-2100; 800-777-5005; www.phillips.com). A monthly newsletter covering many issues related to retirement, such as investment suggestions, tax planning ideas, travel advice, home repair tips, and news from Washington.

Trade Associations and Government Agencies

Administration on Aging (330 Independence Ave., S.W., Washington, DC 20201; 202-619-7501; www.aoa.dhhs.gov/default.htm). The Internet service provides links to government agencies, professional associations, and many other information sources covering health care, financial benefit programs, elder law, and advocacy groups that work on behalf of seniors.

Aging Network Services (4400 East West Hwy., Suite 907, Bethesda, MD 20814; 301-657-4329; www.agingnets.com). Provides referrals to social workers specializing in caring for the aged.

Alliance for Retired Americans (888 16th St., N.W., Washington, DC 20006; 888-373-6497; www.retiredamericans.org). A national advocacy organization that works to protect the health and economic security of seniors on the national, state, and local level.

American Association of Homes and Services for the Aging (2519 Connecticut Ave., N.W., Washington, DC 20008; 202-783-2242; www.aahsa.org). Helps the elderly find appropriate housing. Tracks the accreditation for health facilities and can recommend well-run communities.

American Association of Retired Persons (AARP) (601 E St., N.W., Washington, DC 20049; 202-434-2277; 800-424-3410; www.aarp.org). One of the largest trade associations in the country; offers its members credit cards, discount drug purchase programs, educational seminars, insurance, mutual funds, travel opportunities, and many other services.

American Health Care Association (1201 L St., N.W., Washington, DC 20005; 202-842-4444; www.ahca.org). A federation of 50 state health organizations representing nearly 12,000 nonprofit and for-profit assisted living facilities, nursing and long-term care facilities, and subacute care providers that care for more than one million elderly and disabled individuals nationally.

American Seniors Housing Association (5100 Wisconsin Ave., N.W., Suite 307, Washington, DC 20016; 202-237-0900; www.seniorshousing.org). Addresses the unique challenges of housing the nation's growing population of older adults; has helpful information on its site.

Children of Aging Parents (1609 Woodbourne Rd., Suite 302A, Levittown, PA 19057; 215-945-6900; www.caps4caregivers.org). A national clearinghouse for information, resources, and support for caregivers of the elderly and allied health professionals.

Distance Education & Training Council (1601 18th St., N.W., Washington, DC 20009-2529; 202-332-1386; www.detc.org). The accrediting agency for correspondence schools. Its Directory of Accredited Institutions can tell you where to find a home study course teaching the subject that interests you.

Eldercare Locator (1112 16th St., N.W., Suite 100, Washington, DC 20036; 800-677-1116; www.eldercare.gov). Refers you to appropriate agencies that offer services to senior citizens; for example, can help you find adult day care, home-delivered meals, transportation, home health care, and local centers for seniors.

Hobby Industry Association (P.O. Box 348, Elmwood, NJ 07407; 201-294-1133; www.i-craft.com). A Senior Center in the consumer section for those 55 and over, where you can find tips, projects, and more for a wide range of interests, such as painting, needlecraft, floral crafts, and scrapbooking.

Legal Counsel for the Elderly (Building A, 601 E St., N.W., 4th Floor, Washington, DC 20049; 202-434-2120). A nonprofit legal support center sponsored by AARP that deals with issues of concern to the elderly. Offers legal services by referring consumers to a local attorney member, whose services for the first 30 minutes of consultation are free.

Living Strategies (3 Bala Plaza, Suite 117 East, Bala Cynwyd, PA 19004; 610-667-6545; www.livingstrategies.com). A national network of professional geriatric care managers that assists families with all aspects of aging.

National Alliance for Caregiving (4720 Montgomery Ln., Suite 642, Bethesda, MD 20814; www.caregiving.org). A nonprofit joint venture created to support family caregivers of the elderly and the professionals who serve them.

National Alliance of Senior Citizens (2525 Wilson Blvd., Arlington, VA 22201; fax 703-528-4380). Advocates policies that enhance the retirement years of senior citizens.

National Association of Partners in Education (901 N. Pitt St., Suite 320, Alexandria, VA 22314; 703-836-4880; www.NAPEhq.org). Will connect you with volunteer programs in schools.

National Association of Professional Geriatric Care Managers (1604 N. Country Club Rd., Tucson, AZ 85716; 520-881-8008; www.caremanager.org). Locates certified professionals who assess and coordinate financial, legal, and medical care needs of elderly clients and their families.

National Citizens' Coalition for Nursing Home Reform (1424 16th St., N.W., Washington, DC 20036; 202-332-2275; www.nccnhr.org). An advocacy group that offers a newsletter, legislative information, and a range of publications for consumers and professionals on long-term care issues.

National Council on Aging (409 3rd St., S.W., Suite 200, Washington, DC 20024; 202-479-1200; www.ncoa.org). A nonprofit group specializing in setting standards for operating senior centers and adult day centers, and lobbies on various issues.

Older Women's League (666 11th St., N.W., Suite 700, Washington, DC 20001; 202-783-6686). A group dedicated to the interests of midlife and older women.

Senior Summer School (P.O. Box 4424, Deerfield Beach, FL 33442-4424; 800-847-2466; www.seniorsummerschool.com). Offers active seniors 55 and over an affordable opportunity to enhance their summer at campus locations across the U.S. and Canada.

Travel Discount Services

Several services will help you save a considerable amount of money on travel. For great deals on hotels: Hotelkingdom.com (866-2HOTELS); Hotel Reservations Network (800-964-6835; www.180096hotel.com) offers hotel rooms up to 65 percent off retail rates; Express Hotel Reservations (800-707-3351; www.express-res.com) offers significant discounts on Chicago, New York, and Los Angeles hotels; and Quikbook (800-789-9887; www.quikbook .com) allows you to qualify for big discounts on short notice hotel reservations (typically more than four days) in Atlanta, Boston, Chicago, Los Angeles, New York, San Francisco, Washington, and other cities. Accommodations Express (800-277-1064; www.accommodationsexpress.com) offers hotel rooms in many major U.S. cities. Central Reservations Service (800-548-3311) books in Atlanta, Boston, Miami, New York, Orlando, and San Francisco. Hotel Rooms.com (800-486-7000; www.hotelrooms.com) reserves rooms at hotels in over 200 cities in the United States, the Caribbean, Europe, and Asia; and RMC Travel Center (800-245-5738) books in around 200 American cities.

Other services specialize in booking discounted hotel rooms in certain regions, such as California Reservations (800-576-0003) for most West Coast cities; Citywide Reservations Services (800-468-3593; www.cityres .com) in New England, New York City, Washington, and Montreal; Rooms (800-468-3500; www.hotrooms.com) in Chicago; Capitol Reservations (800-847-4832; www.hotelsdc.com) in Washington, D.C.; San Francisco Reservations (800-677-1500) and Silicon Valley Reservations (877-333-

8996; www.hotelres.com); and San Diego, Phoenix, and Palm Springs Reservations (800-728-3227; www.savecash.com).

iDine Rewards Network (11900 Biscayne Blvd., North Miami, FL 33181; 305-892-3340; 800-438-9013) pays a 20 percent rebate check when you purchase a meal in one of its participating restaurants. You can also get a rebate on various hotels, rental car agencies, and entertainment events. The rebate is figured on the total amount you charge on your credit card, including taxes and tips.

Bestfares.com (1301 S. Bowen Rd., Suite 490, Arlington, TX 76103; 817-860-5761; 800-880-1234; www.bestfares.com) is a magazine loaded with the latest travel bargains on airfares, hotels, car rentals, cruises, and package tours. Author Tom Parsons keeps track of the latest frequent-flier promotions, coupons, and tie-ins to travel companies, allowing you to accumulate frequent-flier miles.

Web Sites

AA.com. American Airlines' Web site <www.aa.com>. Online reservations for your travel can be made. Travel packages are available, and frequent fliers can check on their frequent-flier awards accounts.

Access America <www.accessamerica.com>. Travel insurance covers medical emergencies anywhere in the world, total cost of a canceled trip, collision and comprehensive insurance for a rental car, and accidental death or injury during a flight.

American Institute of Certified Public Accountants <www.aicpa.org>. A section of the site devoted to the AICPA ElderCare Assurance Program. Encourages accountant members to specialize in providing financial services for the elderly.

American Payroll Association-Savings at Work <www.americanpayroll.org/pir99s.html>. Discusses the need for additional savings to boost retirement income and gives advice on how to bring your retirement income to a more comfortable level.

American Society of Travel Agents <www.astanet.com>. Source for finding ASTA member travel agents in your area and has a lot of travel information and advice for consumers.

Arthur Frommer's Budget Travel Online <www.frommers.com>. Contains useful advice on how to use your senior status to achieve reductions in the cost of vacations. Recommends budget vacation packages and facilitates booking to anywhere in the world as a package deal or for your own trip.

Away.com <www.away.com>. Offers vacations focused on adventure travel and outdoor activities—walking, hiking, kayaking, biking, safaris, diving, birdwatching, climbing, trekking, rafting, and horseback riding.

Bid4Vacations.com <www.bid4vacations.com>. You can bid, as at an auction, for the vacation package of your choice from the long list of offered packages, which are listed in such categories as beach vacations and ski vacations.

Caregiving Online <www.caregiving.com>. Associated with the newsletter *Caregiving.* In addition to posting stories from the newsletter, site holds online discussions for home caregivers and makes available an online journal of personal stories.

Cheap Tickets <www.cheaptickets.com>. Specializes in obtaining the lowest-priced airline seats available; also offers low-cost hotels, rental cars, and cruises. Registration required.

Consumer's Checkbook <www.checkbook.org>. Offers the best locally advertised prices on big ticket items, TVs and videos, major appliances, small appliances, home office equipment, sporting goods, tools, cameras and lenses, auto tires, and watches. Requires registration.

Consumer World <www.consumerworld.org>. Lots of news and articles (including maps and calculators) about airline travel, hotels, B&Bs, hostels, home exchanges, and travel destinations.

Delta Airlines <www.delta.com>. Delta's online reservation site where you can plan flights, make reservations, and purchase tickets.

Digitalcity.com <www.digitalcity.com>. Offers shopping, entertainment, and restaurant guides for U.S. cities.

ElderCare Online <www.ec-online.net>. A site for caretakers of the elderly with information on how to care for the elderly, medical issues, home care and independent living, insurance, and legal and financial matters.

Expedia.com <www.expedia.com>. Comprehensive travel and vacation site that offers flights, hotels, rental cars, cruises, and vacation packages. Claims to achieve discounts of up to 15 percent on hotel rooms and flights.

FirstGov for Seniors <www.seniors.gov/retirement.html>. A one-stop shop for seniors maintained by the Social Security Administration; topics include retirement planning, legislation, consumer protection, and tax assistance.

Fodors.com <www.fodors.com>. Lots of travel tips, reviews of hotels and restaurants, and links to online reservation sites.

Hotel Discounts <www.hoteldiscounts.com>. Online booking site for Hotel Reservations Network. Guarantees the lowest rate for any hotel or your money back.

Institute of Certified Travel Agents (ICTA) <www.icta.com>. Locates the nearest certified travel agent in your Zip code. Requires at least five years of travel agent experience plus expertise in tracking bookings outside the computer reservation system.

Janssen Eldercare.com <www.janssen-eldercare.com>. Articles and directories for senior services, such as financial and legal planning, senior care facility locations and evaluation services, options for paying for care, and links to financial and legal advisors.

Knowledge Tours <www.knowledgetours.com>. Offers special World of Knowledge–escorted cruises for over-50s to explore the history and cultures of the regions they visit.

LastMinuteTravel.com <www.lastminutetravel.com>. Specializes in last-minute bookings of airlines, hotels, cars, vacations, and cruises.

Lowestfare.com <www.lowestfare.com>. Specializes in domestic and international fares and also offers cruises and vacation packages.

Mapquest.com <www.mapquest.com>. Offers online maps for any region in the world. Provides driving directions with maps from your address to anywhere you wish to go in the United States, Canada, and Europe.

One Travel <www.onetravel.com>. Offers discounted air fares (sometimes on less well-known airlines), discounted hotels, and rental cars.

Priceline.com <www.priceline.com>. An unusual site that allows consumers to bid for the rates they want to pay for hotel rooms, rental cars, long distance calls, home refinancing, and airline tickets.

ResortQuest International <www.resortquest.com>. Vacation resort rentals available through this site.

Retirement Living <www.retirementliving.com>. Bills itself as the gateway to resources for senior living. Includes links for retirement communities and senior housing, quality-of-care ratings on housing, taxes by state, and state aging agencies.

Retirement Net <www.retirenet.com>. Has links to various nationwide senior facilities, active lifestyle living, golf course living, RV resort living, independent and assisted living, and nursing care.

Senior.com <www.senior.com>. A site for seniors with categories on computing, entertainment, faith, health, home life, money, news, relationships, shopping, insurance, and travel.

Seniorresource.com <www.seniorresource.com>. Has lots of good advice on almost every topic of concern to most seniors. Subjects covered include housing, aging, finance, insurance, humor, and resources available by state.

Seniorsites.com <www.seniorsites.com>. One of the most comprehensive Web sources for information on nonprofit housing and services for seniors, with more than 4,000 listed communities.

SkyAuction.com <www.skyauction.com>. Site lets you bid on worldwide airfare or vacation packages and offers last-minute deals that let you save money.

SWA.com <www.swa.com>. Southwest Airlines Web site offers online reservations and ticket purchases as well as senior fares for those over 65.

Third Age <www.thirdage.com>. A site for over-45s oriented around lifestyles. Offers a variety of forums on money as well as a section on finances heavily skewed toward retirement issues.

Transitions Abroad: Senior Travel Resources <www.transabroad.com>. Offers resources to help seniors get ready to travel abroad.

Trip.com <www.trip.com>. You can book air, rental car, and hotels on this site. Requires registration to book flights, hotels, rental cars, or packages.

TicketPlanet.com <www.ticketplanet.com>. Specializes in obtaining the lowest international air fares and also offers hotel price comparisons.

Travelex Insurance Services <www.travelex.com>. Offers comprehensive travel insurance that covers all travel costs if trip has to be canceled for medical reasons, death in the family, bankruptcy or financial default of the travel package provider, common carrier strike, weather, employer termination, or terrorism at your destination.

Travelocity.com <www.travelocity.com>. Extensive travel site with many special vacation package deals, including cruises. Site finds the lowest fares for your planned flights, hotels, or rental cars.

UAL.com <www.ual.com>. United Airlines Web site, where you can make reservations, purchase your tickets, check on your frequent-flier account, and plan vacations with UAL vacation packages.

US Airways.com <www.usairways.com>. US Airways Web site offers online reservations and ticket purchases. Frequent-flier members can access their mileage accounts.

VacationSpot.com <www.vacationspot.com>. Offers inns, bed and breakfasts, rental condominiums, villas, rental homes, and historic properties.

Wired Seniors.com <www.wiredseniors.com>. Designed for those over 50 and includes information on travel, home and family, health and fitness, entertainment, education, and shopping.

YOUpriceit.com <www.youpriceit.com>. You offer bids on airfares (world-wide). Also has information on hotels, cars, and vacation packages.

Web Site Calculators

The following Web sites offer a variety of calculators, portfolio forecasters, 401(k) plans, bond yields, estate taxes, retirement planners, and more:

www.americanexpress.com	www.money.cnn.com
www.fidelity.com	www.morningstar.com
www.financenter.com	www.troweprice.com
www.financialengines.com	www.vanguard.com
www.investinginbonds.com	

Airline Web Sites

Many airlines allow you to book trips directly on their Web sites, and many give you substantial discounts for doing so. Most airlines post their available inventory on a regular basis, and if they have seats for a destination you want, you can book it online for a discount. Some airlines have specific names for these fares: American calls them NetSAAvers; Northwest calls them Cyber-savers; and US Airways calls them E-savers. An airline would rather sell the seat to you at a discount than have it empty. Here are the Web sites for the major North American airlines, so you can take advantage of discounts:

Aeromexico Airlines <www.aeromexico.com>
Air Canada Airlines <www.aircanada.com>
AirTran Airlines <www.airtran.com>
Alaska Airlines <www.alaskaair.com>
Aloha Airlines <www.alohaairlines.com>
America West Airlines <www.americawest.com>
American Airlines <www.aa.com>
Continental Airlines <www.continental.com>
Delta Airlines <www.delta.com>
Frontier Airlines <www.flyfrontier.com>
Jet Blue (www.jetblue.com>
Mexicana <www.mexicana.com>
Midwest Express Airlines <www.midwestexpress.com>
Northwest Airlines <www.nwa.com>
Pan American Airlines <www.flypanam.com>
Southwest Airlines <www.swa.com>
United Airlines <www.ual.com>
US Airways <www.usairways.com>

Index